Code Generation, Analysis Tools, and Testing for Quality

Ricardo Alexandre Peixoto de Queirós
Polytechnic Institute of Porto, Portugal

Alberto Simões
Polytechnic Institute of Cávado and Ave, Portugal

Mário Teixeira Pinto
Polytechnic Institute of Porto, Portugal

A volume in the Advances
in Computer and Electrical
Engineering (ACEE) Book Series

Published in the United States of America by
    IGI Global
    Engineering Science Reference (an imprint of IGI Global)
    701 E. Chocolate Avenue
    Hershey PA, USA 17033
    Tel: 717-533-8845
    Fax: 717-533-8661
    E-mail: cust@igi-global.com
    Web site: http://www.igi-global.com

Library of Congress Cataloging-in-Publication Data

Names: Queiros, Ricardo Alexandre Peixoto de, 1975- editor. | Simoes,
   Alberto, 1978- editor. | Pinto, Mario Teixeira, 1967- editor.
Title: Code generation, analysis tools, and testing for quality / Ricardo
   Alexandre Peixoto de Queiros, Alberto Simoes, and Mario Teixeira Pinto,
   editors.
Description: Hershey, PA : Engineering Science Reference, an imprint of IGI
   Global, [2019] | Includes bibliographical references and index.
Identifiers: LCCN 2018028320| ISBN 9781522574552 (hardcover) | ISBN
   9781522574569 (ebook)
Subjects: LCSH: Computer programs--Testing. | Computer software--Quality
   control. | Automatic programming (Computer science)
Classification: LCC QA76.76.T48 C63 2019 | DDC 005.3--dc23 LC record available at https://lccn.
loc.gov/2018028320

This book is published in the IGI Global book series Advances in Computer and Electrical Engineering (ACEE) (ISSN: 2327-039X; eISSN: 2327-0403)

British Cataloguing in Publication Data
A Cataloguing in Publication record for this book is available from the British Library.

All work contributed to this book is new, previously-unpublished material.
The views expressed in this book are those of the authors, but not necessarily of the publisher.

For electronic access to this publication, please contact: eresources@igi-global.com.

Advances in Computer and Electrical Engineering (ACEE) Book Series

ISSN:2327-039X
EISSN:2327-0403

Editor-in-Chief: Srikanta Patnaik, SOA University, India

MISSION

The fields of computer engineering and electrical engineering encompass a broad range of interdisciplinary topics allowing for expansive research developments across multiple fields. Research in these areas continues to develop and become increasingly important as computer and electrical systems have become an integral part of everyday life.

The **Advances in Computer and Electrical Engineering (ACEE) Book Series** aims to publish research on diverse topics pertaining to computer engineering and electrical engineering. **ACEE** encourages scholarly discourse on the latest applications, tools, and methodologies being implemented in the field for the design and development of computer and electrical systems.

COVERAGE

- Analog Electronics
- Chip Design
- Computer science
- Digital Electronics
- VLSI Design
- VLSI Fabrication
- Applied Electromagnetics
- Circuit Analysis
- Microprocessor Design
- Algorithms

IGI Global is currently accepting manuscripts for publication within this series. To submit a proposal for a volume in this series, please contact our Acquisition Editors at Acquisitions@igi-global.com or visit: http://www.igi-global.com/publish/.

Titles in this Series

For a list of additional titles in this series, please visit:
https://www.igi-global.com/book-series/advances-computer-electrical-engineering/73675

Advanced Methodologies and Technologies in Network Architecture, Mobile Computing...
Mehdi Khosrow-Pour, D.B.A. (Information Resources Management Association, USA)
Engineering Science Reference • ©2019 • 1857pp • H/C (ISBN: 9781522575986) • US $595.00

Emerging Innovations in Microwave and Antenna Engineering
Jamal Zbitou (University of Hassan 1st, Morocco) and Ahmed Errkik (University of Hassan 1st, Morocco)
Engineering Science Reference • ©2019 • 437pp • H/C (ISBN: 9781522575399) • US $245.00

Advanced Methodologies and Technologies in Artificial Intelligence, Computer Simulation, and Human-Computer Interaction
Mehdi Khosrow-Pour, D.B.A. (Information Resources Management Association, USA)
Engineering Science Reference • ©2019 • 1221pp • H/C (ISBN: 9781522573685) • US $545.00

Optimal Power Flow Using Evolutionary Algorithms
Provas Kumar Roy (Kalyani Government Engineering College, India) and Susanta Dutta (Dr. B. C. Roy Engineering College, India)
Engineering Science Reference • ©2019 • 323pp • H/C (ISBN: 9781522569718) • US $195.00

Advanced Condition Monitoring and Fault Diagnosis of Electric Machines
Muhammad Irfan (Najran University, Saudi Arabia)
Engineering Science Reference • ©2019 • 307pp • H/C (ISBN: 9781522569893) • US $225.00

The Rise of Fog Computing in the Digital Era
K.G. Srinivasa (Chaudhary Brahm Prakash Government Engineering College, India) Pankaj Lathar (Chaudhary Brahm Prakash Government Engineering College, India) and G.M. Siddesh (Ramaiah Institute of Technology, India)
Engineering Science Reference • ©2019 • 286pp • H/C (ISBN: 9781522560708) • US $215.00

For an entire list of titles in this series, please visit:
https://www.igi-global.com/book-series/advances-computer-electrical-engineering/73675

701 East Chocolate Avenue, Hershey, PA 17033, USA
Tel: 717-533-8845 x100 • Fax: 717-533-8661
E-Mail: cust@igi-global.com • www.igi-global.com

Table of Contents

Section 3
Domain-Specific Languages

Detailed Table of Contents

Section 1
Code Quality and Tests

> *Ricardo Santos, E-goi, Portugal*
> *Ivo Pereira, E-goi, Portugal*
> *Isabel Azevedo, Polytechnic Institute of Porto, Portugal*

Detailed documentation and software tests are key factors for the success of a web application programming interface (API). When designing an API, especially in a design first approach, it is relevant to define a formal contract, known as API specification. This document must contain all necessary information regarding the API behavior. Thereby, the specification can be used to dynamically generate API components like documentation, client and server code, and software tests, reducing development and maintenance costs. This chapter presents a study of OpenAPI specification and its application on designing a new RESTful API for E-goi. It also presents a set of solutions for generating documentation, client code libraries, and test cases.

> *Parnasi Retasbhai Patel, Charotar University of Science and*
> *Technology, India*
> *Chintan Bhatt, Charotar University of Science and Technology, India*

Structural coverage analysis for any code is a very common approach to measure the quality of any test suit. Structural coverage determines which structure of the software or which portion is not exercised. This chapter describes two different phases to achieve structural coverage analysis using DO-178B/C standards. Statement coverage is the very basic coverage criteria which involves execution of all the executable statements in the source code at least once. Analysis of structural coverage can be done by capturing the amount of code that is covered by the airborne software. The first phase contains the instrumentation procedure which instruments the source code at execution time, and the second phase is generating a report that specifies which portion of source code is executed and which one is not in the form of a percentage.

Chapter 3

Miguel Jorge Andrade, Polytechnic Institute of Porto, Portugal

Modern work patterns like continuous integration (CI) have an implicit need for testing automation. In current CI solutions, white-box testing is left to the work methodology, typically addressed after code reviews. Code security inspection is often done in specific code reviews focusing on security. SonarQube is a tool that, to a certain extent, can automate white-box design and testing and serve as a guide for formal code reviews. Moreover, this tool can help audit the code for potential security issues. Most web programming today uses components readily available and transparently managed by package managers, like npm for Node.js or Composer for PHP. This use must also be audited at least for potential security problems; yet traditional white-box test design would require a good understanding of the vendor code, which can be difficult/impractical to achieve. This chapter will address SonarQube as a valuable tool to automate white-box and security testing and also provide suggestions on how to manage your vendor branches when there is a need to audit/change the vendor source code.

Section 2
Programming Languages Learning

Chapter 4

Ricardo Alexandre Peixoto de Queirós, Polytechnic Institute of Porto, Portugal

We are assisting the rise of online coding environments as a strategy to promote youth tech employment. With the growing importance of the technology sector, these type of technical training programs give learners emergent tech skills with a big impact and relevance to the current professional market needs. In this realm, MOOCs (massive open online courses) and online coding bootcamps are two increasingly popular options for learners to improve their code development skills and find work within a relatively short amount of time. Among all the features available on these environments, one stands out, which is the code generation. This chapter aims to detail and compare the most popular solutions for both learning contexts based on several criteria such as impact and maturity, user groups, and tools and features. In the features field, the authors highlight the code generation feature as an efficient way to enhance exercise resolution.

Chapter 5

María A. Pérez-Juárez, University of Valladolid, Spain
Míriam Antón-Rodríguez, University of Valladolid, Spain
María I. Jiménez-Gómez, University of Valladolid, Spain
Francisco J. Díaz-Pernas, University of Valladolid, Spain
Mario Martínez-Zarzuela, University of Valladolid, Spain
David González-Ortega, University of Valladolid, Spain

The learning of programming languages and paradigms is complex and requires a lot of training. For this reason, it is very important to detect students' main problems and needs to be able to provide professors with tools that help students to overcome those problems and difficulties. One type of tool that can be used for this purpose is the code validator. This chapter explores the possibilities and impact of using different tools and strategies for learning programming languages and paradigms. To achieve this goal, the authors have conducted a comprehensive search of relevant scientific literature that has been complemented with their experience using a JavaScript code validator and exercises module integrated into the e-learning platform Moodle, with university students during a web programming course.

Alexandre Bragança, Polytechnic Institute of Porto, Portugal
Isabel Azevedo, Polytechnic Institute of Porto, Portugal
Nuno Bettencourt, Polytechnic Institute of Porto, Portugal

Model-driven engineering (MDE) is an approach to software engineering that adopts models as the central artefact. Although the approach is promising in addressing major issues in software development, particularly in dealing with software complexity, and there are several success cases in the industry as well as growing interest in the research community, it seems that it has been hard to generalize its gains among software professionals. To address this issue, MDE must be taught at a higher-education level. This chapter presents a three-year experience in teaching MDE in a course of a master program in informatics engineering. The chapter provides details on how a project-based learning approach was adopted and evolved along three editions of the course. Results of a student survey are discussed and compared to those from another course. In addition, several other similar teaching experiences are analyzed.

Section 3
Domain-Specific Languages

Chapter 7

Rajni Sehgal, Amity University, India
Deepti Mehrotra, Amity University, India

Software often carries the structural deficiencies that make it hard to understand, change, or test; these deficiencies are categorized as a code smell. This code smell affects the performance of software adversely, thereby increase need of maintainability. Refactoring of code helps in reducing the code smell. But refactoring is an expensive process and hence identifies which and how much code need to refactor a challenging task and is termed as refactoring index. In this chapter, entropy approach is proposed to measure the refactoring index of 20 open source software programs. Refactoring index level is given to identify the critical project which urgently required refactoring in order to improve the quality of the project.

Chapter 8

Alberto Simões, Polytechnic Institute of Cávado and Ave, Portugal
Rui Miguel da Costa Meira, Polytechnic Institute of Cávado and Ave,
Portugal

This chapter describes an approach for the implementation of embedded domain-specific languages by using operator overloads and the creation of abstract syntax trees in run-time. Using the host language parser, an AST is created stating the structure of the DSL expression that is later analyzed, simplified, and optimized before the evaluation step. For the illustration of this process, the chapter proposes a domain-specific language for a basic linear algebra system dealing with matrices algebra and its optimization.

Chapter 9

RESTful Web Services Development With a Model-Driven Engineering

Rafael Corveira da Cruz Gonçalves, Polytechnic Institute of Porto,
    Portugal
Isabel Azevedo, Polytechnic Institute of Porto, Portugal

A RESTful web service implementation requires following the constrains inherent to REST architectural style, which, being a non-trivial task, often leads to solutions that do not fulfill those requirements properly. Model-driven techniques have been proposed to improve the development of complex applications. In model-driven software development, software is not implemented manually based on informal descriptions but partially or completely generated from formal models derived from metamodels. A model-driven approach, materialized in a domain specific language that integrates the OpenAPI specification, an emerging standard for describing REST services, allows developers to use a design first approach in the web service development process, focusing in the definition of resources and their relationships, leaving the repetitive code production process to the automation provided by model-driven engineering techniques. The code generation process covers the entire web-service flow from the description and exposure of the endpoints to the definition of database tables.

Preface

INTRODUCTION

Programming is around for some decades. Nevertheless, quality control is not yet a reality. There are different approaches to this problem: code IDEs are able to detect some code smells, and suggest editions to the programmer; code generation, from abstract specifications, can allow the quicker development of code and, if correctly abstracting the generated code, would allow easier implementation, and better generated code quality; code documentation both allows programmers to understand the behavior of the code they use, as it allows other programmers to edit existing code with more confidence, but there is no such thing as good documentation. Tools to allow the generation of documentation allow to assess their completeness, but their quality is still a problem; While code auditing tools are able to analyze code flows, and detect common bad coding practices and code standards try to force programmers to follow a specific set of rules, in order to reduce these bad programming practices, few tools exist that really deal with automatic refactoring of this code; finally, Unit Testing and Feature Testing allows programmers to guarantee that a desired behavior for some code is kept intact during software development, but how to evaluate the coverage of these tests on all possible corner cases is still a main challenge. These are all aspects to be covered on this book, sharing what is being done in the actuality to reduce all these problems.

THE CHALLENGES

In recent years we have witnessed a gigantic process of automating all our day-to-day tasks whether domestic or professional. This complex process requires expert people, machines, and frameworks to support all the code architecture behind this automation. In this sense, coding, once seen as another phase of the software development lifecycle, is now seen as the crucial phase for the quality of the automation process. Being an important and complex phase, it is necessary to provide the programmers with techniques that allow to generate, test and evaluate the code in a simple and practical way. However often these techniques are difficult to apply due to many variables: much disorganized code made by several people with different styles, thus making refactoring difficult and requiring more robust tests, increasing and advanced level of malicious code, among other threats.

DESCRIPTION AND ORGANIZATION OF THE BOOK

This book presents a comprehensive and recent view of the emerging trends, techniques, and tools for code generation, analysis tools, and testing for quality. At the same time, it identifies new trends on this topic from pedagogical strategies to technological approaches. The book has nine chapters organized in three sections. A brief description of each of the sections follows:

Section 1 describes techniques for code refactoring and tests. These novel approaches aim to increase code quality through code generation at project startup thus eliminating delayed and error prone boilerplate code creation. At the same time the refactoring allows developers to improve the internal structure of the code without changing its external behavior. At the same time, it improves code understanding, which facilitates maintenance and avoids the inclusion of defects.

Chapter 1 describes a digital marketing platform API with more than three hundred thousand clients in more than fifty countries. Due to the swift growth of the platform's functionality, its web API documentation and client code libraries became quickly outdated and with unexpected bugs and failures, since there is lack of software tests. This was the main reason for authors to propose a solution capable of successfully generating acceptance tests for their public API based on its specification.

Chapter 2 describes a procedure which ensures that all the covered lines of test suit are given by statement coverage analysis and branches using branch coverage analysis and generate a coverage report. All the specified test cases described in the testing section are tested properly and get appropriate outcomes for statement and branch coverage. The structural coverage analysis provides a sensible approach that balances the DO-178B requirements for structural coverage.

Chapter 3 details how to use SonarQube in an automated manner, more precisely, authors address analysis on security, and how to deal with code from vendor branches. SonarQube is an Open Source quality management platform, dedicated to continuously analyze and measure technical quality, from project portfolio to method. It incorporates a plugin system for extension purposes.

Section 2 enumerates several approaches to foster the teaching-learning process in the domain of computer programming. Since we are dealing with code learning, several techniques are shared to improve learning engagement and integration in learning management systems.

Chapter 4 distinguishes MOOCs (Massive Open Online Courses) and Online Coding Bootcamps as two increasingly popular options for learners to improve their code development skills and find work within a relatively short amount of time. Among all the features available on these environments, one stands out, which is the code generation. This paper aims to detail and compare the most popular solutions for both learning contexts based on several criteria such as impact and maturity, user groups and tools and features.

Chapter 5 presents two educational tools focused on the client-side scripting language JavaScript to support the web development applications learning process for engineering students. The two tools are a Moodle-based JavaScript Code Validator and an exercises module. The experiences were carried out during an academic course with quite positive results.

Chapter 6 presents a three-year experience in teaching MDE in a course of a master program in Informatics Engineering. The chapter provides details on how a project-based learning approach was adopted and evolved along three editions of the course. Results of a student survey are discussed and compared to those from another course. In addition, several other similar teaching experiences are analyzed.

Section 3 promotes the use of Domain Specific Languages (DSL). The DSL are computer languages specialized to a particular application domain. In this case, DSLs are used to as a way to foster code generation and refactoring.

Chapter 7 presents new metrics for refactoring index to prioritize the code smell and find the software that needs maximum refactoring. In this study, refactoring index is calculated for an entire project whereas entropy method can be used for component based system where code smells can be detected from an individual components and components are prioritize according to refactoring need.

Chapter 8 presents a novel technique for the development of embedded DSL through the use of operator overloading. While operator overloading is a common functionality on recent object-oriented languages, the way these operators are used is, in most situations, the simple replacement of the default operator behavior.

Chapter 9 describes the OpenAPI specification (OAS) and presents a custom metamodel, from which a domain specific modeling language was developed. This model is a simplification of the main concepts that integrate the OAS, giving a high-level interpretation of the relationships between them, while supporting the DSL development. This metamodel answers one of the three questions raised by the authors, on what were the main compromises in the specification of a language agnostic model to represent the OAS, since it deliberately leaves out some OAS concepts.

CONCLUSION

This book aims to share new approaches and methodologies for code generation, edition, analysis and testing. At the same time, it identifies new trends on these topics, from pedagogical strategies to technological approaches.

The proposed book could be used as a valuable resource for practitioners and as a reference for research scholars, computer science teachers and students pursuing computer science related subjects and enterprise developers.

Alberto Simões
Polytechnic Institute of Cávado and Ave, Portugal

Mário Teixeira Pinto
Polytechnic Institute of Porto, Portugal

Ricardo Alexandre Peixoto de Queirós
Polytechnic Institute of Porto, Portugal

Acknowledgment

We would like to acknowledge the help of all the people involved in this project and, more specifically, to the authors and reviewers that took part in the review process. Without their support, this book would not have become a reality.

First, we would like to thank each one of the authors for their contributions. Our sincere gratitude goes to the chapter's authors who contributed their time and expertise to this book.

Second, we wish to acknowledge the valuable contributions of the reviewers regarding the improvement of quality, coherence, and content presentation of chapters. Most of the authors also served as referees; I highly appreciate their double task.

Third, we would like to express our thanks to the publishing team at IGI Global for their expert support and guidance, more precisely, to Jordan Tepper, Assistant Development Editor of IGI Global.

This book is dedicated to our families.

Alberto Simões
Polytechnic Institute of Cávado and Ave, Portugal

Mário Teixeira Pinto
Polytechnic Institute of Porto, Portugal

Ricardo Alexandre Peixoto de Queirós
Polytechnic Institute of Porto, Portugal

Section 1
Code Quality and Tests

Chapter 1
Dynamic Generation of Documentation, Code, and Tests for a Digital Marketing Platform's API

Ricardo Santos
E-goi, Portugal

Ivo Pereira
E-goi, Portugal

Isabel Azevedo
Polytechnic Institute of Porto, Portugal

ABSTRACT

Detailed documentation and software tests are key factors for the success of a web application programming interface (API). When designing an API, especially in a design first approach, it is relevant to define a formal contract, known as API specification. This document must contain all necessary information regarding the API behavior. Thereby, the specification can be used to dynamically generate API components like documentation, client and server code, and software tests, reducing development and maintenance costs. This chapter presents a study of OpenAPI specification and its application on designing a new RESTful API for E-goi. It also presents a set of solutions for generating documentation, client code libraries, and test cases.

DOI: 10.4018/978-1-5225-7455-2.ch001

INTRODUCTION

Nowadays, there is a great need to automate processes to achieve increased productivity. This necessity leads many companies to publish part of their internal services on the web, making them available to their clients through Application Programming Interfaces (APIs) (Abelló Gamazo, et al., 2017). Thus, automation is essential for many businesses, like digital marketing, making APIs a core component, since clients often need to automate and customize marketing processes.

However, web API are often black-boxes to its users, since its code is not publicly accessible (Schwichtenberg, 2017). Developers working on their applications rapidly integrate third-party software to build distributed software systems but learning how to use an API properly is not a trivial task (Meng, 2017).

Thereby, one of the most important characteristics of an Application Programming Interface is its technical documentation, which exists to facilitate communication between users and the API. To make an API easy to use it is essential to assure that its documentation is always correct and updated, and it provides clear examples of its usage (Uddin, 2015; Sohan, Anslow, & Maurer, 2015; De, 2017). In fact, the documentation can be very important to understand how to use libraries and frameworks developed by other teams and whose functionalities are easily accessible through APIs (Robillard, 2011).

Still, API documentation is frequently created manually and needs to be updated whenever the API evolves, otherwise it will become obsolete (Abelló Gamazo, et al., 2017), which is a common problem. This often brings maintenance costs to the developers every time a service is created or updated. *Therefore, rather than focusing on automating what's easy, focus on automating the boring parts (unlike you, computers love repetition), the difficult parts (reduce error-prone steps), and the parts that need to happen when you would rather be asleep. As a human, you are better than computers at improvisation and being flexible, exercising judgment, and coping with variations* (Limoncelli, 2018).

Such as for any software, API testing is essential to improve its quality and reduce the costs of developing an application (Tassey, 2002). Yet, sometimes, developing software tests can be even more expensive than building the product itself (Tassey, 2002).

Thus, to maintain an API, including not only its code but also its documentation and software tests, can be a very costly and painful process. Fortunately, some of these maintenance costs can be reduced using an API specification. An API specification establishes a contract and describes the API through a document readable by both humans and machines (Open API Initiative, 2018), allowing the generation of documentation dynamically through that contract. The API is forced to follow the contract defined by its specification, so it is possible to generate client and server code, documentation and tests.

In this chapter, it will be provided examples on E-goi's public API. E-goi is a digital marketing platform with more than three hundred thousand clients in more than fifty countries (although E-goi's center of attention is in Brazilian, Portuguese, Spanish and Colombian market). As a digital marketing platform, this software allows its clients to create marketing campaigns for different channels, including email, Short Message Service (SMS), voice messages, fax, web push and mobile push. After creating a contact list and filling it with relevant contacts, the list can be divided in different segments, ready to receive different sorts of campaigns. E-goi also provides its users with tools like automation workflows, forms and landing pages that, like campaigns, can be created from scratch, edited from many templates (either E-goi templates or already existing templates previously created by clients).

Due to the swift growth of the platform's functionality, its web API documentation and client code libraries became quickly outdated. Additionally, the frequent evolution faced by E-goi public API often leads to unexpected bugs and failures, since there is lack of software tests. The reason why these tests are insufficient, and documentation and client code libraries are frequently outdated is that they have high maintenance costs, which could be mitigated with a dynamic generation of these artifacts, based on an API specification.

BACKGROUND

In this section, OpenAPI 3.0 (Open API Initiative, 2017) will be analyzed, giving an overview of the specification. Representational State Transfer (REST) architectural style, which was first described by Fielding (Fielding, 2000), will also be studied since OpenAPI Specification (OAS) is a specification language built for REST API (Open API Initiative, 2018).

Aiming to improve web scalability, it was proposed REST architectural style that comes along with six constraints, which are (Massé, 2011):

- **Client-Server:** Clients and servers are implemented and deployed separately, if both are in conformance with uniform interface constraint.
- **Uniform Interface:** All components interacting in a web application must conform with a uniform interface, which requires identification of resources, manipulation of resources through representations, self-descriptive messages and hypermedia as the engine of application state (HATEOAS).
- **Layered System:** Intermediary applications, such as proxies, may exist between clients and servers if they agree with the same uniform interface.

- **Cache:** Acts on responses, reducing latency and therefore improving the overall performance of a web application.
- **Stateless:** Servers do not have knowledge about the client's application state, obligating clients to send contextual information when communicating with the server.
- **Code-On-Demand:** Servers can temporarily transfer executable programs, like scripts or plugins to their clients, so that the client is able to understand and execute the code. This is the only optional constraint.

These constraints are important as an architectural style defines *the vocabulary of components and connectors that can be used in instances of that style, together with a set of constraints on how they can be combined* (Garlan, 1993).

According to Richardson Maturity Model (RMM), web services can have different levels of maturity (Richardson, 2013; Webber, 2010; Massé, 2011).

Level 0: It is the most basic level of a web service. In this level, services have a single Uniform Resource Identifier (URI) and use only one Hypertext Transfer Protocol (HTTP) method (Webber, 2010).

Level 1: The level one is the URI level, where many URIs are present (having individual resources instead of a single endpoint) but still using only one HTTP method (Webber, 2010).

Level 2: The level two comes by with the employment of multiple URI and the usage of HTTP methods (Webber, 2010).

Level 3: Level three (hypermedia level) can be hit by accomplishing the previous levels' constraints and adding links to other resources, allowing the transition between application states (Webber, 2010).

Then, after reaching the hypermedia level, it is possible to say that an API is RESTful and RMM is useful to state what it means. When only level 1 or 2 is reached the term "pragmatic REST" (Mulloy, 2013) is used, in opposition to "pure REST" (Costa, 2014), because of the emphasis on practical issues aspects when developing services that follow the REST architecture style.

There are many open source specification languages for REST API, including OAS (Open API Initiative, 2018), REST API Modeling Language (RAML) (RAML, 2018) and API Blueprint (Apiary, 2017). In this chapter, only OpenAPI will be analyzed because of its large adoption in comparison to the others. That is proved on Figure 1, which shows four bar plots, comparing community size for each repository project on Github, based on the number of users watching, starring, forks and contributors.

OpenAPI Specification is led by the Open API Initiative (OAI). It defines a standard interface, which acts as a contract like interfaces in lower-level programming

Figure 1. API Blueprint, OAS and RAML community comparison
Based on GitHub

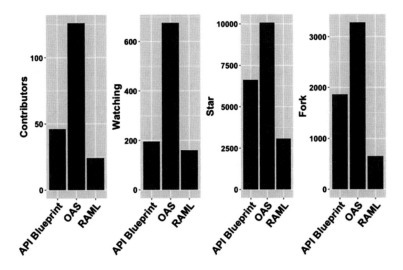

languages, allowing the discovery of a web API functionality by humans and machines without the need of consulting source code, additional information or inspecting network traffic (Open API Initiative, 2018). Through a properly defined OpenAPI description, it is possible to generate documentation, client and server code and software tests with a minimal amount of implementation logic (Open API Initiative, 2018). Although a design-first approach is preferred in API development (Massé, 2011), OAS permits both design-first and code-first development processes and consents two different specification formats: JavaScript Object Notation (JSON) and YAML Ain't Markup Language (YAML) (Open API Initiative, 2018).

The last released version of OpenAPI Specification is 3.0.1 version. As OpenAPI uses semantic versioning 2.0.0 (Open API Initiative, 2017), the OpenAPI structure will remain the same for all patch versions existent in 3.0 minor version. According to semantic versioning 2.0.0 (Preston-Werner, s.d.), there are three types of changes:

- **Major:** Changes that are incompatible with the current API.
- **Minor:** New functionalities that are backward-compatible.
- **Patch:** Backward-compatible bug fixes.

Being so, an API version takes the form of $x.y.z$, where x corresponds to a major version, y to a minor version, and z to a patch (Preston-Werner, s.d.).

Thereby, OpenAPI 3.0 differs slightly from its previous major version. As it is possible to verify through Figure 2, it has many elements, identified by the following keywords:

- *info*: Basic API information.
- *servers*: Uniform Resource Locator (URL) of API servers.
- *security*: Authentication and authorization.
- *paths*: Available API resources.
- *tags*: Tags used to group operations.
- *externalDocs*: Links for external documentation.
- *components*: Reusable components (which are *responses, parameters, examples, requestBodies, headers, links, callbacks, schemas* and *securitySchemes*).

Another important detail about OpenAPI is the vast number of tools that support the specification. Before its 3.0 version, OpenAPI was known as Swagger. It was renamed upon the release of 3.0 version in 2015 and Swagger became the set of tools that implement the specification (Pinkham, 2017). Among these tools, there are Swagger UI, which can automatically generate an interactive page of documentation and Swagger Codegen, that generates client code libraries and server code. Usage examples of these tools is shown in this chapter.

Figure 2. OpenAPI 3.0 structure
Adapted from (ErnstFriedman, 2017)

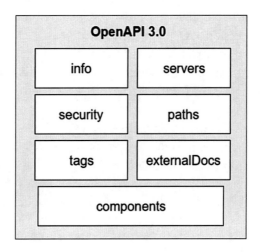

API SPECIFICATION AND DYNAMIC GENERATION OF ARTIFACTS

The focus of this chapter is to understand how artifacts like documentation, client code and software tests can be generated using an OpenAPI specification. Then, it is necessary to understand how to design an API using OpenAPI. So, the rest of this chapter provides examples on how to design and describe an API using Open API Specification, in a design-first approach, as well as some solutions that can be used to dynamically generate objects considering the supplied OpenAPI examples.

Despite being based on E-goi's public API, not all existent operations are defined. Also, not all components are complete due to its complexity and hypermedia links are not descripted for the same reason. Instead, shorter samples are provided so that readers can easily understand how to use OpenAPI Specification. Also, E-goi's new API hasn't been yet deployed to a public stable version and some changes might occur.

API Specification

Describing a REST API, especially public APIs that are intended to be used by clients, must be a delicate and cautious process. In this section, small extracts of an OpenAPI definition are provided and explained. The full specification regarding the partial descriptions presented in this document is displayed in the appendix 1.

API Basic Information

First, it is necessary to indicate the OpenAPI version and it is possible to describe the API's basic information, including its title, description, terms of service, contacts, license and current version, as it is shown in the following code written in YAML.

```
openapi: 3.0.1
info:
title: Public API
description: New E-goi's public API
termsOfService: https://e-goi.com
contact:
 name: (+351) 300 404 336
license:
 name: E-goi
version: 1.0.0
```

Resources and Operations

Then, OpenAPI Specification allows the definition of resources and operations. That definition contains a set of tags that may be used to group related operations, a summary, a description, a unique identifier, its parameters and responses. Since some parameters and other schemas may be reused, it is often a good practice to define them outside the operation scope and invoke them using the *ref* keyword. Responses contain a status code, a description and a content, which can be in various media formats. Again, the *ref* keyword can be used in a response to reference a schema defined in a global scope. The next code example displays a summarized version of E-goi's public API operation to retrieve all contact lists of an account.

```
paths:
/lists:
 get:
 tags:
 - Lists
 summary: Get all lists
 description: Returns all lists
 operationId: GetAllLists
 parameters:
 - $ref: '#/components/parameters/limit'
 responses:
 '200':
 description: OK
 content:
 application/json:
 schema:
 type: array
 items:
 $ref: '#/components/schemas/list
```

Parameters

As we can see in the following code example, for each parameter it must be indicated its name, the location where that parameter must be sent and its schema, which contains the constraints of the parameter. It may also be included a description and the *required* keyword, which takes a false Boolean value by default.

```
parameters:
 limit:
 name: limit
 in: query
 description: Number of items to return
 required: false
 schema:
 type: integer
 minimum: 1
 example: 20
```

Schemas

A schema can be defined and reused not only inside parameters but also inside responses. For instance, a response may contain a set of properties where it is possible, for each one, to indicate some constraints and information like a description, a type, an example and an enumerate. The next snippet shows a response schema where a list contains an *id*, a *title* and a *status* that can be *active, inactive* or *blocked*.

```
schemas:
list:
 description: Success response schema for this operation
 properties:
 id:
 description: Id of the list
 type: integer
 example: 1
 title:
 description: Title of the list
 type: string
 example: Title
 status:
 description: Status of the list
 type: string
 enum:
 - active
 - inactive
 - blocked
 example: active
```

Apikey Authentication

An OpenAPI description may also contain different kinds of authentication. It is possible to define different security schemes, like it was done with parameters and schemas. These security schemes may be reused inside operations through *security* keyword, as well as it can be invoked in a global scope, as shown in the example bellow.

```
security:
- Apikey: []
components:
parameters:
  ...
schemas:
  ...
securitySchemes:
 Apikey:
 type: apiKey
 name: Apikey
 in: header
```

Documentation

One of the biggest capabilities of OpenAPI is the automatic generation of documentation. A dynamically generated documentation could be implemented from scratch, but it is not necessary since Swagger provides Swagger UI (Swagger, 2018). Taking the specification already presented as an example, it is possible to render an interactive documentation page, illustrated on Figure 3.

As shown in Figure 4, it is possible to complete the request parameters and execute the operation. Then, the server will answer with a response that should be coherent with the response defined, which is shown in Figure 5.

Although it is desirable that the server response is in conformance with the specified response, Swagger UI still presents the server response even if the response schema is not well defined. For that reason, it is essential to have acceptance tests, which will be covered later in this chapter.

It is also possible for the users of Swagger UI to see the schemas defined in the OpenAPI description and its details, like presented in Figure 6.

Figure 3. Swagger UI 3 generated documentation page

Figure 4. Example of request

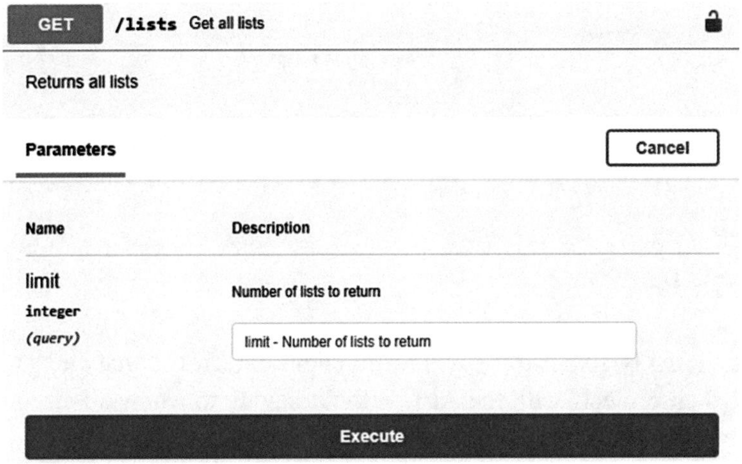

Figure 5. Example of response description

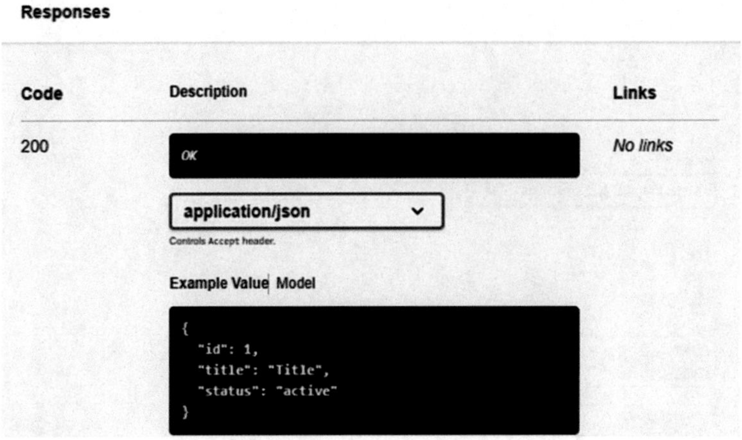

Figure 6. Example of a model schema

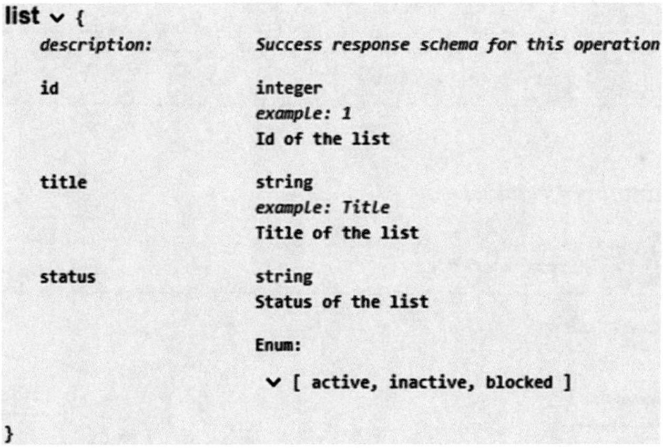

Client Code

Some public APIs, like E-goi's API, offer client libraries so that clients can easily integrate their projects with the API, without having to worry about logic related to web implementation.

Swagger offers a framework, called Swagger Code Generator (Swagger, 2018), or simply Swagger Codegen, which is capable of automatically generate client code libraries in many languages through an API specification. However, Swagger Codegen has not released a stable version supporting OpenAPI Specification 3.0, yet (Swagger, 2018).

Although the last stable version of Swagger Codegen is version 2., version 3 is already being developed. While the generation of client could be implemented manually, Swagger Codegen is a powerfull tool, capable of generating code for many languages and frameworks and widely used by known companies like Autodesk, Cisco, IBM, Red Hat and Upwork (Swagger, 2018). Thereby, in appendix 2, it is provided the OpenAPI definition which was built before converted to OAS 2.

Swagger Codegen command line interface application takes many different flags to customize the generation of the code. Among the most important flags there are:

- **-a <authorization> or --auth <authorization>:** Authorization headers for retrieving data from an API through Swagger Codegen.
- **-c <configuration file> or --config <configuration file>:** Additional configuration that vary according to the programming language. Can be used to, for example, to select a specific HTTP client.
- **-i <spec file> or --input-spec <spec file>:** Location for the specification file.
- **-l <language> or --lang <language>:** Language or framework of the generator.
- **-o <output directory> or --output <output directory>:** Location of the output files.
- **-s or --skip-overwrite:** Flag used to skip file overwrite.

Using these parameters, it is possible to generate a client code library with a simple command. For example, the command java -jar swagger-codegen-cli.jar generate -i https://api.e-goi.com/rest-lphp-o/path/to/file would generate a PHP client library for E-goi's API.

Besides the generated client code, Swagger Codegen also generates documentation files on how to use the the library. A good code example should be executed with minimal effort (Montandon, 2013); thereby good code examples often areconcise, being explained step by step, with inline comments and links to external resources when necessary (Nasehi, 2012).

Code examples generated Swagger Codegen meet these requirements. A *readme* file is generated, containing all requirements and steps necessary to install the library into the client application. Additionally, this file contains information about authorization and links to every existent API endpoint. These links are references for other generated files related to API resources, which are generated with a clear example, for each operation, on how to use the client library. Each operation reference files for schemas and parameters are also generated, with each attribute clearly descripted as in the specification.

Generated PHP Client Library

The following PHP code example shows how to call the client library, where the developer only needs to insert his key, to instantiate a client and to call an existing method (passing parameters if necessary). This is a code example provided by Swagger Codegen, organized in logical chunks and with inline comments to help the user using the library.

```php
<?php
require_once(__DIR__ . '/vendor/autoload.php');
// Configure API key authorization: Apikey
$config = Swagger\Client\Configuration::getDefaultConfigurati
on()
 ->setApiKey('Apikey', 'YOUR_API_KEY');
$apiInstance = new Swagger\Client\Api\ListsApi(
 new GuzzleHttp\Client(),
 $config
);
$limit = 56; // int | Number of items to return
try {
 $result = $apiInstance->getAllLists($limit);
 print_r($result);
} catch (Exception $e) {
 echo 'Exception when calling ListsApi->getAllLists: ',
$e->getMessage(), PHP_EOL;
}
?>
```

Tests

When using an API specification, it is fundamental to assure that the documentation provided to the clients after every API change is correctly implemented by the back-end (De, 2017). To achieve this, acceptance tests can be used, verifying whether the defined contract is well implemented by the API. Acceptance tests are software tests that match the acceptance criteria defined by a customer, testing if the requested functionality was delivered correctly (Finsterwalder, 2001). In this case, the acceptance criteria are the responses that customers using the public API expect to see.

When developing or evolving systems, requirements constantly change and, in most cases, these changes affect other documentation artifacts (Hotomski, 2018).

The changes that customers expect to see are the ones defined in the specification, since it was used to build the documentation page. Thereby, the API will be tested against these acceptance tests, built over the OpenAPI definition.

The automation of these tests can lead to a significant reduction of maintenance costs and it is less prone to errors caused by overlooking in a manual testing process (Finsterwalder, 2001). However, they can be less effective than manual tests with additional costs and efforts that do not bring benefits (Amannejad, 2014). Test code, as any code in general, is susceptible to design problems, and different possibilities must be pondered. Many concerns in this area have led to what has been designed as "Software Test Code Engineering" (Yusifoğlu, 2015; Garousi, 2016).

Alternatives for the Generation of Acceptance Tests

Various approaches can be used to generate acceptance tests based on an OpenAPI specification. For instance, the tests could be generated directly into the API being tested. As the Unified Modeling Language (UML) component diagram in Figure 7 shows, this application is executed through the console that consumes an OpenAPI specification. The controller instantiates an object of *Specification* and injects that dependency into a generator, responsible for generating the tests in the API. The usage of adapter design pattern (Vlissides, 1995) is important and the *Test Framework Adapter* is used to enable the generator to build tests for multiple test frameworks.

Another solution for this problem is to build a Test API. Instead of generating the tests for each API with its own test framework, it is possible to provide a web API where all the tests are stored, which requires only one test framework and consequently only one adapter, as the logical view present in Figure 8 shows.

Figure 7. Test generator component diagram

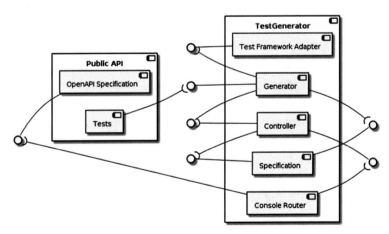

Figure 8. Test API component diagram

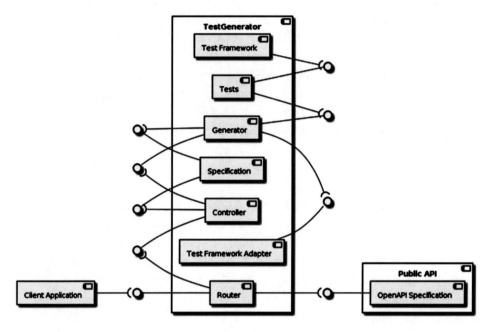

Each approach can be used for multiple APIs, having its advantages and disadvantages. Using a test generator console application can be more specific for the target API, generating tests that can be easily extended by developers. However, it is necessary to develop an adapter for each new test framework and the generator must be installed on the API server.

On the other hand, a web service API with the capability of storing and executing tests requires only implementation for one test framework, since it works independently from the web API being tested. Consequently, the rest of this section will focus on the design and implementation of the Test API.

Solution

To generate tests, a specification with valid syntax is not enough, since some methods may require parameters. A complete specification often includes example values that are used as parameters for the tests. However, a specification is valid even if the user does not provide any examples. Still, these tests can be generated based on the defined constraints of each parameter. These constrains include the data type, maximum or minimum values, enumerates and regular expressions. Then, the Test API can generate data to match the defined constraints, creating valid parameters to execute the operations and testing it against the defined response.

But, to avoid test smells and to assure the reliability of the tests, it is important to guarantee that there is not randomness or any source of non-determinism (Bowes, 2017). Thereby, when generating data from constraints, it is important to use a fixed value. Then, with the purpose of generating one acceptance test for each operation, it is used the first value that satisfies the constraint.

Still, to fully automate the acceptance testing process it is necessary to fulfill the requirements of each operation that is being tested. Operations that delete a resource cannot originate a test on its own, since they require a service that mocks the entity to be executed first. For example, before testing an operation that deletes a specific contact list, it is necessary to create a contact list, by requesting a *post* method to *lists* resource. Also, operations that create resources often need to retrieve (through a *get* method) the created entity, to verify its data.

There are various solutions to solve this problem. HATEOAS could be used to navigate between different resource states, finding the appropriate method to create the entity. Although, this method would rely heavily on the API hypermedia design, which is not desirable, since the Test API should be a scalable application, capable of producing automated testing for different types of REST APIs if these API provide a well formed OpenAPI definition. It could also be used OpenAPI links, which work in a way comparable to HATEOAS. However, the purpose of using OpenAPI links is to use the response of an operation as input for another, which means a delete method would have to supply an empty input to a create method.

As an alternative, upon calling the Test API, it can be provided not only the specification, but also an additional configuration file, where all API operations are listed and associated with their required dependencies. The mentioned file could be written in JSON format, with the following structure:

```
{
"/lists/{id}": {
 "specificationDependencies: [
 "CreateList"
 ]
}
}
```

As it is possible to see on the JSON example already presented, the configuration file may contain the resources present in the specification as well as their dependencies, that can be a reference for other operations identified by the OpenAPI keyword *operationId.*

However, since *tests should not dictate the code* (Bowes, 2017), the mentioned service dependencies should not be forced to exist in production code and, therefore, in API specification. Accordingly, these dependencies don't inevitably need to be references to other operations in the API. Instead they can be references to external services, which can have the sole purpose of testing. As the following JSON example illustrates, it is possible to define external dependencies. Unlike the dependencies that exist in the specification, these require additional data (which is used to call the service), consisting in its URL, HTTP method, query parameters, headers and body parameters.

```
{
"/lists/{id}": {
 "externalDependencies": [
 {
 "URL": "protocol://domain-or-ip:port/path",
 "httpMethod": "POST",
 "query": {},
 "headers": {
 "Accept": "application/json",
 "Content-Type": "application/json"
 },
 "body": {
 "title": "Title"
 }
 }
 ]
 }
}
```

It is also important to note that for levels deeper in the resource hierarchy, for example */lists/{listId}/segments/{segmentId}*, there may be more than one dependency (in this case the creation of a contact list and the creation of a list segment). A partially generated file can be requested from the Test API, identifying all existing resources that require an *id*, so the developer only needs to include the desired dependencies for each resource.

Finally, after being provided with an OpenAPI definition and a configuration file containing all the necessary dependencies for each resource, the Test API can dynamically create acceptance tests. The following code is a sample of a generated test case for the operation to delete a contact list, using PHPUnit as test framework. The private method *dependencyCreateList* is also generated based on the configuration file supplied, and it is used to solve dependencies required for testing the delete method.

```
public function testDeleteList(){
  // dependencies
  $listId = $this->dependencyCreateList('DeleteList');
  // delete request
  $request = new Delete('/lists/' . $listId);
  $response = $request->call();
  // assert server response
  $this->assertResponse($response);
}
private function dependencyCreateList($operation){
  // post request
  $request = new Post('/lists');
  $response = $request->call();
  // obtain id from specification
  $id = $this->getIdFromResponse($operation, $response);
  return $id;
}
```

Each resource has its own test class. Then, to reuse common implementation it is important to create an abstract superclass with common implementation. The function *getIdFromResponse*, shown in the presented snippet, is an example of common implementation across many test cases. This method is responsible for retrieving the path parameter from the operation and get the correspondent *id* from the response. However, errors made by developers upon defining the configuration file may occur. Regarding that scenario, if the developer indicates a reference to a dependency that does not exist, this system will reject the configuration provided.

The already presented test is a success scenario, but tests should also cover failures (Bowes, 2017). This means that for each operation more than one acceptance test must be created.

Taking for example the *get* request to */lists?limit=20*, tests should answer questions like (De, 2017):

1. What is the default API behavior when no query parameters are passed?
2. What is the API behavior when the right query parameter with the right value is passed?
3. What is the API behavior when the parameter name passed is incorrect?
4. What is the API behavior when the parameter does not have any value?
5. What is the API behavior when the parameter value is incorrect?
6. What is the API behavior when multiple query parameters are passed in the right combination?

7. What is the API behavior when multiple query parameters are passed in incorrect combinations?
8. What is the default data format for the API response when no information about the requested data format is passed?
9. What is the data format for the API response for both success and error conditions?
10. What is the HTTP response status code for different success and error conditions?
11. What is the API response for unexpected HTTP methods, headers, and URLs?

To answer these questions, it is necessary to create many acceptance tests for each operation. For both questions 2, 3 and 4, an acceptance test is needed for each existing parameter. The answer to question 5 follow the same perspective; however, for situations where the parameter assumes few values, it is possible to generate a test for each existing value. For example, the status that a list can assume in E-goi are active, inactive or blocked. Then, generating non-matching data, based on the constraints provided, the system would create three tests, one for each value present in the specified enumerate. Question 6 and 7 can also be responded if the API description contains enough information about the combinations of parameters (OpenAPI provides proper keywords to define different types of combinations). About the remaining questions, the information contained in the specification is enough to generate tests to validate data formats and other meta information.

FUTURE RESEARCH DIRECTIONS

OpenAPI Specification is constantly evolving, and all the mentioned tools and solutions need to go along with it. To state the work that is currently being developed within Open API Initiative and Swagger community, the number of open and closed issues for each project is shown in Table 1 (Open API Initiative, 2018; Swagger, 2018; Swagger, 2018).

Table 1. OpenAPI, Swagger UI and Swagger Code Generator Issues

	Open Issues	Closed Issues
OpenAPI	338	664
Swagger UI	236	2932
Swagger Codegen	1362	2644

As informed in this chapter, Swagger Code Generator is not yet capable of using OpenAPI Specification 3.0. Swagger Codegen last stable version is version 2.3.1. Both versions 2.4.0 and version 3.0.0 are being developed but their release dates haven't been defined yet. Version 3.0.0 will come with major changes, and will, therefore, supporting OpenAPI Specification 3.0 (Swagger, 2018).

Although the presented solution for the generation of acceptance tests solves the stated problems related to the lack of tests, there is still room for improvements. The integration of this API with a Graphical User Interface (GUI) would turn this solution user-friendly, since writing the configuration file necessary for the test generation is susceptible to human mistakes. In a GUI, the system could suggest possible dependencies and it could also allow the user to perform requests for external endpoints, saving these requests as dependencies. It would also be useful for the user to define additional values, besides the examples present in the specification, to the parameters to be tested.

Also, some external dependencies can introduce delays when running on test cases (Bowes, 2017). For that reason, it is important to mock these dependencies (Bowes, 2017). Being so, future research on the Test API must consider the creation of mocks for testability.

CONCLUSION

Documentation and software tests are critical components of any API. Also, an API specification used in a design driven approach can be useful to improve software quality in a web API. Acting as a contract for the API it can guarantee that API components, such as documentation and client code, can rely on that source, since every change on the specification will be reflected in the API and all its components.

As API specifications may not be coherent with the back-end implementation, acceptance tests can be created to test the interconnection between the API and its specification. The generation of all the mentioned artifacts can bring significative reduction of maintenance expenses.

Although there are already many open source tools implementing OpenAPI Specification, like Swagger UI and Swagger Code Generator, there is a lack of open source tools to generate software tests. For that reason, this chapter proposed a solution to overcome this problem, capable of successfully generating acceptance tests. Yet, it is important to note that it is still necessary to do other types of software tests and manual testing. The intent of the presented solution is not to replace these tests but rather guaranteeing that the specification is always coherent with the back-end implementation.

For E-goi's public API, this work will avoid documentation and client libraries to become obsolete, which was one of the biggest problems faced by clients. Tests will also play an important role, since they will force the API to follow its definition every time the API evolves. Also, this work brings benefits to E-goi developers, as all the mentioned artifacts are generated dynamically through the specification, without much effort.

ACKNOWLEDGMENT

This research was supported by E-goi, since the company provided hardware and facilities to the researchers.

REFERENCES

Abelló Gamazo, A., Ayala Martínez, C. P., Farré Tost, C., Gómez Seoane, C., Oriol Hilari, M., & Romero Moral, Ó. (2017). A Data-driven approach to improve the process of data-intensive API creation and evolution. In *International Conference on Advanced Information Systems Engineering (CAiSE 2017)* (pp. 1-8). Essen, Germany: CEUR-WS.org.

Amannejad, Y. a. (2014). A Search-Based Approach for Cost-Effective Software Test Automation Decision Support and an Industrial Case Study. In *Software Testing, Verification and Validation Workshops (ICSTW), 2014 IEEE Seventh International Conference on* (pp. 302-311). Cleveland, OH: IEEE.

Apiary. (2017). *API Blueprint*. Retrieved from GitHub: https://github.com/apiaryio/api-blueprint

Bowes, D. a. (2017). How good are my tests? In *Emerging Trends in Software Metrics (WETSoM), 2017 IEEE/ACM 8th Workshop on* (pp. 9-14). Buenos Aires: IEEE.

Costa, B. a. (2014). Evaluating a Representational State Transfer (REST) Architecture: What is the Impact of REST in My Architecture? In *Software Architecture (WICSA), 2014 IEEE/IFIP Conference on* (pp. 105-114). Sydney: IEEE.

De, B. (2017). API Management. In B. De (Ed.), *API Management* (pp. 15–28). Berkeley, CA: Apress. doi:10.1007/978-1-4842-1305-6_2

ErnstFriedman, J. (2017). *Open API Initiative Announces Release of the OpenAPI Spec v3 Implementer's Draft*. Retrieved from Open API Initiative: https://www.openapis.org/blog/2017/03/01/openapi-spec-3-implementers-draft-released

Fielding, R. T. (2000). *Architectural Styles and the Design of Network-based Software Architectures* (Doctoral dissertation). University of California, Irvine, CA.

Finsterwalder, M. (2001). Automating acceptance tests for GUI applications in an extreme programming environment. *Proceedings of the 2nd International Conference on eXtreme Programming and Flexible Processes in Software Engineering*, 114-117.

Garlan, D. a. (1993). An Introduction to Software Architecture. In *Advances in Software Engineering and Knowledge Engineering* (pp. 1–39). World Scientific. doi:10.1142/9789812798039_0001

Garousi, V., & Felderer, M. (2016). Developing, verifying and maintaining high-quality automated test scripts. *IEEE Software*, *33*(3), 68–75. doi:10.1109/MS.2016.30

Hotomski, S. a. (2018). Keeping Evolving Requirements and Acceptance Tests Aligned with Automatically Generated Guidance. In *International Working Conference on Requirements Engineering: Foundation for Software Quality* (pp. 247-264). Springer. 10.1007/978-3-319-77243-1_15

Limoncelli, T. A. (2018). Documentation is Automation. *Communications of the ACM, 61*(6), 48–53. doi:10.1145/3190572

Massé, M. (2011). *REST API Design Rulebook: Designing Consistent RESTful Web Service Interfaces.* O'Reilly Media, Inc.

Meng, M. a. (2017). Application Programming Interface Documentation: What Do Software Developers Want? *Journal of Technical Writing and Communication.*

Montandon, J. E. (2013). Documenting apis with examples: Lessons learned with the apiminer platform. In *Reverse Engineering (WCRE), 2013 20th Working Conference on* (pp. 401-408). Koblenz: IEEE.

Mulloy, B. (2013). *Web API design.* Academic Press.

Nasehi, S. M. (2012). What makes a good code example? A study of programming Q&A in StackOverflow. In *Software Maintenance (ICSM), 2012 28th IEEE International Conference on* (pp. 23-34). Trento: IEEE.

Open API Initiative. (2017). *OpenAPI Specification.* Retrieved from GitHub: https://github.com/OAI/OpenAPI-Specification/blob/master/versions/3.0.1.md

Open API Initiative. (2018). *OpenAPI Specification.* Retrieved from GitHub: https://github.com/OAI/OpenAPI-Specification

Pinkham, R. (2017). *What Is the Difference Between Swagger and OpenAPI?* Retrieved from Swagger: https://swagger.io/blog/difference-between-swagger-and-openapi/

Preston-Werner, T. (n.d.). *Semantic Versioning 2.0.0.* Retrieved from Semantic Versioning 2.0.0: https://semver.org/spec/v2.0.0.html

RAML. (2018). *The RESTful API Modeling Language (RAML) Spec.* Retrieved from Github: https://github.com/raml-org/raml-spec

Richardson, L. A. (2013). *RESTful Web APIs: Services for a Changing World.* O'Reilly Media, Inc.

Robillard, M. P., & DeLine, R. (2011). A field study of API learning obstacles. *Empirical Software Engineering, 16*(6), 703–732. doi:10.100710664-010-9150-8

Schwichtenberg, S. A. (2017). From Open API to Semantic Specifications and Code Adapters. In *Web Services (ICWS), 2017 IEEE International Conference on* (pp. 484-491). Honolulu, HI: IEEE.

Sohan, S., Anslow, C., & Maurer, F. (2015). A case study of web API evolution. In *2015 IEEE World Congress on Services* (pp. 245-252). New York: IEEE. 10.1109/SERVICES.2015.43

Swagger. (2018a). *Swagger Code Generator*. Retrieved from Github: https://github.com/swagger-api/swagger-codegen/tree/3.0.0

Swagger. (2018b). *Swagger UI*. Retrieved from Github: https://github.com/swagger-api/swagger-ui

Tassey, G. (2002). *The economic impacts of inadequate infrastructure for software testing*. National Institute of Standards and Technology.

Uddin, G., & Robillard, M. P. (2015). How API documentation fails. *IEEE Software*, *32*(4), 68–75. doi:10.1109/MS.2014.80

Vlissides, J. A. (1995). *Design patterns: Elements of reusable object-oriented software*. Reading, MA: Addison-Wesley.

Webber, J. A. (2010). *REST in practice: Hypermedia and systems architecture*. O'Reilly Media, Inc. doi:10.1007/978-3-642-15114-9_3

Yusifoğlu, V. G. (2015). Software test-code engineering: A systematic mapping. *Information and Software Technology*, *58*, 123–147. doi:10.1016/j.infsof.2014.06.009

ADDITIONAL READING

Garousi, V., & Küçük, B. (2018). Smells in software test code: A survey of knowledge in industry and academia. Journal of Systems and Software, 138, 52-81.Hunter, K. L. (2017). *Irresistible APIs: designing web APIs that developers will love*. Manning Publ.

Hotomski, S., Charrada, E. B., & Glinz, M. (2017, September). Aligning Requirements and Acceptance Tests via Automatically Generated Guidance. In *2017 IEEE 25th International Requirements Engineering Conference Workshops (REW)* (pp. 339-342). IEEE.

Hylli, O., Ruokonen, A., Mäkitalo, N., & Systä, K. (2016, December). Orchestrating the Internet of Things Dynamically. In *Proceedings of the 1st International Workshop on Mashups of Things and APIs* (p. 4). ACM.

Myers, G. J., Sandler, C., & Badgett, T. (2011). *The art of software testing*. John Wiley & Sons.

Peng, C., & Bai, G. (2018). Using Tag based Semantic Annotation to empower Client and REST Service Interaction. In *the 3rd International Conference on Complexity, Future Information Systems and Risk (COMPLEXIS 2018)* (pp. 64-71).

Surwase, V. (2016). REST API Modeling Languages-A Developer's Perspective. *IJSTE-International Journal of Science Technology & Engineering, 2*(10), 634–637.

KEY TERMS AND DEFINITIONS

Acceptance Tests: Software tests that verify if the requirements defined by a customer are achieved.

API: Set of tools to create applications that access other services.

API Design First: Methodology where the API is designed, producing a document which will serve as basis for implementation.

API Specification: Document that contains all important information about a web API and reflects its behavior.

Automated Software Testing: Tests that are controlled by a software and can be repeated periodically.

RESTful: Capability of applying REST architectural style.

Web API: API available in the web.

APPENDIX 1

Below, it is presented in full the OpenAPI specification, in its 3.0.1 version, used as example along this chapter, written in YAML.

```
openapi: 3.0.1
info:
title: Public API
description: New E-goi's public API
termsOfService: https://e-goi.com
contact:
 name: (+351) 300 404 336
license:
 name: E-goi
version: 1.0.0
servers:
- url: https://api.e-goi.com/rest
paths:
/lists:
 get:
 tags:
 - Lists
 summary: Get all lists
 description: Returns all lists
 operationId: GetAllLists
 parameters:
 - $ref: '#/components/parameters/limit'
 responses:
 200:
 description: OK
 content:
 application/json:
 schema:
 type: array
 items:
 $ref: '#/components/schemas/list'
 post:
 tags:
 - Lists
 summary: Create list
```

```
description: Creates and returns a list
operationId: CreateList
requestBody:
content:
application/json:
schema:
$ref: '#/components/schemas/listRequest'
responses:
200:
description: OK
content:
application/json:
schema:
$ref: '#/components/schemas/list'
/lists/{id}:
get:
tags:
- Lists
summary: Get list by id
description: Returns a list given its id
operationId: GetList
parameters:
- $ref: '#/components/parameters/id'
responses:
200:
description: OK
content:
application/json:
schema:
$ref: '#/components/schemas/list'
put:
tags:
- Lists
summary: Update list
description: Updates and returns a list
operationId: UpdateList
parameters:
- $ref: '#/components/parameters/id'
requestBody:
content:
```

```
application/json:
schema:
$ref: '#/components/schemas/listRequest'
responses:
200:
description: OK
content:
application/json:
schema:
$ref: '#/components/schemas/list'
delete:
tags:
- Lists
summary: Deletes a list
description: Deletes a list given its id
operationId: DeleteList
parameters:
- $ref: '#/components/parameters/id'
responses:
'204':
description: OK
security:
- Apikey: []
components:
parameters:
 limit:
 name: limit
 in: query
 description: Number of items to return
 required: false
 schema:
 type: integer
 minimum: 1
 example: 20
 id:
 name: id
 in: path
 description: Unique numeric identifier
 required: true
 schema:
```

```
     type: integer
     minimum: 1
   schemas:
    list:
    description: Success response schema for this operation
    properties:
    id:
    description: Id of the list
    type: integer
    title:
    description: Title of the list
    type: string
    example: Title
    status:
    description: Status of the list
    type: string
    enum:
    - active
    - inactive
    - blocked
    example: active
    listRequest:
    description: Request schema for this operation
    properties:
    title:
    description: Title of the list
    type: string
    example: Title
   securitySchemes:
    Apikey:
    type: apiKey
    name: Apikey
    in: header
```

APPENDIX 2

Below, it is shown a full OpenAPI Specification 2.0 (formerly known as Swagger Specification), written in YAML, used to generating client code libraries along with Swagger Code Generator.

```
swagger: '2.0'
info:
  contact:
    name: (+351) 300 404 336
  description: New E-goi's public API
  license:
    name: E-goi
  termsOfService: 'https://e-goi.com'
  title: Public API
  version: 1.0.0
host: api.e-goi.com
basePath: /rest
schemes:
  - https
paths:
  /lists:
    get:
      parameters:
        - description: Number of items to return
          in: query
          minimum: 1
          name: limit
          required: false
          type: integer
      responses:
        '200':
          description: OK
          schema:
            items:
              $ref: '#/definitions/list'
            type: array
      tags:
        - Lists
```

```
      description: Returns all lists
      operationId: GetAllLists
      summary: Get all lists
   post:
     parameters:
       - in: body
         name: body
         schema:
           $ref: '#/definitions/listRequest'
     responses:
       '200':
         description: OK
         schema:
           $ref: '#/definitions/list'
     tags:
       - Lists
     description: Creates and returns a list
     operationId: CreateList
     summary: Create list
 '/lists/{id}':
   delete:
     parameters:
       - description: Unique numeric identifier
         in: path
         minimum: 1
         name: id
         required: true
         type: integer
     responses:
       '204':
         description: OK
     tags:
       - Lists
     description: Deletes a list given its id
     operationId: DeleteList
     summary: Deletes a list
   get:
     parameters:
       - description: Unique numeric identifier
```

```
          in: path
          minimum: 1
          name: id
          required: true
          type: integer
      responses:
        '200':
          description: OK
          schema:
            $ref: '#/definitions/list'
      tags:
        - Lists
      description: Returns a list given its id
      operationId: GetList
      summary: Get list by id
    put:
      parameters:
        - description: Unique numeric identifier
          in: path
          minimum: 1
          name: id
          required: true
          type: integer
        - in: body
          name: body
          schema:
            $ref: '#/definitions/listRequest'
      responses:
        '200':
          description: OK
          schema:
            $ref: '#/definitions/list'
      tags:
        - Lists
      description: Updates and returns a list
      operationId: UpdateList
      summary: Update list
definitions:
  list:
```

```
      description: Success response schema for this operation
      properties:
        id:
          description: Id of the list
          type: integer
        status:
          description: Status of the list
          enum:
            - active
            - inactive
            - blocked
          type: string
        title:
          description: Title of the list
          type: string
  listRequest:
    description: Request schema for this operation
    properties:
      title:
        description: Title of the list
        type: string
securityDefinitions:
  Apikey:
    in: header
    name: Apikey
    type: apiKey
security:
  - Apikey: []
x-components:
  parameters:
    id:
      description: Unique numeric identifier
      in: path
      minimum: 1
      name: id
      required: true
      type: integer
    limit:
      description: Number of items to return
```

```
in: query
minimum: 1
name: limit
required: false
type: integer
```

Chapter 2
Structural Coverage Analysis Methods

Parnasi Retasbhai Patel
Charotar University of Science and Technology, India

Chintan Bhatt
Charotar University of Science and Technology, India

ABSTRACT

Structural coverage analysis for any code is a very common approach to measure the quality of any test suit. Structural coverage determines which structure of the software or which portion is not exercised. This chapter describes two different phases to achieve structural coverage analysis using DO-178B/C standards. Statement coverage is the very basic coverage criteria which involves execution of all the executable statements in the source code at least once. Analysis of structural coverage can be done by capturing the amount of code that is covered by the airborne software. The first phase contains the instrumentation procedure which instruments the source code at execution time, and the second phase is generating a report that specifies which portion of source code is executed and which one is not in the form of a percentage.

1. INTRODUCTION

Software is the crucial thing which is used everywhere in our society from education to medical and business. Some of the devices are operatable on basis of softwares. In order to increase the quality, software testing is important. Testing is one of the most important phase of software life cycle. Software testing is a process of finding errors to reduce the damage and improve the reliability, dependency and quality

DOI: 10.4018/978-1-5225-7455-2.ch002

of software (Zander, Schieferdecker, & Mosterman, 2011). Different standards are provided to check the criticality of software.

From the last few decades, control and coverage have been employed in most of functional areas of aerospace industries including navigation, flight control and other avionics softwares. Testing of developed code is core part of software development to protect civil aviation safety and reliability of software for airborne equipments. It is most important to check the correctness and accuracy of code for any software to avoid software failures and accidents. Each requirement contains one or more test-cases to prove its correctness.

DO-178B/C and DO-278 are used to assure safety of avionics software and control systems. DO-178B/C provides guidance and standards for software development, verification, configuration management and the interface to approval authorities. It prescribes a procedure which is being followed in the software development of airborne systems by developers. Based on a safety criteria DO-178B provides different levels which are shown in Table 1.

2. TESTING TECHNIQUES

Testing involves mainly two techniques such as black box testing and white box testing.

2.1 Black Box Testing

In this type of testing only functional specifications are required. Internal software structure is not required in this kind of software testing strategy.

Table 1. Levels according to failure conditions

Level	Failure Conditions	Coverage Criteria
A	Catastrophic failure condition or cascading system failure	MC/DC, Branch & Statement Coverage
B	Hazardous failure condition	Branch & Statement Coverage
C	Major system failure	Statement Coverage
D	Minor system failure	None
E	No effect on system	None

2.2 White Box Testing

In this type of testing, all requirements with functional specifications are required along with proper knowledge of software or system. White box testing is also known as structural testing or glass box testing which involves structural coverage criteria which are further discussed. Structural coverage analysis is one of the testing methods of white box testing.

From given figure testing is mainly divided into two parts from that one is static testing and second is dynamic testing. Static testing further divided into a static analysis, data flow, control flow, inspection and technical reviews. Dynamic Testing divided into main three parts from that first is structural testing, second is specification testing and third is experience based testing.

Structural testing again divided in statement coverage, branch coverage, MC/DC coverage, path coverage, function coverage and line coverage.

Specification testing divided into boundary value analysis testing, decision table & use-case testing.

Experience-based testing is divided into two parts from first is error guessing and second is exploratory testing.

Figure 1. White box testing taxonomy

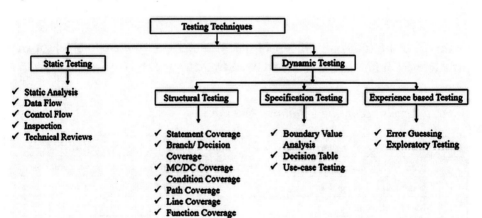

3. STRUCTURAL COVERAGE

Structural Coverage determines that which structure of the software or which portion is not exercised. Structural Coverage Analysis for any test code is one of the approaches to measure the quality of any test suit. Depending upon the RTCA standards, DO-178B defines different software quality assurance levels for structural coverage. Table 2 describes different types of structural coverage according to DO-178B levels.

There are three main different metrics/ criteria considered within DO-178B which are considered as Statement coverage, Decision coverage & Modified Condition/Decision coverage. Figure 2 shows all three coverage criteria with their level importance prescribed by DO-178B standards.

3.1 Statement Coverage

Statement coverage is a criteria which involves execution of all exercised statements at execution time of test suit at least once.

Machine instructions are considered as a statement for any test suit which is written in assembly language.

Table 2. Software quality assurance levels for structural coverage

Level	Coverage Criteria	Measures
A, B, C	Statement Coverage	Each statement of source code is evaluated
A, B	Branch/ Decision Coverage	Each branch condition/decision is evaluated
A	Modified Condition/Decision Coverage (MC/DC)	Every entry and exit points are evaluated Each branch & each condition in decision are evaluated

Figure 2. Structural coverage levels described by DO-178B standards

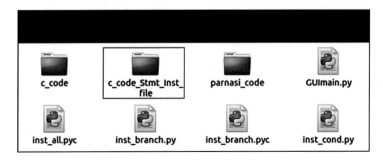

Statement coverage gives the outcome in form of percentage in a manner of executed statements from the total number of statements of test suit. Achieving higher statement coverage is related to increase software reliability.

3.2 Branch and Decision Coverage

Decision coverage is considered as each and every entry point and exit point of test suite has been exercised at least once ate execution time. Every decision in the source code has considered all possible at least once.

All branches are tested at least once. Statement coverage does not provide a solution for branches or multiple conditions which is solved in branch coverage. Boolean expressions are tested in branch coverage.

A decision without a Boolean operator is considered as a condition. If a condition appears more than once in a decision, each possibility considers as a specific condition.

3.3 Modified Condition and Decision Coverage (MC/DC)

MC/DC can be defined as,

- Every entry and exit point of test suit has been exercised at least once at execution time.
- Every condition within a decision has been taken all possible outcomes at least once.
- Every decision in test suit has been taken all possible outcomes at least once.
- Each condition within a decision has been shown independently in decision's outcomes.

3.4 Calculate a Structural Coverage

The structural coverage can be calculated as below given equation which is for statement coverage. It is same for branch and MC/DC coverage according to their executed branches and conditions with decision outcomes.

Box 1.

$$Structural\ Coverage = \frac{Number\ of\ Executed\ Statements * 100}{Total\ Number\ of\ Statements}$$

Consider a following example,
Test Code:

```
1.if (A > 1) && (B = 0)
2.      C:= C / A;
3.if (C = 2) || (B > 1)
4.      C:= C + 1;
```

Scenario 1

By selecting $A = 2$, $B = 0$, and $C = 4$ as input to this code suit, each statement is executed and exercised at least once as below:

$C: = C/A$

$C: = 4/2 = 2$

Now z's new value is 2 so another if condition becomes true and exercised like,

$C:= C+1 = 3$

So here, Statement Coverage $= 4/4 *100 = 100\%$
Here we get 100% statement coverage because every line is exercised at list once.

Scenario 2

But now if we consider $C = 5$ as input than only first two statements are executed because for A=2 and B=0, the 'if' condition becomes true but for C=5 it becomes false so only statement 1 & 2 are executed, but that does not determine that statement 3 & 4 are not exercised.

$C: = C/A$

$C: = 5/2 = 2.5$

So here, Statement Coverage $= 2/4 *100 = 50\%$
Here we get 50% statement coverage because half of the code lines are exercised.
Branch Coverage/ Decision coverage required two test cases from which one is for a true outcome and another is for a false outcome. In above example [(C=2)

or (B>1)], test cases (FF) and (TF) will bring the decision outcome between true and false. Here (B>1) is not tested in scenario-1 so coverage is not 100% coverage.

It gives 50% of coverage for scenario-1 and scenario-2 both.

In MC/DC, each condition gives independent effect to the outcome. Here minimum n+1 test case is there for n inputs. For above example [(C=2) or (B>1)], so we have minimum three test cases such as (TF), (FT), (FF).

Consider one other real-time example in which a flight has four engines and all four have to work properly to take off the flight.

The self-check module will check the status of all four engines of flight and then return if the flight can take off. The flight must be able to take off with at least one of the engine-1 or engine-2 and one of the engine-3 or engine-4 on.

Test Code:

```
int takeoff(int e1, int e2, int e3, int e4){
                            if (e1 || e2) && (e3||e4)
{
                                return 1;
                                }
                            else {
                                return 0;
                                }
                            }
```

Test cases are required to get 100% structural coverage are specified in below Table 3. These test cases are derived from the same procedure which is discussed above for all three coverage criteria such as only one test case is required for statement coverage as it checks only statements of test code, two test cases are required for branch coverage as they check both TRUE and FALSE outcome of test code and five test cases are required for MC/DC coverage as it contains n+1 test cases.

Table 4 specify all its five test cases which determined for MC/DC coverage for all four engines.

Table 3. Required test cases according structural criteria

Coverage Criteria	% of Coverage	Required Test Cases
Statement Coverage	100%	1
Branch Coverage	100%	2
MC/DC Coverage	100%	5

Table 4. Test cases to get 100% coverage for MC/DC

Test Case	Engine 1	Engine 2	Engine 3	Engine 4	Result
1	1	0	1	0	1
2	1	0	0	1	1
3	0	1	0	1	1
4	1	0	0	0	0
5	0	0	0	1	0

4. LITERATURE SURVEY

DO-178B provides guidance to developers for getting certification for airborne systems and equipment with software requirement suit. A number of documents are available for structural coverage.

The primary objective of structural coverage analysis verifies all requirements and determines which portion of test suit is exercised and which is not. DO-178B provides different criticality levels that must be achieved by any test software. In structural coverage, automated test data generation is a most important feature of software testing procedure. Structural coverage testing can be done using following testing methods:

- Concolic Testing
- Random Testing
- Search Based Testing
- Control Flow Testing

According to Rapita system ltd., who publishes a white paper: "Seven Roadblocks to 100% Structural Coverage (and how to avoid them)", specify the number of reasons that why it may not be possible to achieve 100% structural coverage. In practice, these usually conspire to make it very rare to achieve full coverage. To reduced effort for certification activities, different tools offer different file format like CSV, text, XML, HTML files (RAPITA Systems Ltd, n.d.).

Requirement-Based Testing (RBT) is one of the structural coverage techniques. RBT is used to achieve structural coverage testing by a combination of requirement based testing outcomes and their coverage analysis. The code which is not covered is analyzed using a number of other criteria. This combination of testing results and analysis provides the actual structural coverage (Gifford, 1996).

According to Zhu's software test units for coverage, they have main two program groups. These two program groups are based on the structural criteria of different test adequacy. First is the control flow criteria and second is data flow criteria. These two kinds of criteria are combined and extended to give another dependent coverage criteria. Most sufficient criteria for both of these group is flow graph model of program structure. However, a few control flow criteria are defined as test requirements in terms of code rather than using any other software abstract model (Zhu, Hall, & May, 1997).

According to Namin's, they provide a solution in which they determine how the size of code and coverage both are individually given their impact on the test suit for overall software. They generate different test suits of some fixed size and measures the relationship between coverage and fixed size of test suits. Increasing test suit's size which direct cause to achieve higher efficiency and higher coverage outcomes (Namin & Kakarla, 2011).

According to the CarFast's approach, they measure the speed with statement coverage, is achieved both in the number of test runs of the application under test the AUT test with multiple test case inputs such as multiple time execute the same application with different input test cases and measures their execution time. While the passed time provides the absolute value of the time it takes to reach a certain level of coverage. Measuring the number of iterations, which essentially means that achieving coverage goals with a number of test cases (Park, Hussain, Taneja, Mainul Hossain, Grechanik, & Quing Xie, 2012).

According to Komal Anand, she develops an approach in which MC/DC coverage increase automatically. She used Concolic tester tool (CREST) and a transformer (SOP) which based on a sum of the product. She provides main four steps in her mechanism in which one part include Modified Quine McCluskey method which is applied to it. It is a method to manual minimize a Boolean function and improve a performance. She calculated MC/DC for C code and got variation of MC/DC coverage up to 3.81% (Anand, 2014).

According to Arun Kumar Sahani, he proposed a framework to improve analysis for branch coverage based on Java programs. He provides working principles for Java program code transformer and JCUTE of a framework. According to his results, this tool provides 17.21% more branch coverage than existing available tools. This branch coverage is covered with an average time of 28156.9 milliseconds of computations. But his concept was not in distributed manner because computation time must be less in a distributed manner which is one of the main concepts in a real-time application. He also has to develop a transformer which performs independently.

This tool performs only for branch coverage so he mentioned MC/DC coverage to the module as a future work (Sahani, 2015).

According to authors, they optimized test cases by using CFG (Control Flow Graph) in which they covering source code so that all possible paths which contain Boolean expressions and conditions are covered and according to that new test cases can be generated. In this approach, test cases are automatically generated and reduce a cost and effort of testing the procedure. In their first step, they generate test cases randomly and then apply the genetic algorithm on them. The genetic algorithm produces new optimized test cases. A particular set of test cases detects faults from source code as much as they can. It also improves a quality of test cases. In future may be genetic algorithm is used to make every technique which is used in testing. Only one disadvantage is the whole mechanism developed for branch and conditional coverage. It cannot be able to perform and generate test cases for MC/DC coverage (Srivastaval & Dwivedi, 2015).

According to all the authors, they specify in the paper that they got the minimum data sets to satisfy MC/DC coverage criteria based on a decision tree concept. They provide a genetic algorithm which is able to solve all the problems which are occurred while generating a data. After examination of the result, they prove that their provided mechanism is more effective. Their mechanism was not well performed for more complex Boolean expressions and complex decisions so they provide a future enhancement as to improve an algorithm and genetic algorithm to get more effective results (Xin, Wei, Feng-yu, & Qi-jun, 2015).

According to authors, level-A has to undergo complex structural coverage analysis to ensure that code has to be used and fulfill the requirement based testing. They provide structural coverage analysis's main two particular issues from that first is source code to object code traceability and second is data coupling and control coupling analysis. They provide RT-tester source-code-to-object-code traceability analyzer (RTT-STO) and RT-tester data and control coupling analyzer (RTT-STO). These two are developed for low-level verification of avionics system's Airbus (Brauer, Dahlweid, & Peleska, 2015).

According to authors, they successfully measure the feasibility of test cases which are generated automatically from the functional requirements and testing a target software in avionics. They provide requirement based coverage criteria and automated procedure for functional requirement based testing. They provide their methods and integrated it with the testing procedure. Their developed tool is used for industrial case studies. As a future work, they want to implement the mechanism for reactive systems (Sun, Brain, Kroening, Hawthorn, Wilson, Schanda, Javier, Jimenez, Daniel, Bryan, & Broster, 2017).

According to authors, they evaluate a random testing technique to provide coverage according to MC/DC coverage criteria. They tested one hundred of logical expressions with different size. Also, generate 256 of test cases with a particular size in which they are from 2 to 1024 test cases and all are randomly generated. All these are evaluated using different structural coverage analysis tools such as CodeCover, TestWell CTC++ & CCM. They also derive that increment of test cases which are randomly generated also gives a high level of coverage for MC/DC coverage. Also, derived that the obtaining result can be useful for integration random testing to increase the effectiveness of software testing for all complex logical structures with all other approaches (Vilkomir, Alluri, Kuhn, & Kacker, 2017).

Basic Concepts

1. **Condition:** A Boolean statement which contains Boolean operators is called as a condition. It contains && (AND) and || (OR) and XOR Boolean operators within a statement.
2. **Decision:** A Boolean operator with zero, one or more than one Boolean operator can be considered as a decision. We can also be called it as a predicate. If a decision has 0 Boolean operators than it can be considered as a Condition.
3. **Group Condition:** A Boolean expression which contains more than one conditions and which are comparable with each other are considered as group condition.

Example:

Expression ((A == 1) && (B>4)) || ((C<10) && (D == 0)).

Here four conditions are used separately.

Coverage Terminologies

1. **Instrumentation:** Instrumentation is the process to insert an additional test suit to the input test suit at the execution time to determine some information or data which is used to get structural coverage.

Instrumentation can be done at source level or object level instrumentation which done before the execution of test suits. Instrumentation can also be done at execution time but it is rarely used to obtain details for coverage report.

2. **Merge:** Ability to run test suit in different environments in different parts and then combine all outcomes in coverage report is considered in the merge. Most of the coverage tools support offline merge feature.

5. FRAMEWORK OVERVIEW

Our framework is designed to be flexible and implement the statement and branch coverage test cases.

For Statement Coverage analysis the ideal infrastructure would be considered as:

1. Probe Instrumentation
2. Deployment of Structured Code Coverage instrumented application
3. Automatically collect coverage data during execution
4. Merge & Final Report generation

Basic functionalities are shown in Figure 3:

In step-1, assume that a tester gives a C folder as an input file which is parsed by the parser which automatically generates three new log files along with one main instrumented code file.

In step-2, coverage report is generated. This is done using the previously generated instrumented file and log files.

Here we have two different parsers are used from which one is for instrumentation procedure to parse the original file and another is to parse the instrumented file for generating a report. Coverage reports can be generated for each file of the folder. Consider the figure 4.

5.1 Probe Instrumentation Technique

Instrumentation is done at the beginning of any function definition /condition declaration. Consider the Figure 5 which describes the instrumentation procedure for our approach for statement coverage. In this procedure, tester gives a C file as input to the mechanism described for statement coverage in section 5.2.

Figure 3. Basic functionalities

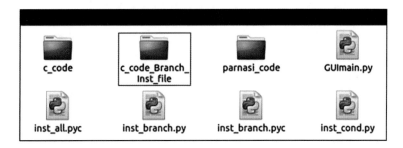

Figure 4. Framework for structural coverage

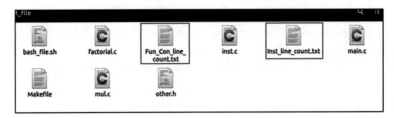

Figure 5. Process of instrumentation

```
#include<string.h>
#include<stdio.h>
#include "other.h"
int main()
{
int a, b;
char operator;
printf("Insert two numbers: ");
scanf("%d %d", &a, &b);
        if (a>b || a==0|)
        {
        printf(" %d + %d = %d \n", a, b, sum(a, b));
        }
        else if (a<b)
        {
        printf(" %d * %d = %d \n", a, b, mul(a, b));
        }
        else
        {
        printf("Nothing.. ");
        }
return 0;
}
```

At the time of program compilation, a parser checks the function definition and condition declaration to insert an instrumented function after the next of function definition and condition declaration statements.

Here the instrumentation is done at the starting of the function definition and condition declaration to get the exact portion of that particular function or condition's criteria of a line of code. Here we apply a simple mechanism in which parser just check for function definition and condition declaration and if it found then add the instrumentation function to next of the line and if not then just pass for the report generation part.

Instrumentation function contains the logic of gathering a line count of executed probes. Using that probe count, we get the actual portion which is executed. At the run-time, there are three other log files are generated from which one file contains instrumented line counts, the second file contains function definition and condition declaration line counts and the third file contains brace match counts which are used to determine executed portion of test suit (Patel, Bhatt, & Talati, 2018).

Figure 6 illustrates this concept with a simple C program. Here two programs from which program(a) is the original 'C' code and program(b) is the instrumented code in which Ins_Probe(); is the instrumented function which is inserted at the execution time of the code. It gives the actual count number of executed line of the test suit at a run-time.

5.2 Report Generation

Report generation is the graphical representation of test suit which differentiates the executed code and unexecuted code. Instrumented file with other log files is used to analyze the code with original source code and gives the actual output. Consider the Figure 7 which describes the process for generating a report. In this phase, tester has the one original C code folder, one instrumented code folder and other three

Figure 6. Example of probe instrumentation for C code

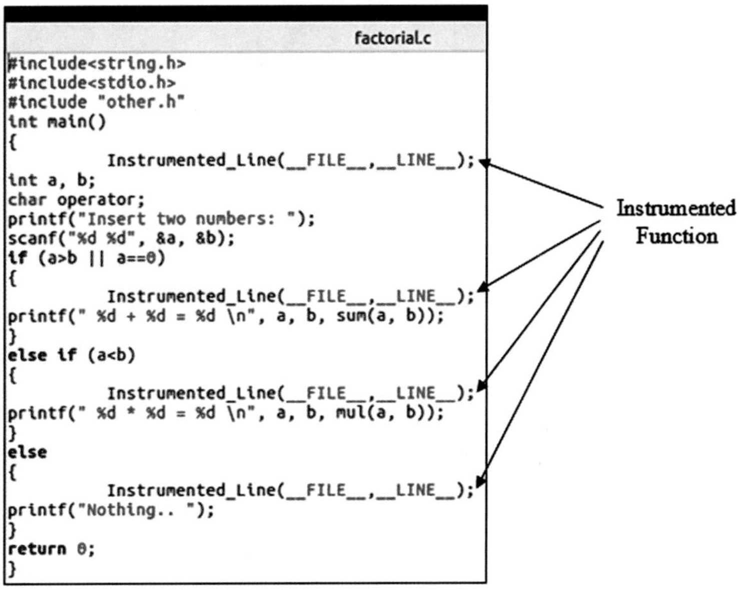

Figure 7. Process of generating a report

log files from which one contains the instrumented line counts which specify the instrumented line numbers which are further compared with executed instrumented counts, second contains the function definition/ condition declaration line counts and third contains executed probes line counts which give actually executed probes at the time of all program execution of input folder. Instrumented folder, instrumented line count file and function definition/ condition declaration line count files are parsed by the report parser which maps the counts of these files with original C code files.

At the time of instrumentation process, instrumentation is done by inserting a function at a particular location which gives the executed instrumented location in other files. This file is considered here as applied mechanism for given test suit. We get the report in the .html file format in which executed portion is displayed in green colour notation and an unexecuted portion is displayed in red colour notation. In HTML report format percentages are also shown which specifies that how much lines are executed in form of percentage at execution time (Patel, Bhatt, & Talati, 2018).

5.3 Analysis of Coverage

Above discussed procedure is a general mechanism for structural coverage analysis. Analysis of coverage is used to give obtained percentage by generated test cases. In our approach, this analysis is used to check that any other test cases are required or not for obtaining more coverage. Consider given algorithms used for generating coverage report and its analysis.

6. RESULT

Implementation of this structural coverage tool is done according to the procedure which we discussed in earlier sections.

Algorithm 1. Statement coverage analyser

```
Input: P, Test Suit                    // Folder containing
multiple C programs with test cases
Output: Statement Coverage        // Obtained % for statement
coverage
Begin
       /* Identifying location for probe Instrumentation */
for each statement in s ∈ P do
                    List_T ← line_count
                    if fun_con or looping_stmt or con_stmt
in s then
1.             s´ ← insert_fun (filename, line_count)
                    end if
end for
/* Run Instrumented Code & determine the Outcomes */
for probe-inst-stmt in s´ ∈ P do
2.       list1 ← line_count
                    for exe_line_count s ∈ P do
3.             list2 ← line_count
                             if list1 == list2 then
4.                       List_E ← line_count
                           end if
                    end for
end for
       /* Calculate Statement Coverage */
5.       Statement Coverage ← [Size(List_E)/Size(List_T)] × 100%
```

6.1 Basic GUI

Consider a figure 8 which contains a basic GUI of SCA tool. It contains main 3 options for coverage criteria.

- **Input Folder:** Select one folder as an input which contains multiple 'C' code files. Here we select "c_code" folder for instrumentation and report generation procedure.

Algorithm 2. Branch coverage analyser

```
Input: P, Test Suit                  // Folder containing
multiple C programs with test cases
Output: Branch Coverage       // Obtained % for branch
coverage
Begin
        /* Identifying location for probe Instrumentation */
for each statement in s є P do
        if && or || in s then
1.        s´ ← insert_fun (filename, line_count)
2.        list1 ← add_to_list(s)
end if
                end for
/* Run Instrumented Code & determine the Outcomes */
        for each predicate in list1 do
                for each condition in con є P do
                        if con evaluates to TRUE then
1.        True_flag ← TRUE
end if
        if con evaluates to FALSE then
2.                Flase_flag ← FALSE
end if
if both TRUE and FALSE flags are TRUE then
3.                List_E ← add_to_list(con)
end if
4.        List_T ← add_to_list(con)
                        end for
                end for
        /* Calculate Statement Coverage */
5.        Branch Coverage ← [Size(List_E)/Size(List_T)] × 100%
```

6.2 Instrumentation Procedure

Click on instrumentation button to create a new instrumented folder. After the instrumentation procedure new folder is generated which contains all instrumented files of original source programs.

Figure 8. Basic GUI

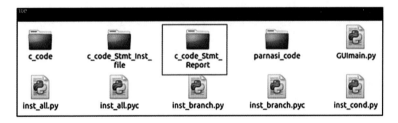

Figure 9. Select a folder

In Figure 10 and Figure 11 show both newly generated folders namely "c_code_Stmt_Inst_file" and "c_code_Branch_Inst_file". These both are generated for statement instrumentation and branch instrumentation respectively.

Instrumented folder contains other log files which are further used for report generation procedure. It also contains one log file which is used to execute an instrumented function from each instrumented 'C' files of the folder.

Below figure shows a difference between original source code and instrumented code of original code.

We can see the difference between the original source file and instrumented file by both the given figures, Figure 13 and Figure 14. In Figure 14 one new line

Figure 10. Instrumented folder for statement coverage

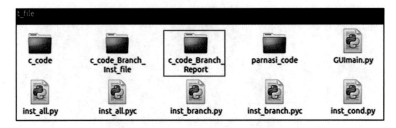

Figure 11. Instrumented folder for branch coverage

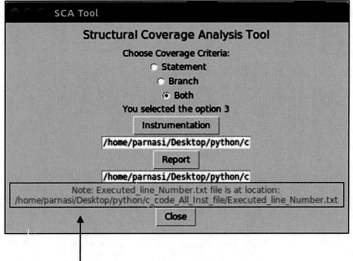

Shows path for an unknown or new user who wants to run a
code & generate a report of an already instrumented folder
without instrumentation procedure

Figure 12. Getting other log files with instrumented folder

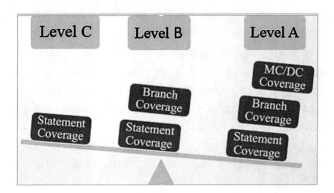

Figure 13. Original source code

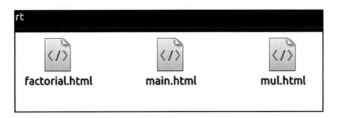

Figure 14. Instrumented code of original source code

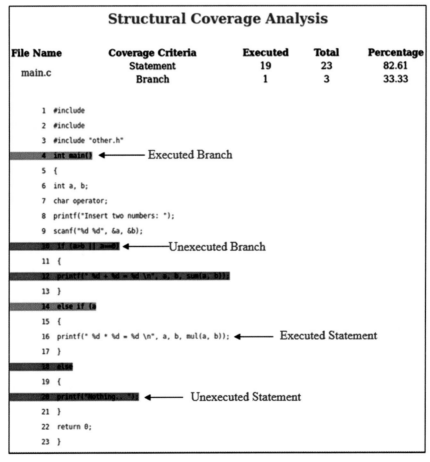

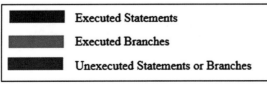

is inserted at a particular location which is one C function "Instrumented_Line(__FILE__,__LINE__)" and used to gather the information at run-time.

After the execution, we get the executed probe's log file which is shown in below figure with a red mark. This file contains line counts of all the executed probes along with its appropriate file name.

6.3 Generate Coverage Report

For coverage report select one 'C' folder

Click on report button to create new report folder. After the report generation, procedure new folder is generated which contains all .html files of original source programs.

From the Figure 17 and Figure 18, we can see that a new folder is generated at report generation phase which contains all html files of original source programs.

Both newly generated folders namely "c_code_Stmt_Report" and "c_code_Branch_Report". These both are generated for statement report and branch report folders respectively.

Figure 15. Getting executed probe file

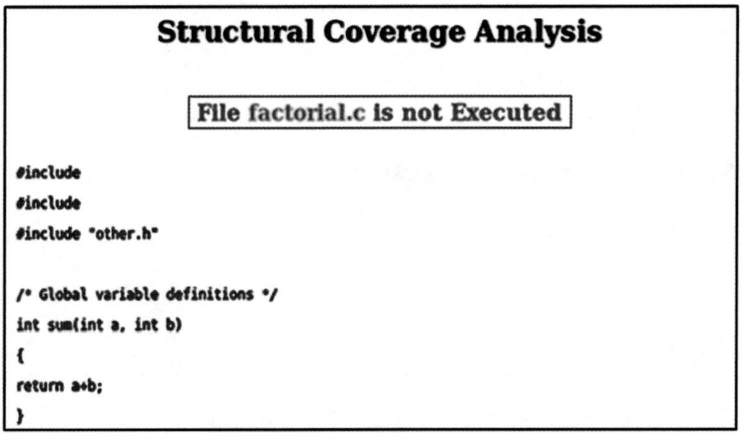
Structural Coverage Analysis
File factorial.c is not Executed
#include
#include
#include "other.h"
/* Global variable definitions */
int sum(int a, int b)
{
return a+b;
}

Figure 16. Selecting folder for report generation

Step: 1
Instrumentation
Step: 2
Generate Coverage
Report

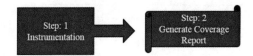

Figure 17. Report folder for statement coverage

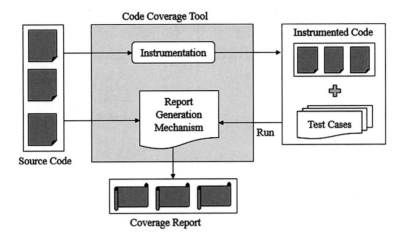

Figure 18. Report folder for branch coverage

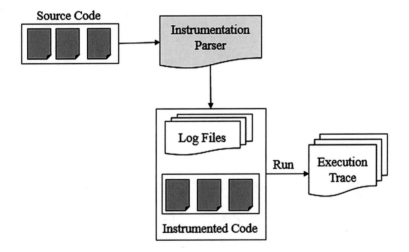

After the execution, SCA tool looks like a figure given below. Figure 19 shows the final GUI of SCA tool after completion of both phases.

Generated Report in HTML Format. Here below figure shows the ".html" files of original source code program files.

Consider Figure 21 which shows HTML file format.

Above figure shows one of the html file formats for both statement and branch coverage of original source code programs. Here "main.c" is one of the files from original C files. After the instrumentation and report generation phase html file is

Figure 19. SCA tool after the execution of test programs

(a) Original C code	(b) Instrumented C code:

If (condition)
    begin
      Proc1;
   end proc 1
else
    begin
   Proc2;
   end pr2c 1
(end if)
	If (condition)
	    begin
	       Ins_Probe();
	      Proc 1;
	     end proc 1
	  else
	       begin
	       Ins_Probe();
	       Proc 2;
	      end proc 2
	(end if)

Figure 20. HTML files

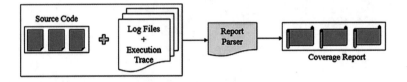

Figure 21. HTML file for statement and branch coverage

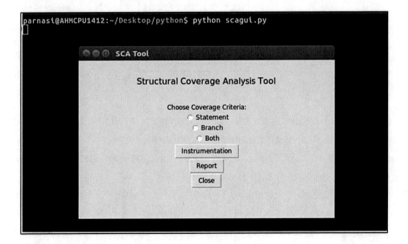

58

generated. Here percentage for statement coverage is 82.61% and for branch coverage, it is 33.33% shown in the outcome. The green code in below file indicates the code which is executed at run-time and redline code indicated as a not executed code at run-time. The yellow line indicates branches which are executed at run-time. A total number of branches and statements are also mentation in below file format.

Figure 22 shows the unexecuted file format. The file which is not executed at the time of execution, code of that file cannot be considered in coverage procedure.

7. CONCLUSION

The discussed procedure ensures that all the covered lines of test suit are given by statement coverage analysis and branches using branch coverage analysis and generate a coverage report. All the specified test cases described in the testing section are tested properly and get appropriate outcomes for statement and branch coverage.

The structural coverage analysis provides a sensible approach that balances the DO-178B requirements for structural coverage. Statement testing forces the developer to reason carefully before complete implementation of the design specification. It reveals an error in the hidden code but doesn't reveal missing code or statement.

Statement coverage doesn't reveal the missing statement or code. It specifies an error in the hidden code. It cannot provide the solution for branching conditions but these can be retrieved using branch coverage. Coverage is expensive in terms of both money and time required to perform testing in avionics software.

Figure 22. Not executed file

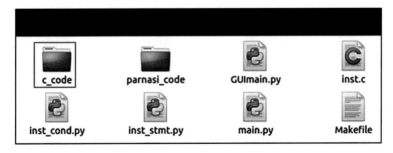

8. FUTURE ENHANCEMENT

All above-discussed procedure is done for statement coverage and branch coverage analysis.

Develop MC/DC coverage with their appropriate functionality and with the combination of these statement and branch coverage analysis.

Develop a mechanism to fulfill all the requirements for other two criteria such as decision coverage and MC/DC coverage and complete tasks which are listed below:

- Deactivated Code
- Impossible combinations of events
- Compiler-introduced errors

REFERENCES

Alemerian K. A., (2013). *Evaluation of Software Testing Coverage Tools: An Empirical Study*. Academic Press.

Anand, K. (2014). *Automatic Test Case Generation Using Modified Condition/Decision Coverage Testing* (Master's thesis). National Institute of Technology, Rourkela, India.

Bhatt, D. (2017). A Survey of Effective and Efficient Software Testing Technique and Analysis. *Iconic Research and Engineering Journals (IREJOURNALS)*.

Brauer, J., Dahlweid, M., & Peleska, J. (2015). *Tool-Supported Structural Coverage Analysis for DO-178C Compliant Software*. Academic Press.

Charles, O. (1997). *Application of test hypotheses to a definition of coverage* (Ph.D. thesis). Henri Poincare University - Nancy 1, Nancy, France.

DOT/FAA/AR-06/54. (2007). *Software Verification Tools Assessment Study*. Air Traffic Organization Operations Planning Office of Aviation Research and Development.

Gifford, W. (1996). Structural Coverage. *Analytical Methods*, 15.

Key benefits of Structural Coverage Analysis for DO-178B Systems. (n.d.). Retrieved from https://www.rapitasystems.com/blog/4_key_benefits_structural_coverage_DO-178B_systems

Li, N. (2014). *Evaluation of Modified Condition/Decision Coverage in Testing a Web Server* (Research thesis).

Namin, S., & Kakarla, S. (2011). The use of mutation in testing experiments and its sensitivity to external threats. *ISSTA*, 342–352.

Pachauri, A., & Srivastava, G. (2012). Program Test Data Generation for Branch Coverage with Genetic Algorithm: Comparative Evaluation of a Maximization and Minimization Approch, *ITCS, SIP, JSE-2012. CS & IT, 4*, 443–454.

Park, S., Hussain, I., Taneja, K., Mainul Hossain, B. M., Grechanik, M., & Xie, Q. C. F. (2012). *CarFast: Achieving Higher Statement Coverage Faster*. Retrieved from https://www.cs.uic.edu/~drmark/index_htm_files/CarFast.pdf

Patel, P., Bhatt, C., & Talati, D. (2018). Structural Coverage Analysis with DO-178B Standards. In *International Conference on Advanced Computing, Networking and Informatics (ICANI)*. Springer.

Rapita Systems. (n.d.). Retrieved from https://www.rapitasystems.com/

RAPITA Systems Ltd. (n.d.). *Seven Roadblocks to 100% Structural Coverage (and how to avoid them)*. Retrieved from https://www.danlawinc.com/wp-content/uploads/2016/12/MC-WP-007-51-LR-Roadblocks-to-100pc-Coverage.pdf

Sahani, A. K. (2015). *A Novel Approach to Improve Concolic Testing* (Master's thesis). National Institute of Technology, Rourkela, India.

Shahid, M., & Ibrahim, S. (2011). An Evaluation of Test Coverage Tools in Software Testing. *International Conference on Telecommunication Technology and Applications, Proc. of CSIT (IACSIT)*, 5.

Shelke, S., & Nagpure, S. (2014, July 1). The Study of Various Code Coverage Tools. *International Journal of Computer Trends and Technology*, *13*(1), 46–49. doi:10.14445/22312803/IJCTT-V13P110

Srivastaval, J., & Dwivedi, T. (2015). Software Testing Strategy approach on source code applying conditional coverage method. *International Journal of Software Engineering and Its Applications*, *6*(3), 25–31. doi:10.5121/ijsea.2015.6303

Statement and Branch Coverage Examples. (n.d.). Retrieved from https://www.istqb.guru/how-to-calculate-statement-branchdecision-and-path-coverage-for-istqb-exam-purpose

Statement Coverage in Software Testing. (n.d.). Retrieved from https://www.guru99.com/learn-statement-coverage.html

Structural Coverage Analysis for Safety-Critical Code. (n.d.). Retrieved from http://mys5.org/Proceedings/2015/Day_3/2015-S5-Day3_1415_Bhattacharya.pdf

Sun, Y., Brain, M., Kroening, D., Hawthorn, A., Wilson, T., Schanda, F., . . . Broster, I. (2017). *Functional Requirements-Based Automated Testing for Avionics*. arXiv:1707.01466v1

Szugyi, Z., & Porkolab, Z. (2013). Comparison of DC and MC/DC Code Coverages. *Proceedings of the Twelfth International Conference on Informatics*. 10.15546/aeei-2013-0050

Thakur, M. S. (2017). Review on Structural Software Testing Coverage Approaches. *International Journal of Advance research, Ideas and Innovations in Technology*, 281-286.

VectorCAST Interactive Tutorial. (n.d.). Retrieved from https://www.vectorcast.com/sites/default/files/downloads/pdf/vcast_interactive_tutorials.pdf

Vilkomir, S., Alluri, A., Kuhn, D. R., & Kacker, R. N. (2017). Combinatorial and MC/DC Coverage Levels of Random Testing. *IEEE International Conference*, 61-68. 10.1109/QRS-C.2017.19

Xin, F., Wei, Z., Feng-yu, Y., & Qi-jun, L. (2015). Test Data Automatic Generation Based on Modified Condition/Decision Coverage Criteria. *International Conference on Computer Science and Intelligent Communication (CSIC)*.

Zander, J., Schieferdecker, I. K., & Mosterman, P. (2011). Model-Based Testing for Embedded Systems. *Computational Analysis, Synthesis, and Design of Dynamic Systems.*

Zhu, H., Hall, P. A. V., & May, J. H. R. (1997). Software unit test coverage and adequacy. *ACM Computing Surveys*, 29(4), 366–427. doi:10.1145/267580.267590

Chapter 3

White–Box Testing Automation With SonarQube:
Continuous Integration, Code Review, Security, and Vendor Branches

Miguel Jorge Andrade
Polytechnic Institute of Porto, Portugal

ABSTRACT

Modern work patterns like continuous integration (CI) have an implicit need for testing automation. In current CI solutions, white-box testing is left to the work methodology, typically addressed after code reviews. Code security inspection is often done in specific code reviews focusing on security. SonarQube is a tool that, to a certain extent, can automate white-box design and testing and serve as a guide for formal code reviews. Moreover, this tool can help audit the code for potential security issues. Most web programming today uses components readily available and transparently managed by package managers, like npm for Node.js or Composer for PHP. This use must also be audited at least for potential security problems; yet traditional white-box test design would require a good understanding of the vendor code, which can be difficult/impractical to achieve. This chapter will address SonarQube as a valuable tool to automate white-box and security testing and also provide suggestions on how to manage your vendor branches when there is a need to audit/change the vendor source code.

DOI: 10.4018/978-1-5225-7455-2.ch003

INTRODUCTION

Testing code has been one of the most recurring practices to assure software quality and is a fundamental pillar of any software development methodology. Today this can be regarded as a widespread and adopted practice (Kochhar, Bissyande, Lo, Jiang 2013). It is followed in about 50% of Open Source projects available in GitHub and is part of any syllabus on software engineering. Testing is mostly addressed by unit testing, and other Quality Assurance (QA) methodologies are usually delegated to the software development methodology. One of the most recognized and effective (McConnell, 2016) QA methods is code reviews, or "peer code reviews". Code reviews take time, and even if it's recognized that they will save time in the project lifetime, they are often postponed or even ignored in small projects.

Historically, white-box testing or, to a certain extent, static code analyses, require a team to be available at some point in time, to execute the code review task, make corrections and design new tests, based on the code knowledge and project propose (Ostrand, 2002). On a Continuous Integration (CI) project and specifically in a Continuous Delivery project this action should be done more often, but this would be frequently infeasible, either to have a team reviewing each commit, or even if just reviewing before any production update.

This is where automated static code analysis is valuable (Zampetti, Scalabrino, Oliveto, Canfora, Penta, 2017).

There are several tools available that can help developers, language specific tools, multi-language tools and also on-line services. This chapter will address one specific tool, SonarQube. Other tools could be used to obtain the same results: hopefully the insights gained on analyzing a specific tool can also be helpful on addressing the same workflows with other tools, or assist in designing custom tools.

SonarQube provides preconfigured rules that check committed code to look for "code smells" and other patterns like potential bugs or security issues. These are just to detect potential problems, they do not assure a real problem exist, yet these rules can be combined to "score" a potential problematic commit, and force the build to fail. These rules can be independently written, but often they are sourced from a rules repository. These repositories are categorized by programming language and function. As an example, a project manager can enforce a certain indentation or code style for a project. In SonarQube These rules have associated an expected problem resolution time, which can be added to achieve a "technical debt" measure for the project. These analyses can be automated and triggered by commits in a CI environment. Different sets of rules, called "Quality Profiles", can be applied depending on the nature of the project. A second SonarQube concept is the "Quality Gate". This is an aggregation of several computed measures, like the number of code smells, total technical debt, the severity of issues found, code coverage on new code, etc. The project manager can define thresholds on these measures to pass or fail the project, making the build pass or fail accordingly.

This chapter will be focusing on how to use SonarQube in an automated manner, specifically addressing analysis on security, and how to deal with code from vendor branches.

SonarQube

SonarQube® software (previously called Sonar) is an Open Source quality management platform, dedicated to continuously analyze and measure technical quality, from project portfolio to method. It incorporates a plugin system for extension purposes. It is the main product of the Sonarsource company with headquarters in Geneva, Switzerland.

Architecture

The SonarQube Platform is made of 4 components (SonarQube, 2018):

1. One SonarQube Server starting 3 main processes:
    a. a Web Server for developers, managers to browse quality snapshots and configure the SonarQube instance
    b. a Search Server based on Elasticsearch to back searches from the UI
    c. a Compute Engine Server in charge of processing code analysis reports and saving them in the SonarQube Database
2. One SonarQube Database to store:
    a. the configuration of the SonarQube instance (security, plugins settings, etc.)
    b. the quality snapshots of projects, views, etc.
3. Multiple SonarQube Plugins installed on the server, possibly including language, SCM, integration, authentication, and governance plugins
4. One or more SonarQube Scanners running on your Build/Continuous Integration Servers to analyze projects

Integration

1. Developers code in their IDEs and use SonarLint to run local analysis.
2. Developers push their code into their favourite SCM: git, SVN, TFVC, ...
3. The Continuous Integration Server triggers an automatic build, and the execution of the SonarQube Scanner required to run the SonarQube analysis.

4. The analysis report is sent to the SonarQube Server for processing.

5. SonarQube Server processes and stores the analysis report results in the SonarQube Database, and displays the results in the UI.

6. Developers review, comment, challenge their Issues to manage and reduce their Technical Debt through the SonarQube UI.

7. Managers receive Reports from the analysis.

8. Ops use APIs to automate configuration and extract data from SonarQube.

9. Ops use JMX to monitor SonarQube Server.

Alternatives

There are several alternatives to SonarQube, a comprehensive list is available in Wikipedia "List of tools for static code analysis" page (Wikipedia, 2018). This is a fairly comprehensive list containing multi-language analysis tools, language specific tools and SaaS services. Key factors for SonarQube are:

- **Open Source:** Mostly valuable because the SonarQube developing team accepts contributions. Plugins or "quality profiles" can be proposed and shared among users.
- **Multiple Programming Languages:** Out of the box, it can readily analyze most common programming languages and there are also plugins available for several other languages. It can also deal with projects with more than one coding language.
- **Local and Server Deployment:** SonarQube is easily installed locally and in a server environment, Java being the only dependency. There are recent SaaS services like codacity.com or gitlab.com regarded as good alternatives, but they require your code to be out of your servers, and that requirement is often not possible to attend, especially in a corporate environment. Sonarsource also provides free and paid SaaS solutions.
- **Available APIs:** Well document engine and web APIs are crucial to accomplish a good integration within a CI stack.
- **Professional Services:** Sonarsource provides several levels of optional professional services. Also, other companies can provide professional (paid) plugins for specific tasks, like obsolete or less used programming languages, or quality profiles to specific tasks, e.g. web development security rules for PHP.
- **Known Release Cycle:** The road-map for future SonarQube development is known in advance, and they provide timely releases and an LTS (Long Term Support) version. A stable and known release cycle is especially important on the CI server side.

Historically, static code analysis tools were language-specific. If the project was a Java project then it would use a set of Java analysis tools. If PHP then a set of PHP analysis tools were used, and so on. This required specialized development teams to set-up the initial project for each language. Also, as several tools were sourced from different vendors, knowledge about these tools needed to be maintained and kept current. On top of these tools, designing or adapting specific tools for each project was common. Arguably this is still the most effective way to address very specific needs, but it is not, by far, the most efficient. Using a tool like SonarQube enables developers to address generic projects with almost no set-up and, on the CI server side, only some configuration is needed for adding new projects or changing existing ones. Also, it can easily manage projects with more than one programming language, which is becoming more common every day, specifically in web development and mobile development.

This does not invalidate the use of specific tools for specific project needs, that can be integrated server-side, alongside SonarQube. There are several plugins available written for this integration propose.

Having a common QA tool for code, also have the advantage of providing a common interface for the team members, coders, testers, QA, project managers, across several different projects.

Continuous Integration

First, let's address testing automation in a continuous integration environment. Although SonarQube tool can be used independently, professional development is usually done in an environment of several integrated tools. Current common development environments are designed for continuous integration and continuous delivery. These environments are usually built or heavily adapted by development teams, and, albeit they are usually unique solutions, some common components and tool choices can be identified:

- **Version Control Systems:** Subversion, GIT.
- **Continuous Integration Server:** Jenkins, Travis, Gitlab CI, Hudson.
- **Automation Scripting Tools:** Ansible, Salt, Puppet, Chef.
- **Issue and Project Tracking:** Redmine, GitLab, Jira, GitHub.

Alongside this base of tools, several other tools are usually integrated, making a CI environment a somewhat complex set of integrated tools. It is no trivial task to maintain these environments, keeping components updated and well-integrated. This why component choices usually favor: widely adopted components, comprehensive and well document APIs, predictable release cycles and long-term support options.

See figure 1 for an example of an integrated CI environment. The figure summarizes a web development stack. In this example, the "Custom integration layer" changes according to the target language, framework or product. The "Continuous Integration Server", Jenkins in this case, is responsible for the orchestration of the complete stack. The automation is usually attained by the use of custom scripts written in an automation language (Ansible, SaltStack, Puppet, etc.). Not all the tools depicted will be used on every project, but selected as needed. In this example, all the tools shown are Open Source.

Isolated Usage

SonarQube is easily installed in all major operating systems, Java being the only requirement. There are also available plugins for integration with most major IDEs or editors. Developers can immediately take advantage of the tools analysis capability. Usually, the analysis can be automated in the developer's platform using the build tool environment (Ant, Maven, CMake, Gradle, etc.), or run the language scanner by hand, when coding for scripting languages (JavaScript, PHP, Python etc.). Analysis can use a pre-shared set of Quality Profiles and Quality Gate definitions, and/or include the developer unique rule sets.

USAGE

Setting-up a new project in SonarQube is as simple as declaring where the sources files are. Optionally your unit test and code coverage reports directory should be set, and also language-specific options (by programming language). In a CI environment, this is probably already automated by project creation scripts. An analysis can immediately take place if there is source code available.

Rules

Rules are the smallest component of SonarQube. They are grouped to form Quality Profiles and are the basis for other metric calculations, used to analyze projects and design Quality Gates. Rules are created by the languages plugins and are run against source code, generating issues on specific conditions. Those issues are then used to compute remediation cost and technical debt. There are three basic types of rules: Reliability and Maintainability rules, from which zero false positives are expected, and Security rules, which may produce some false positives. Figure 2 shows an example of a rule on SonarQube web interface.

Figure 1. Example for a continuous integration stack

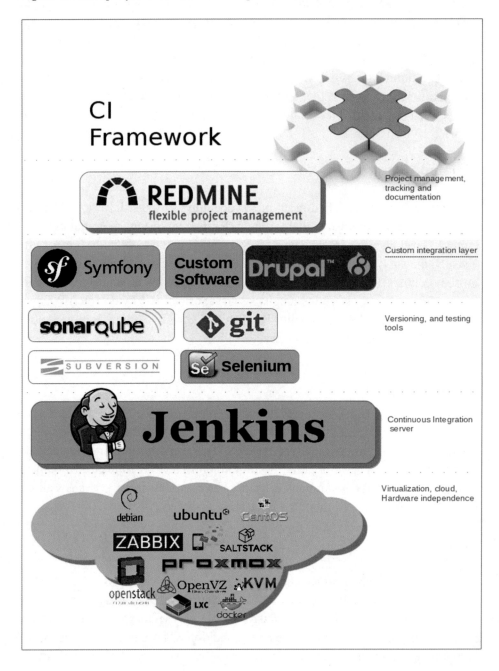

Figure 2. Example of a rule

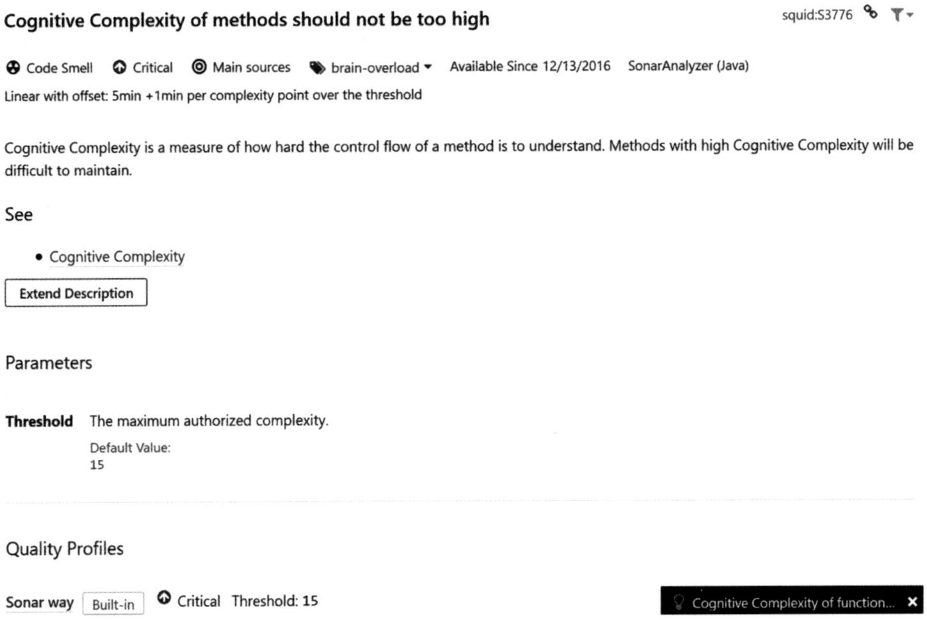

Cognitive Complexity of methods should not be too high

squid:S3776

✛ Code Smell   ⬦ Critical   ◎ Main sources   🏷 brain-overload ▾   Available Since 12/13/2016   SonarAnalyzer (Java)

Linear with offset: 5min +1min per complexity point over the threshold

Cognitive Complexity is a measure of how hard the control flow of a method is to understand. Methods with high Cognitive Complexity will be difficult to maintain.

See

- Cognitive Complexity

[Extend Description]

Parameters

Threshold   The maximum authorized complexity.
         Default Value:
         15

Quality Profiles

Sonar way   [Built-in]   ⬦ Critical   Threshold: 15   💡 Cognitive Complexity of function... ✕

Figure 3. Some rules for a Java quality profile

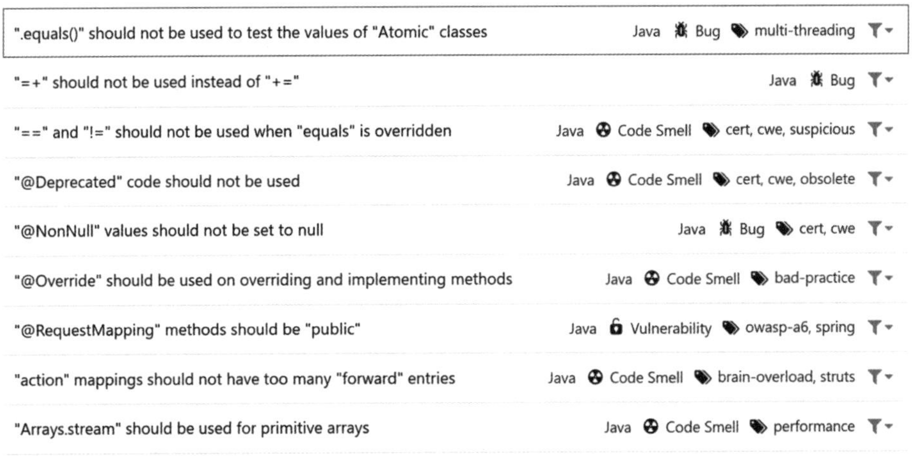

".equals()" should not be used to test the values of "Atomic" classes	Java 🐛 Bug	🏷 multi-threading ▾
"=+" should not be used instead of "+="	Java 🐛 Bug	▾
"==" and "!=" should not be used when "equals" is overridden	Java ✛ Code Smell	🏷 cert, cwe, suspicious ▾
"@Deprecated" code should not be used	Java ✛ Code Smell	🏷 cert, cwe, obsolete ▾
"@NonNull" values should not be set to null	Java 🐛 Bug	🏷 cert, cwe ▾
"@Override" should be used on overriding and implementing methods	Java ✛ Code Smell	🏷 bad-practice ▾
"@RequestMapping" methods should be "public"	Java 🔒 Vulnerability	🏷 owasp-a6, spring ▾
"action" mappings should not have too many "forward" entries	Java ✛ Code Smell	🏷 brain-overload, struts ▾
"Arrays.stream" should be used for primitive arrays	Java ✛ Code Smell	🏷 performance ▾

Rules are organized and categorized according to:

- **Language:** the language to which a rule applies.
- **Type:** Bug, vulnerability or code smell rules.
- **Tag:** It is possible to add tags to rules in order to classify them and to help discover them more easily.
- **Repository:** The engine that contributes rules to SonarQube.
- **Default Severity:** The original severity of the rule - as defined by the plugin that contributes this rule.
- **Status:** Rules can have 3 different statuses:
  - **Beta:** The rule has been recently implemented and we haven't gotten enough feedback from users yet, so there may be false positives or false negatives.
  - **Deprecated:** The rule should no longer be used because a similar, but more powerful and accurate rule exists.
  - **Ready:** The rule is ready to be used in production.
- **Available Since:** date when a rule was first added on the SonarQube instance. This is useful to list all the new rules since the last upgrade of a plugin for instance.
- **Template:** display rule templates that allow to create custom rules.
- **Quality Profile:** inclusion in or exclusion from a specific profile.

Customizing Rules From Existing Rules

Custom rules can be created from existing rules, and then edited. This makes possible to "fine-tune" some rules parameters. Creating completely new rules is also possible and a very important feature. This topic will be addressed in the CUSTOM RULES section.

Quality Profiles

Quality Profiles can be viewed simply as a particular set of rules. When configuring a new project, probably the first step is to check/choose which Quality Profiles will be used. You can then chose to make your own Profile (cloning an existing one) and select which code rules should or should not be used in your project. You can add new rules to the profile or remove/deactivate some rules. Figure 3 is a screenshot of SonarQube displaying some rules of a Java quality profile.

Developers can use any amount of Quality Profiles, even though it is recommended to have as few Quality Profiles as possible to ensure consistency across the projects in the organization. Quality Profiles start by being a copy of some of the standard Built-in Quality Profiles and then customized. A useful available feature is "Inheritance". Project managers can set-up a base profile, functioning as a "root", with a core set of rules. Then, depending on the project being worked on, a child profile can be created. Once it's created, you can change parent to inherit from Root, then add some other rules.

Quality Gates

Secondly, a Quality Gate can/should be defined and adapted to the specific project. This is normally just a few metrics, but it can also be more complex. A Quality Gate is the best way to enforce a quality policy in the developer's organization and is generally used to tag the build as "failed" from the SonarQube component.

In order to fail or pass the Quality Gate, a set of Boolean conditions based on measure thresholds are defined. Each build will be measured and classified by the Quality Gate. Some example conditions can be:

- No new blocker issues
- Code coverage on new code greater than 80%
- Etc.

Ideally, all projects would be verified against the same Quality Gate, but that's not always practical. For instance, you may find that:

- Technological implementation differs from one application to another (you might not require the same code coverage on new code for Web or Java applications).
- You want to ensure stronger requirements on some of your applications (internal frameworks for example).
- Project requirements changed.
- Etc.

You can set a level for "Warning" and "Error" for each Quality Gate. Usually, your CI server will have associated actions to the Quality Gate result. The most common action would be to fail the build if the Quality Gate fails, and generate some alert emails. SonarQube has also a notification mechanism that can be used to this effect, but usually this is not needed/used in a CI environment. Figure 4 illustrates a quality gate set-up in SonarQube web interface.

Figure 4. SonarQube quality gate example

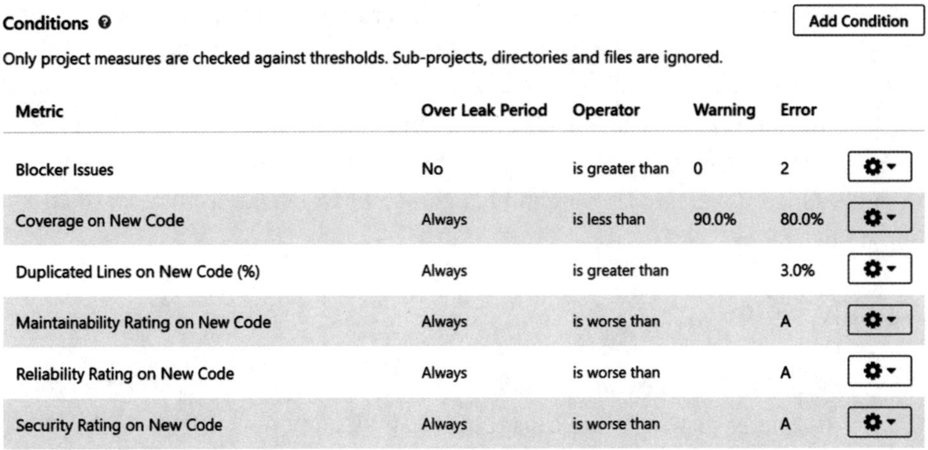

Conditions ⊘   **Add Condition**

Only project measures are checked against thresholds. Sub-projects, directories and files are ignored.

Metric	Over Leak Period	Operator	Warning	Error	
Blocker Issues	No	is greater than	0	2	⚙ ▾
Coverage on New Code	Always	is less than	90.0%	80.0%	⚙ ▾
Duplicated Lines on New Code (%)	Always	is greater than		3.0%	⚙ ▾
Maintainability Rating on New Code	Always	is worse than		A	⚙ ▾
Reliability Rating on New Code	Always	is worse than		A	⚙ ▾
Security Rating on New Code	Always	is worse than		A	⚙ ▾

Run Analysis

In a CI environment, a new analysis will be triggered with each commit to the server. SonarQube has the ability to export/import project settings (provided via plugin). With this option, developers have a way to run the analysis in their own environment prior to committing. There are also available plugins to most common IDEs (IntelliJ, Eclipse, NetBeans, Atom, VS code etc.). Running SonarQube in the developing environment can also help developers in a more interactive way. After the analysis is run, several metrics will be immediately available on the SonarQube web interface. Examples of these are presented in Figure 5, Figure 6, and Figure 7

Figure 5. Project summary analysis result

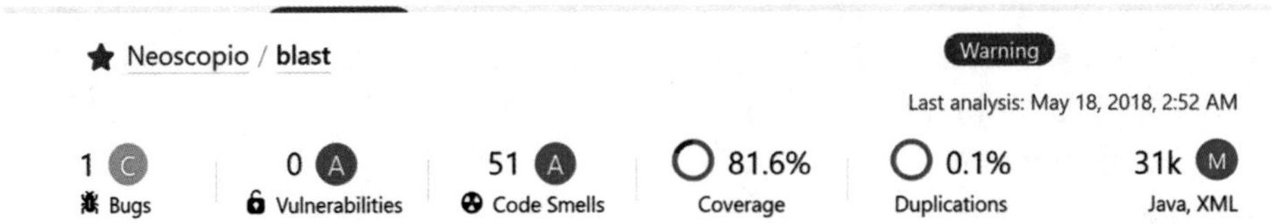

⭐ Neoscopio / blast   Warning
Last analysis: May 18, 2018, 2:52 AM

1 Ⓒ	0 Ⓐ	51 Ⓐ	◯ 81.6%	◯ 0.1%	31k Ⓜ
🐞 Bugs	🔓 Vulnerabilities	⊕ Code Smells	Coverage	Duplications	Java, XML

Figure 6. Quality gate summary

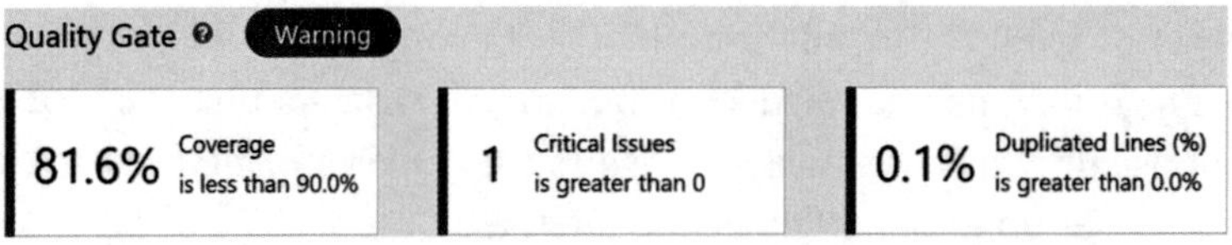

Quality Gate ⊘   Warning

81.6% Coverage is less than 90.0%	**1** Critical Issues is greater than 0	**0.1%** Duplicated Lines (%) is greater than 0.0%

Figure 7. Detected code smells

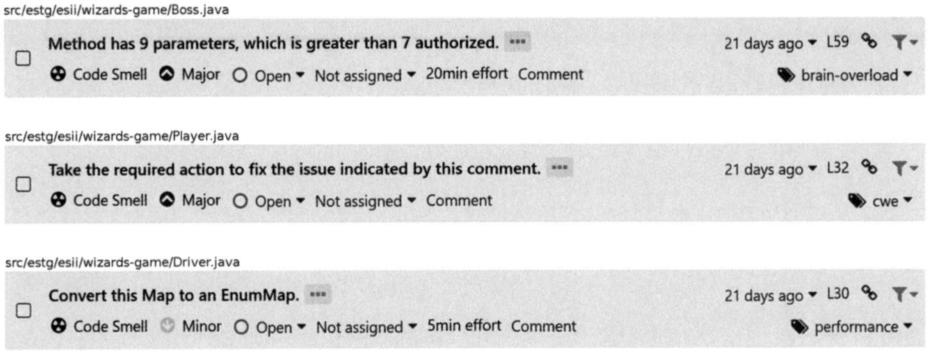

src/estg/esii/wizards-game/Boss.java

| | **Method has 9 parameters, which is greater than 7 authorized.** *** | 21 days ago ▾ L59 ⚬ ▼▾ |
| | ⊕ Code Smell ⚠ Major ○ Open ▾ Not assigned ▾ 20min effort Comment | 🏷 brain-overload ▾ |

src/estg/esii/wizards-game/Player.java

| | **Take the required action to fix the issue indicated by this comment.** *** | 21 days ago ▾ L32 ⚬ ▼▾ |
| | ⊕ Code Smell ⚠ Major ○ Open ▾ Not assigned ▾ Comment | 🏷 cwe ▾ |

src/estg/esii/wizards-game/Driver.java

| | **Convert this Map to an EnumMap.** *** | 21 days ago ▾ L30 ⚬ ▼▾ |
| | ⊕ Code Smell ◌ Minor ○ Open ▾ Not assigned ▾ 5min effort Comment | 🏷 performance ▾ |

Scope of Analysis: Types of Files and Data

The outcome of the analysis will be quality measures and issues (instances where coding rules were broken). However, what gets analyzed will vary depending on the language:

- On all languages, "blame" data will automatically be imported from supported SCM providers. Git and SVN are supported automatically. Other providers require additional plugins.
- On all languages, a static analysis of source code is performed (Java files, COBOL programs, etc.)
- A static analysis of compiled code can be performed for certain languages (.class files in Java, .dll files in C#, etc.)
- A dynamic analysis of code can be performed on certain languages.
- Unit Tests results and Code Coverage reports are integrated if available

Unrecognized Files

By default, only files that are recognized by a language plugin are loaded into the project during analysis. For example, if your SonarQube instance has the Java and JavaScript plugins on board, all .java and .js files will be loaded, but .xml files will be ignored. This behavior can be changed by setting up analysis parameters and general configuration. Parameters to configure project analysis can be set in multiple places. Here is the hierarchy of parameters:

- Global analysis parameters, defined in the UI, apply to all the projects
- Project analysis parameters, defined in the UI, override global parameters

- Project analysis parameters, defined in a project analysis configuration file or an analyzer configuration file, override the ones defined in the UI
- Analysis/Command line parameters, defined when launching an analysis, override project analysis parameters

Please refer to SonarQube documentation on Analysis Parameters.

ISSUES

Issues are the result of some rule failing. SonarQube raises an issue every time a piece of code breaks a coding rule.

Each issue has one of five severities:

- **Blocker:** Bug with a high probability to impact the behavior of the application in production: memory leak, unclosed JDBC connection, ... The code MUST be immediately fixed.
- **Critical:** Either a bug with a low probability to impact the behavior of the application in production or an issue which represents a security flaw: empty catch block, SQL injection, ... The code MUST be immediately reviewed.
- **Major:** Quality flaw which can highly impact the developer productivity: an uncovered piece of code, duplicated blocks, unused parameters, ...
- **Minor:** Quality flaw which can slightly impact the developer productivity: lines should not be too long, "switch" statements should have at least 3 cases, ...
- **Info:** Neither a bug nor a quality flaw, just a finding.

Associated with each rule is also an estimated "time to fix" the corresponding issue. These measures will amount to the Technical Debt of the project.

Within each issue created, SonarQube can show the associated problematic code, highlighting the problematic lines immediately from the web interface. Refer to Figure 8 for an example.

Technical Review

To each issue found, a state can then be associated. Confirm, False Positive, Won't Fix, Change Severity, and Resolve fall into this category, which presumes an initial review of an issue to verify its validity.

Figure 8. Associated problematic code highlight

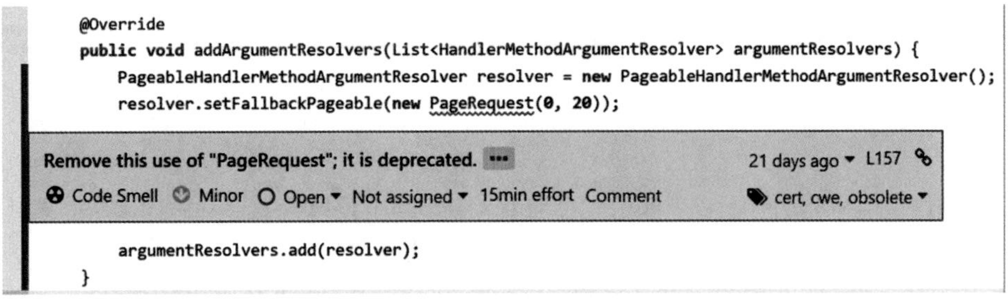

```
@Override
public void addArgumentResolvers(List<HandlerMethodArgumentResolver> argumentResolvers) {
    PageableHandlerMethodArgumentResolver resolver = new PageableHandlerMethodArgumentResolver();
    resolver.setFallbackPageable(new PageRequest(0, 20));
```

Remove this use of "PageRequest"; it is deprecated. •••	21 days ago ▾ L157 ⚲
⊕ Code Smell ◎ Minor ○ Open ▾ Not assigned ▾ 15min effort Comment	🏷 cert, cwe, obsolete ▾

```
    argumentResolvers.add(resolver);
}
```

- **Confirm:** By confirming an issue, you're basically saying "Yep, that's a problem." Doing so moves it out of "Open" status to "Confirmed".
- **False Positive:** Looking at the issue in context, you realize that for whatever reason, this issue isn't actually an issue because there is not actually a problem.
- **Won't Fix:** Looking at the issue in context, you realize that while it's a valid issue it's not one that actually needs fixing.
- **Change Severity:** This is the middle ground between the first two options. Yes, it's a problem, but it's not as bad a problem as the rule's default severity makes it out to be. Or perhaps it's actually far worse. Either way, you adjust the severity of the issue to bring it in line with what you feel it deserves.
- **Resolve:** If you think you've fixed an open issue, you can Resolve it. If you're right, the next analysis will move it to closed status. If you're wrong, its status will go to re-opened.

If you tend to mark a lot of issues false positive or won't fix, it means that some coding rules are not appropriate for your context. So, you can either completely deactivate them in the quality profile or use issue exclusions to narrow the focus of the rules so they are not used on specific parts (or types of object) of your application. Similarly, making a lot of severity changes should prompt you to consider updating the rule severities in your profiles.

As you edit issues, the related metrics (e.g. New Bugs), will update automatically, as will the Quality Gate status if it's relevant.

Issue Management

SonarQube provides several features and functionality to manage issues and associated workflows. In a CI environment, this functionality can be elsewhere, namely in a more dedicated Issue Tracker software solution. In this case, when an issue is assigned, it will be exported to the corresponding application and treated there. When the corresponding issue is closed, the CI server will resolve the initial issue in SonarQube.

Technical Debt

Technical debt is a term originally introduced to justify to non-technical stake holders the development effort on non-visible features (Kruchten, Nord, Ozkaya, 2012). It can be more technically defined as the implied effort of additional rework caused by implementing the work to transform a currently flagged solution (e.g. code smell) into a better approach. Technical debt affects productivity by making code hard to understand, fragile, time-consuming to change, difficult to validate, and creates unplanned work that blocks progress. Unless managed, technical debt can accumulate and hurt the overall quality of the software and the productivity of the development team in the long term.

The cost of never paying down this technical debt is clear; eventually the cost to deliver functionality will become so slow that it is easy for a well-designed competitive software product to overtake the badly-designed software in terms of features. In my experience, badly designed software can also lead to a more stressed engineering workforce, in turn leading higher staff churn (which in turn affects costs and productivity when delivering features). Additionally, due to the complexity in a given codebase, the ability to accurately estimate work will also disappear. In cases where development agencies charge on a feature-to-feature basis, the profit margin for delivering code will eventually deteriorate (Ali, 2016).

SonarQube will show you the Technical Debt for your project in effort time, i.e. days and hours. An 8-hour day is assumed when values are shown in days (There is a configuration parameter to change this, but is deprecated). SonarQube will also show you a Technical Debt Ratio as a percentage. This ratio is the ratio between the cost to develop the software and the cost to fix it. The Technical Debt Ratio formula is:

Remediation Cost / Development Cost

There is also another metric, Maintainability Rating: This is calculated using SQALE (SQALE, 2017) (Software Quality Assessment based on Lifecycle Expectations), methodology and is complex. A somewhat simplified idea is to tell you that if this ratio, Debt vs. cost to rewrite, considering the total cost of the project since start, grows too high, maybe it's a good time to rewrite the application instead of spending time reimbursing your debt. SQALE is an open method that can be freely applied to any software project, and it might worth a look, especially in long-life projects. Please refer to the link in the references section.

At the basis of all the Technical Debt calculations is an estimate of resolution time predefined on the rules. Project managers should be monitoring if Technical Debt grows, and, if this is the case, develop a sense of the growth rate. Since all calculations have at its base values of estimations, The total Technical Debt should be considered no more than approximate. Still, the metric change rate can be of great value in determining issues with project environment alterations that can occur for many reasons, from significant requirement changes to changes in the developer's team.

Other Metrics

SonarQube provides other metrics useful to convey a quick overview of the complete project health. The web interface also includes meaningful graphics to help at this propose. Also, there are several plugins which can insert their own metrics to be used in analysis and/or Quality Gates. Some other standard metrics worth mentioning are:

- **Duplications:** Density (%), Duplicated Lines, Duplicated Blocks, Duplicated Files
- **Size:** Lines of Code, Lines, Statements, Functions, Classes, Files, Directories, Comment Lines, Comments (%)
- **Complexity:** Cyclomatic Complexity (score), Cognitive Complexity (score)

Cognitive Complexity™

This is a recent metric developed by Sonarsource company with the objective to measure complexity caused by nesting code, better than the measure given by the Cyclomatic Complexity score. The method is based on the Cyclomatic Complexity measure method and uses human judgement to score structures differently based where they occur. The method first version was originally published in 2016 (Campbell, 2018) and, as such, there isn't much literature on practical results for this metric. The Sonarsource describes the metric as follows:

- Cyclomatic Complexity uses a mathematical model to assess methods, producing accurate measurements of the effort required to test them, but inaccurate measurements of the effort required to understand them.

- Cognitive Complexity breaks from the practice of using mathematical models to assess software maintainability. It starts from the precedents set by Cyclomatic Complexity, but uses human judgement to assess how structures should be counted, and to decide what should be added to the model as a whole. As a result, it yields method complexity scores which strike programmers as fairer relative assessments of maintainability than have been available with previous models.

Unit Tests and Code Coverage

The project can also be configured to include Unit Test results and Code Coverage results. On the latter, the web interface can highlight which parts of the code are covered by Unit Tests and which parts are not.

Act on Analysis

Generally, each build will be successful, even if some potential bugs/issues are found and are still below the Quality gate threshold parameters. Eventually, some build will fail, because some major issue was found, or just by an accumulation of issues. Developers will normally fix some issues until the Quality Gate threshold is met. Project managers can analyze the build history and the general project progression since start. This analysis can provide valuable insight into the project. The failed tests and the failed rules history can become a starting point for a code review and/ or the design of new tests or the addition/removal of rules to the quality profile. SonarQube "technical debt" value, complexity, size and duplication metrics, and their evolution, along with some graphical analysis, will provide project managers with a readily estimate of project health, cost and time.

In a CI environment, there will be other areas of intervention. For example, an increase in security issues, even if resolved, could trigger a security audit to a web application (automated or not). A scheduled security audit can use the reverse path, leading to the addition of more security related rules. An increase in code complexity might anticipate a code review. Moreover, on long-running development projects, requirements will change, like language version compatibility (Java, Python, JavaScript, PHP etc.), target operating systems and their versions (Like Android, Linux, Windows etc.), target web browsers and their versions, and so on. Rules and Quality Profiles can be viewed as dynamic in these cases. This means project managers should timely review and adapt the project Quality Profiles, adding and removing rules.

Automatic Code Generation

Some rules on code syntax or style could be corrected automatically, server-side. Refactoring code has been lately moved almost exclusively to the IDEs/editors on the developer's side. The code-refactoring features present in new IDEs and editors are evolving at a speedy pace, and it seems the IDE is the right place to do code refactoring, as it is immediately correctable. Refactoring code server-side is a deprecated practice in favor of IDE refactoring.

CUSTOM RULES

One of the interesting aspects of SonarQube design is the ability to add custom rules to the analysis. SonarQube provides two ways to accomplish this: Use of XPath rules to navigate language's Abstract Syntax Tree (AST) using the SonarQube web interface and to code the rules via a Java plugin. Unfortunately, they are language dependent and one or both methods might not be available for a specific language. If both are available, the Java API will be more fully featured than what's available for XPath and is generally preferable. The SonarQube documentation and repository provides information and several code examples for most languages. This is a compelling feature, an organization can code their own specific internal rules and coding standards and distribute the plugin among collaborators. On the other hand, if the new rules are generic, SonarQube encourages contributing the rules to the project having a high probability of being included in the specific language plugin in a future version.

SECURITY PROFILES

Security rules are treated somewhat differently than other coding rules. As a rule of thumb, coding rules cannot give a false positive. If an issue is raised, then it is an issue. Of course, you are free to ignore it or disable the rule. This requirement is relaxed on security rules, as this is, by their nature, a difficult task. As an example, a rule can establish that all input should be escaped, but of course might not be necessary or convenient in some situations. The SonarQube documentation mentions this:

The idea is that the rule will flag anything suspicious, and leave it to the human security auditor to cull the false positives and sent the real issues for remediation. Such rules are tagged with "security" and off by default.

Security by Default

Securing code has been historically an afterthought at most for many software projects, leading to catastrophic results in some well-known cases, even for the largest and popular software companies. Securing code was never more necessary than now. Recent European legislation (General Data Protection Regulation GDPR) will heavily penalize companies that fail to provide (and demonstrate) necessary precautions when dealing with personal user data, from customers, employees, and citizens in general.

A commonly used solution/reasoning to postpone security audits and upgrades was to keep everything behind a controlled environment, e.g. behind a corporate firewall. The rationale here is that the exposure is vastly reduced to a few known actors working in a well-defined environment. This, in fact, reduces exposure to security risks (Dadheech, Choudhary, Bhatia, 2018), but this method is not well fitted for today's environments and users. The Number of users with justifiable access to the internet and several application environments in a local network is growing, and their access (mobile, laptops) are not easily secured. Recent cases of ransomware all across the globe are just an example of how one cannot blindly trust corporations "demilitarized" zones.

Some common security requirements can sometimes be achieved by the use of well-known developing frameworks. Still, this is not enough for large software projects, and it may not even be possible.

Security awareness is not top-of-mind for most developers. Historically developers are interested in features and functionality and even if this is changing, security knowledge about possible attack vectors is vast and constantly being updated, so security is an area of its own merits and specialists. This makes it more valuable to be able to have security profiling tools that can help detect potential problems. Having these rule sets shared and readily available, incorporating new rules in a timely fashion is of the uttermost importance.

Some experts in this area are providing professional (free and paid) SonarQube security plugins. There are also SaaS code analysis services, but as mentioned earlier, that might not be an acceptable choice. As an example of a SonarQube security plugin for PHP, look at http://www.ripstech.com. A recent review on software security focused methods revealed that the most frequently used approaches are static analysis and dynamic analysis that provide security checks in the coding phase (Mohammed, Niazi, Alshayeb, Mahmood, 2017).

OTHER PROFILES

Profiles can also be used to enforce coding standards. If your organization has established coding style and practices, these can be coded as a plugin. This can also be used to check adherence to other projects coding styles and practices. As an example, if you were to develop a module for Drupal CMS and intended to make it publicly available, there is a SonarQube plugin that can check this specific project coding style.

VENDOR BRANCH ANALYSIS

A recent common practice in web and mobile software development is to use not only a development framework but also several components, probably managed by package managers, resolving and installing other dependencies. This can easily amount to a vendor branch composed of many different components from as many different sources. Usually, these components have widespread use and are well known, but this is unpredictable. Since your project will be heavily dependent on third-party code, your quality assurance procedures and specifically your security analysis should consider your vendor branch code. This can seem a herculean task, since your vendor branch code will, almost certainly, start much larger than your specific source code.

As mentioned before, you can expect some quality assurance code (mostly unit tests) for the components on your vendor branch, yet, depending on your requirements, running a SonarQube scan can easily detect several problems. These can be of several natures, let's address some of the possibilities:

- **No Unit Tests or Insufficient Code Coverage:** If you are relying on some expected behaviors of some component functionality, you should at least have unit testing for these uses. If they aren't available or if they are insufficient, you can write them in your own project test directory or directly in the vendor branch test directory. If the latter is available, and your tests are generic, you should also consider contributing them upstream. Depending on your project nature and legal contracts, this may not be possible, but if it is, contributing upstream will benefit your project in the long run if/when new versions are available. Contributing unit tests is usually well accepted when the upstream project is already using unit testing, but it can be more difficult if this is not the case. Either way is fairly easy to maintain your own unit tests for vendor branch code.

- **Code Smells, Bugs:** These can be ignored for the most part, unless you find an actual unequivocal bug. As before, bug patches can be contributed upstream, benefiting your project in the long run, and are usually well accepted, although requiring an additional bug description in a project manager (often GitHub). If you can't or won't make a pull request, keeping your changes and updating to newer component versions, can be tricky. A way to accomplish this will be presented later in this chapter.
- **Security Concerns:** If you find a potential security problem, you should at least replicate the issue upstream, even if you cannot contribute a patch. Most security issues should be clear, but some can be tricky to treat upstream. Correcting them can also be a non-trivial task, requiring changing vendor code in a significant way. This and the next topics are on the same level in terms of vendor branch maintainability for software projects.
- **Complexity:** You may find a high Cyclomatic Complexity score or a high score of the new "cognitive complexity" metric. Correcting for this in your vendor branch is generally not necessary, yet some caution is advisable; if your project is depending in complex methods or functions, developers should specifically look for the code coverage report for those methods, and consider writing additional tests for those methods if coverage is insufficient. In case a complex remediation is found necessary, developers should consider overriding the method completely, or rename the function name and rewrite a new one. This will provide better resilience against conflicts in vendor branch future updates.
- **Added Functionality:** Sometimes, after a code review, it can be apparent that some new feature is needed in one of your vendor components. Most often than not, these needs will be specific to your project and not generic enough to be contributed upstream. In these cases, project managers should consider a trade-off: Implementing the functionality in the project source code root, even if not optimal, or significantly alter the component source code. In the latter, vendor component unit test cases, and regression test cases should be carefully designed if you plan to update the component in the future.

Managing Local Changes to Vendor Branches

If you made local changes to the vendor branch code and wrote the appropriate unit/regression test cases, then, if you update the component and reapply your patches, your tests will detect any upstream changes that would affect your functionality. Making sets of patches and reapplying on components updates can/will become arduous to manage, as patches grow and component changes over time. This is a good reason to push your changes upstream, but for specific project needs that would not be possible. Fortunately, there is a better way: Keeping a local source control management (SCM) branch of your changed vendor components tree in use, alongside with your modified version. When you want to update a modified component, then you should "diff" the current and new version of the unmodified vendor code, and apply the differences to your own local main vendor branch. This procedure doesn't take into account the removal and addition of new files, so this possibility should be accounted for. Both Git and Subversion have features and tools to deal with this, and detailed information on this vendor branches update procedure can be found in the official Subversion documentation on the topic "Vendor branches".

The main advantage with this procedure is that it can be automated: If there are no source code conflicts, the "diff" would apply cleanly, and your unit/function/ regression tests should assure some confidence that everything is ok. SonarQube rules will run on the new patched vendor code and the process is repeatable. In case of code conflicts this will not be true and require immediate intervention or to postpone the update to a later time. Either way, you can at least test automatic updates for local changed vendor components.

CONCLUSION

The SonarQube tool was introduced and some guidelines that can automate white-box testing, specifically in a CI environment. Some key features are worth to emphasize, as they arguably are of great value to testing and quality assurance of a software project, namely: Open Source, Large adoption, Multi-language, extensible, server-side, cloud and client-side, easy configuration, easy integration. These set of features makes SonarQube a worthy replacement for language-specific testing stacks. Using this tool gives project managers access to a set of predefined, language-specific rules and rule sets. This feature can be thought of as a collective descriptive memory of best coding practices. The Open Source and community nature of the SonarQube project make this feature very dynamic and responsive, and hopefully even more dynamic and responsive in the future, as adoption grows. Professional services are readily available and not limited to the Sonarsource company who manages the SonarQube, but also from any other professionals who are experts in particular areas. Most importantly is the automation capabilities this tool can provide. Out-of-the-box it allows white-box best coding practices to be automated; continuous use provides insights for code-reviews and the design of new test cases; new rule sets can be defined and shared across an organization, simplifying and automating project setups.

Most of the insights shared in this chapter originate from knowledge acquired managing real-world software projects, from small size projects to large and long-running projects for companies, private, and government institutions across more than ten years of professional experience. Teaching and observing these concepts both at professional work environments and at a higher education level provided some insights on ease of use, future adoption of CI and automated testing. Specifically, on an academic level, it is abundantly evident that introducing SonarQube on to software development leads to much better coding practices, mostly attributed to the automatic "scoring" of code. In a professional environment, this relation is also evident, albeit it can benefit from some prior training.

REFERENCES

Ali, J. (2016). *Mastering php design patterns. Mastering PHP Design Patterns.* Packt Publishing Limited.

Campbell, A. G. (2018, September 10). *Cognitive Complexity, A new way of measuring understandability.* Retrieved October 18, 2018, from https://www.sonarsource.com/docs/CognitiveComplexity.pdf

Dadheech, K., Choudhary, A., & Bhatia, G. (2018). De-Militarized Zone: A Next Level to Network Security. *2018 Second International Conference on Inventive Communication and Computational Technologies (ICICCT).* 10.1109/ICICCT.2018.8473328

Kochhar, P. S., Bissyande, T. F., Lo, D., & Jiang, L. (2013). Adoption of Software Testing in Open Source Projects--A Preliminary Study on 50,000 Projects. *2013 17th European Conference on Software Maintenance and Reengineering.* doi:10.1109/csmr.2013.48

Kruchten, P., Nord, R. L., & Ozkaya, I. (2012). Technical Debt: From Metaphor to Theory and Practice. *IEEE Software, 29*(6), 18–21. doi:10.1109/MS.2012.167

McConnell, S. (2016). *Code complete.* Redmond, WA: Microsoft Press.

Mohammed, N. M., Niazi, M., Alshayeb, M., & Mahmood, S. (2017). Exploring software security approaches in software development lifecycle: A systematic mapping study. *Computer Standards & Interfaces, 50*, 107–115. doi:10.1016/j.csi.2016.10.001

Ostrand, T. (2002). White-Box Testing. In J. J. Marciniak (Ed.), Encyclopedia of Software Engineering. Academic Press. doi:10.1002/0471028959.sof378

SonarQube. (2018). *Architecture and Integration - SonarQube Documentation.* Retrieved October 18, 2018, from https://docs.sonarqube.org/display/SONAR/Architecture+and+Integration

SQALE. (2017, July 1). Retrieved October 18, 2018, from https://en.wikipedia.org/wiki/SQALE

Wikipedia. (2018). *List of tools for static code analysis.* Retrieved October 18, 2018, from https://en.wikipedia.org/wiki/List_of_tools_for_static_code_analysis#Multi-language

Zampetti, F., Scalabrino, S., Oliveto, R., Canfora, G., & Penta, M. D. (2017). How Open Source Projects Use Static Code Analysis Tools in Continuous Integration Pipelines. *2017 IEEE/ACM 14th International Conference on Mining Software Repositories (MSR)*, 334-344.

KEY TERMS AND DEFINITIONS

CI: Continuous Integration.
CMS: Content Manage System.
QA: Quality Assurance.
SaaS: Software as a Service.
SCM: Source Control Management.
UI: User Interface.

Section 2
Programming Languages Learning

Chapter 4
A Survey on Computer Programming Learning Environments

Ricardo Alexandre Peixoto de Queirós
Polytechnic Institute of Porto, Portugal

ABSTRACT

We are assisting the rise of online coding environments as a strategy to promote youth tech employment. With the growing importance of the technology sector, these type of technical training programs give learners emergent tech skills with a big impact and relevance to the current professional market needs. In this realm, MOOCs (massive open online courses) and online coding bootcamps are two increasingly popular options for learners to improve their code development skills and find work within a relatively short amount of time. Among all the features available on these environments, one stands out, which is the code generation. This chapter aims to detail and compare the most popular solutions for both learning contexts based on several criteria such as impact and maturity, user groups, and tools and features. In the features field, the authors highlight the code generation feature as an efficient way to enhance exercise resolution.

INTRODUCTION

Learning computer programming can be a lonely, complex, and demotivating process (Ala-Mutka, 2007), (O'Kelly & Gibson, 2006), (Robins & Rountree, 2003). These issues have been addressed in the last years, with the appearance of several on-line learning environments trying to leverage coding education and make it accessible to

DOI: 10.4018/978-1-5225-7455-2.ch004

everyone, even those with absolutely no coding experience or knowledge (Verdú et al., 2012), (Xavier & Coelho, 2011). These environments come in various formats ranging from non-interactive approaches (e.g. YouTube channels, blogs, books) to integrated and interactive solutions (e.g. intelligent tutors, on-line coding providers).

Nowadays there is an enormous demand on the technology sector to be up to date with the latest frameworks and languages. Regardless whether you are a coding newbie or a mature developer, you have several options, besides a computer science degree, to improve your programming skills. In this realm, MOOCs (Massive Open Online Courses) and Online Coding Bootcamps are two increasingly popular options for learners to improve their development skills and find work within a relatively short amount of time. While these two are excellent alternative learning contexts, the two options still have very distinct differences (Church, 2016).

A MOOC is an online course, usually available without charge, where learners can choose their own learning pace and direction. MOOCs are free educational courses often delivered by renowned university professors that typically feature a mix of downloadable readings, quizzes, discussion boards, video content and peer-to-peer assessment. The goal of MOOCs is to reach a much larger audience than traditional courses can accommodate. Often, MOOCs offer certificates for a fee which are awarded on successful completion of a course, and transferable college credit.

An Online Coding Bootcamp, on the other hand, is an intensive and paid course, usually eight to twelve weeks in duration, which offers hands-on training, career guidance and job assistance. These types of platforms involve a greater time commitment for the learner and are more suitable for who wants to quickly master a specific language (or stack) and get a technical job.

Both type of environments offers several features to foster code practice. One of the most important is the code generation feature. In fact, several environments deliver skeleton code that the students should complete to meet the problem requirements. Other feature typically used is the delivery of buggy programs. In this case the students would have to find logic errors in the program thus stimulating valences as debugging and testing. The rationale is simple: with the delivery of skeleton or buggy programs, the "problem-solving" issue is softened and the students' working memory is free to build a new mental model of the problem to solve.

In this paper we will focus our attention on both learning contexts. In Section 2 we review the existent learning environments. In Section 3 we focus on the code generation techniques of the learning environments. Finally, we summarize the contributions of this research.

SURVEY

In the next subsections we compare the most popular solutions for both learning contexts based on criteria such as impact & maturity, user groups, tools and features (MoocLab, 2015).

Impact and Maturity

In this study we tried to measure the impact of MOOCs and Online Bootcamps in the coding teaching-learning process. Although relatively recent, several of these initiatives have been growing with the contribution of educational institutions and communities of developers (CourseReport, 2016). Table 1 compares the studied MOOCs on a set of parameters measuring their impact and maturity, namely, the date of creation, the number of courses available and their costs, the number of users and the evidence provided by the platform that the course has been completed.

All platforms studied have been created in the last decade which shows the emergence of this area and the importance of computer programming as a key competency for the professional market. Looking at the large number of courses that each platform hosts, we can also conclude that the platforms are very active and have an enormous growth potential. For instance, EdX was created in 2012 by the Massachusetts Institute of Technology and Harvard University, and in four years has more than 2300 faculty and staff teaching over 950 courses.

Table 1. MOOC Platforms impact and maturity comparison

	Date	#Courses	Cost	Users	Cert.
EdX	2012	950	F/P	7M	Yes
Coursera	2012	1800	F/P	17M	Yes
Udacity	2012	130	F/P	1.6M	Yes
CodePlayer	2012	-	F	-	None
Code Academy	2011	23	F	25M	Badges
Code.org	2013	5	F	40M	None
TreeHouse	2011	269	P	202m	Badges
CodeSchool	2012	60	P	2M	Badges

EdX and Coursera present a greater number of courses than other platforms since they are not exclusively dedicated to programming courses. For instance, the Coursera MOOC platform has courses in the most varied subjects, such as Sciences, Technology, Arts & Humanities, IT, Social Sciences, Business and Education. In fact, Coursera is the largest MOOC platform partnering with top universities and organizations and offering a huge variety of on-line courses.

In terms of users, all platforms have millions of users who enroll in their courses. CodeAcademy is a fantastic example of community of practice. The platform offers free coding classes covering the core programming concepts and syntax in HTML & CSS, JavaScript, jQuery, PHP, Python and Ruby. All courses are self-paced allowing learners to progress at their own rate with a focus on learning through actively coding. Each lesson is made up of a series of interactive coding exercises, which allow learners to practice coding inside a web browser, and each exercise is accompanied by a written explanation. Achievements are rewarded with badges and users are able to share projects with the rest of the community and even potential employers. Community is also an important factor for Code.org that launched, in December 2013, the "Hour of Code Challenge" on its website to teach computer science to school students, challenging them to complete short programming tutorials

Regarding the cost of the courses, there are few platforms totally free. Most of the platforms offer a hybrid model plan with two flavors: 1) free and paid courses or 2) courses with a blend of some free introductory topics and exercises and other (more advanced) paid resources. Typically, a paid course is eligible for certification. For instance, Edx supports verified certificates (minimum cost $50 to $150) which ensures the course successful completion. EdX also supports other type of certificates such as honor code certificates for distinctive performances and XSeries certificates that are specialization programs consisting of series of related modules/courses in a specific subject.

Table 2 compares the studied Online Bootcamp environments on a set of parameters measuring their impact and maturity.

The set of criteria used is composed by: the date of creation of the Bootcamp, the number of courses running, the tuition paid by the learner for the course, the workload required to complete the program (in weeks) and the documentation or evidence provided by the Bootcamp that the course has been completed (e.g. project portfolio, course certificate).

Bootcamp is a new fresh theme. All the examples were born in the last five years. In fact, Coding bootcamps made their debut with Dev Bootcamp, founded in 2012. In 2014, 6,740 developers have graduated from coding bootcamps and grew to 10,333 graduates in 2015. As of June 2016, there are 91 coding bootcamps in the US and Canada.

Table 2. Online Bootcamp platforms impact and maturity comparison

	Date	#Cour.	Tuit.	Leng.	Accred.
Hack Reactor	2012	6	$17,78	12	Portfolio
Bloc	2013	5	$14,49	12-36	Portfolio
ThinkFul	2012	4	$733	12-24	Portfolio
Coding Dojo	2012	5	$7,50	14	Portfolio
CareerFoundry	2013	4	$1,69	12-24	Portfolio
DesignLab	2013	2	$299	4-6	P./Cert.
FireHose	2012	8	$4,00	12-36	Portfolio
SkillCrush	2014	3	$399	12	Certif.

The educational model in bootcamps is typically organized in courses ("learning pathways" or "learning tracks"). Each learning path (e.g. Web Development) is organized in lessons (e.g. HTML/CSS, JavaScript, and Ruby) that students must assist. These lessons, typically made up of video lessons, are combined with daily challenges. Also, new lessons can be purchased separately depending of the tuition model of the bootcamp.

In this study, we can conclude that bootcamps offer paid online courses from a few hundred to thousands of dollars. According to a 2016 market research report, tuition ranges from free to $21,000 for a course, with an average tuition of $11,451. Despite these prices, learners adhere to this new paradigm due essentially to the chances of get an employment.

Courses in bootcamps range from 8 to 36 weeks, but most courses are in the 10-12 weeks range with an average of 12.9 weeks. Some bootcamps Courses run for 3 to 6 months, depending on the learner's time commitments, with an estimated weekly workload of 10-20 hours. This versatility has brought more people to the bootcamps solving one of the great criticisms related to this type of teaching that was considered too intense and rigid.

Finally, the accreditation of bootcamps is made primarily by the delivery of a project portfolio. In the coding realm, the portfolio could be a set of projects held in a GitHub account. Some bootcamps offer job assistant and Career Coaching as part of the program or as a paid extra.

User Groups

The studied environments (both MOOCs and bootcamps) provide an infrastructure for different types of users and have in mind different types of courses. Table 3 lists a comparison on MOOCs platforms regarding its type.

Table 3 compares the studied MOOCs on a set of parameters related with user groups.

Most of the platforms are best suited for High School students, professionals and people with general interest.

However, based on this study, most of the platforms serve essentially as a good primer for self-starting coders offering a taste of the main coding languages at basic and intermediate levels. These platforms can also be used for programmers with some experience, but who need some recycling in the most emerging technologies. Udacity plays a slightly different role in this set, as it offers self-paced on-line courses focusing mainly on vocational technology courses for professionals, teaching skills that industry employers are looking for.

Regarding the subject of the courses, and except for EdX and Coursera, all the platforms studied here, focus exclusively on the learning of computer programming languages. These platforms have a common goal: help people to learn basic skills related with front-end technologies like HTML5, CSS3, JavaScript. Treehouse and CodeSchool extend the curriculum of their courses offering training in the responsive design area. Other languages are not forgotten. For instance, CodeAcademy offers courses to share skills using PHP, Python, Ruby, Ruby on Rails, SQL and Java languages.

Table 3. MOOC platforms user groups comparison

	End Users	**Subjects**	**Language**	**Level**
EdX	Acad./Prof.	Generic	English	B/I
Coursera	Acad./Prof.	Generic	Multiple	B/I
Udacity	Prof.	Tech.	English	B/I
CodePlayer	Acad.	Coding	English	I/A
Code Academy	Acad./Prof.	Coding	English	B/I
Code.Org	Acad./Prof.	Coding	Multiple	B
TreeHouse	Acad./Prof.	Coding	English	B/I/A
CodeSchool	Acad.	Coding	English	I/A

As said before, subjects are very diverse ranging from sciences, Technology, IT, Social Sciences, Business to Arts & Humanities. The type of learning is mostly academic with some professional education courses. Regarding languages, the studied MOOC platforms offer courses in English. Finally, most of the courses are suitable for self-starting learners and do not require any prior and specific knowledge. However, there are platforms, more focused in the teaching of computer programming skills that require some coding knowledge.

Table 4 compares the studied Online bootcamps on a set of parameters related with user groups.

Coding bootcamps are more suitable for professionals who want to change career, get an IT job or simply refresh an emergent technological subject. Other users take the courses to learn a specific language or stack to build a app or company. In this case, the choice of a mentor is essential, so he can adapt the course to the user needs.

Some courses are intended for experienced developers who are looking to quickly pick-up new technologies. These courses require learners to be proficient in MVC/OOP stack, have basic algorithm knowledge, be comfortable with HTML, JavaScript and CSS, and be familiar with the installation of applications on Mac/Windows/Linux.

Most online bootcamps courses are focused on the learning of front-end (FE) and back-end (BE) Web languages. One of the most popular courses are those related with the combination of the two previous stacks, usually called full stack (FS). The term full-stack means developers who are comfortable working with both back-end and front-end technologies. In this realm, MEAN is the most popular being defined as a full-stack development toolkit that combines the most powerful technologies for

Table 4. online Bootcamp platforms user groups

	End Users	Subjects	Level
Hack Reactor	Prof.	FE/BE/FS/UX/MO	B/I/A
Bloc	Prof.	FE/BE/FS/UX/MO	B/I/A
ThinkFul	Acad./Prof.	FE	B/I
Coding Dojo	Acad./Prof.	FE/BE/FS/UX	B/I/A
CareerFoundry	Prof.	FE/BE/UX	B/I
DesignLab	Acad./Prof.	UX	B
FireHose	Prof.	FE/BE/FS	B/I/A
SkillCrush	Prof.	FE/BE/UX	B/I

JavaScript development. MEAN is a collection of JavaScript-based technologies - MongoDB, Express.js, AngularJS, and Node.js - used to develop web applications from the client and server sides to databases. These courses cover the four elements of the MEAN stack and prepares users for building real-time apps, creating custom JS libraries, and mastering the MVC Frameworks -- front and back-end.

Other popular courses are related to the development of mobile (MO) apps, for Android and iOS, and to design, more precisely User eXperience (UX) that could be defined as a process of fostering user satisfaction with an app by improving the usability and accessibility provided while interacting with the application.

Features and Tools

The studied environments (both MOOCs and bootcamps) adopt different features based on a set of tools and services. In this subsection, we compare both types of environments based on different aspects. Regarding MOOCs, we analyze what type of features they must engage and retain learners such as, collaborative and gamification tools, learning paths, type of instructions, and others. In Online Bootcamps we stress the existence of mentoring, job assistance tools, and others. Table 5 compares the studied MOOCs on a set of parameters measuring their features and tools.

Most of the MOOCs offer learning paths with a list of courses to work through. This feature is very important, especially for those new to programming. Despite the existence of paths, the studied MOOCs don't offer a very rigid structure allowing learners to choose several learning paths during the course.

The materials of the courses come in several flavors and are organized in two types: 1) expository resources, such as videos (the most popular format) and HTML/

Table 5. MOOC platforms features and tools comparison

	Path	Esp. Res.	Eval. Res.	Social
EdX	Yes	Videos	Quiz	F/D
Coursera	Yes	Videos	Quiz/Puz	UP/F/D
Udacity	Yes	Videos	Quiz	Forum
CodePlayer	No	Videos	No	Com/Rec
Code Academy	Yes	ICE	ICE	Ach/Badges
Code.Org	Yes	Videos	ICE/Puz	Levels
TreeHouse	Yes	Videos	ICE/Puz	Badges
CodeSchool	Yes	Videos	ICE	F/Badges

PDF tutorials and 2) evaluation resources, such as interactive code exercises, quizzes and puzzles. Almost all the platforms offer transcript videos as a way to disseminate knowledge. These videos include the resolution step-by-step of exercises. This way, learners gain some theoretical/practical skills that can be later consolidated and applied in coding challenges. These challenges can be run inside of interactive coding exercises components (ICE) giving feedback and support to the learner during the resolution of the exercise (e.g. CodeAcademy, Treehouse). Most of these components are based on cloud IDEs (e.g. Cloud9, Codeanywhere) and integrate some tools like resources sequence, chat and video visualization.

Regarding gamification and social features, most platforms adhere to the same components, such as forums (F), learning dashboards (D), user profiles (UP), comments (COM), recommendation (REC), levels and badges.

For instance, CodePlayer offers a different approach to learning code by playing code like a video, helping people to learn front-end technologies quickly and interactively. The platform also includes a commenting tool and links to related walkthroughs. CodeAcademy includes a user progress dashboard informing of the current state of the learner regarding its progress in the courses. This platform enhances the participation in the courses by also including achievements (ACH) that are rewarded with badges and users are also able to share completed projects with the rest of the site community and potentially showcase their skills to employers.

Other important information is, excepting Code.org, all the platforms have a strong presence in the mobile world, with app versions for Android and iOS.

Table 6 compares the studied Online bootcamps on a set of parameters related with features and tools.

Table 6. Online bootcamp platforms features and tools comparison

	Type	Mentor	Job	Gamif.
Hack Reactor	Session	Yes	Yes	Chat/Badges
Bloc	Session	Yes	Yes	Chat/Badges
ThinkFul	Session	Yes	Yes	Chat/Badges
Coding Dojo	Session	Yes	No	Badges
CareerFoundry	Session	Yes	Yes	Badges
DesignLab	Session	Yes	No	Badges
FireHose	Session	Yes	No	Badges
SkillCrush	On demand	No	No	Badges

Online bootcamps courses have two kinds of courses: session-based and on-demand. The former has a scheduled start and an end date. The later allow users to study on their own schedule. Most of the platforms analyzed use the session-based style.

Mentoring is a well-known feature of online bootcamps. Mentoring usually consists of a number of 1 to 1 session with an expert. Users are assigned a personal mentor offering support and guidance via several hours weekly virtual (or presential) meetings, and study units are supported by mentor-lead daily chat-rooms. For instance, in Bloc and ThinkFul platforms, learners work alongside a remote mentor and benefit from up to 3 virtual mentor meetings a week, depending on the course length, and practice coding with their mentor in real-time by screen sharing.

Some providers also offer course graduates career coaching and/or job placement. Through existing connections with recruiters and employers, some platforms assist graduates in finding employment with organizations. From the studied platforms only Hack, Bloc, Thinkful and CareerFoundry have a job assistant tool.

After the completion of the bootcamp learners earn a Bootcamp completion badge which can be displayed on the learner resume, on-line profile and on website to show employers about the completion of the training that qualifies the learner for a job. For instance, in Bloc platform student engagement is enhanced by gamification and rewards. Also, collaborative tools are used to enhance participation and augment retention. Hack Reactor includes chat rooms (opened 24/7) that allow students to interact with each other socially or to go over assignments.

Survey Analysis

Regardless of the learning context, an Integrated Learning Environment (ILE) is the common approach to mimic a physical classroom and to give instructors the right tools to help learners to progress in the course and achieve success. Mostly used tools and services are the following: code editors, resources navigators, internal assessment tools, forums, chats, job assistant tools, coaching and mentoring services and gamification tools. Nevertheless, depending of the learning context (MOOC or Bootcamp), the ILE is equipped differently with specific tools. In this subsection we discuss the main features associated to the ILEs (resource sequencing, gamification and code edition and evaluation), and for each one, we describe how they are used in both learning contexts.

An ILE shares courses in the form of a sequence of resources. These resources are usually categorized in two groups: expositive (e.g. videos, HTML/PDF tutorials) and evaluative (e.g. quizzes, interactive exercises). Most of the times, these resources are organized in units (or modules) and sequenced in a fixed way. You cannot switch between modules, only if you have completed the previous module. The completion of the module will unlock the next one, giving the concept of game levels. There are some exceptions. For instance, CodePlayer does not have any rigid sequence of resources. The learner chooses one resource, and, at the end, several resources are recommended based on the resource's similarity.

However, one must say that MOOCs are less structured than Bootcamps which are more rigid and focused. Thus, a resources navigator tool should adjust to the learning context. In other words, a resource navigator should have the flexibility enough to adapt to both flavors. In addition, a resource navigator should be able to receive input from a recommendation service, so the initial resources sequence could adapt to the learner progress and profile.

The flexibility of both learning contexts is different. An on-line coding bootcamp usually requires a time commitment of 6 to 8 weeks. This means that the learner will need to leave work (or work overtime) to cover this period. On the other hand, a MOOC is a much more flexible option allowing the apprentice at the learner's pace. This approach has its drawbacks, since completion rates can be as low as 13% (Onah, Sinclair & Boyatt, 2014). This is the main reason for the appearance of the so-called gamification tools that have an ultimate and common goal: to augment the retention rate. In both learning contexts, gamification tools are associated to the learners rewarding through badges for the completion of a course, module or a specific challenge. Some platforms also provide a set of collaboration tools (e.g. forums, chat, comments) to enhance learner's participation and peer assessment.

Evaluation is a huge and sensible topic. Most of the platforms dedicated to computer programming learning use a sandbox-based tool or code editor to allow learners to test their code. Usually, code editors (e.g. Cloud9) are personalized and interactive. In the learning of web technologies, as the code is written a preview of the Web app is displayed in another window. This feature gives the learner an interesting perspective of the job done and can guide him through the resolution of the challenge by helping in the choice of the best approaches to finish the exercise. The evaluation is made internally (both static and dynamic) and visual indicators are given to inform on the success of the resolution of the exercise. In some platforms (e.g. CodeAcademy), a skeleton of the resolution is provided, and the challenge is divided into several steps. As the learner completes each step the platform gives a positive feedback, offering the learner a sense of accomplishment and confidence. Despite all these features, the editors lack other types of evaluation such as modelling languages (e.g. UML, ER).

CODE GENERATION FEATURE

Some of these environments allow the resolution of exercises from scratch or based on a previous generated code version. These versions can be of two flavors:

- **Skeleton Programs:** Will accelerate the beginning of exercises resolution by the students and facilitate their problem understanding. With the structure included, students can now focus on the core of the problem and abstract their foundations.
- **Buggy Programs:** Include logic and/or execution errors. These types of programs can stimulate students to debug and test their programs. Often this is a forgotten practice which leads to malfunctioning programs.

Both types of generated code are based on a complete annotated program solution provided by the teacher. The annotations are formally described within an annotation type and processed by an annotation processor. This processor is responsible for a set of actions ranging from the creation of dummy methods to the exchange of operator types included in the source code.

After the creation of the annotation type and processor the teacher must code the solution program that will use the annotation type previously created. The following code excerpt shows an annotated solution program coded by the teacher for the sum problem.

```
@ProcessorInterface(comment = " Complete the method !",
removeBody = true)
public static long sum (long num1, long num2)
{
  return num1 + num2;
}
```

Upon compilation the compiler with the help of the registered annotation processors will generate several source files accordingly with the syntax of the annotations found in the source code and the associated semantic in the annotation processor. The next code excerpt shows a possible source file:

```
public static long sum (long num1, long num2) {
 // Complete the method!
}
```

For buggy programs, operators and values are exchanged (for instance) in order to produce programs with logic/execution errors. The next example shows an annotated factorial function:

```
public static long factorial(long num) {
  @ProcessorInterface(changeValue=">")
    if(num <= 1)
      return 1;
    else
      @ProcessorInterface(changeOperator)
      return num * factorial(num - 1);
}
```

The compiler will produce the following buggy code that the student should correct:

```
public static long factorial(long num) {
  if(num > 1)
    return 1;
  else
    return num * factorial(num + 1);
}
```

Regardless of the code generation type, some studies (Lister et al., 2004) and (McCracken et al., 2001) prove that these types of files will engage novice students on initiating the resolution of exercises and on stimulating them to test more effectively their solutions while using in a regular basis the debugger tools.

CONCLUSION

Nowadays, computer program environments are typically used to foster programming skills. In this realm, MOOCs (Massive Open Online Courses) and Online Coding Bootcamps are two increasingly popular options for learners to improve their code development skills and find work within a relatively short amount of time.

Based on a survey, we conclude that both learning contexts have their own advantages/disadvantages and several specificities regarding a common goal: to share tech contents and promote practice to master a complex domain: the computer programming learning. In this context, learners should select the best learning environments, depending on personal goals, available money and deadlines.

Regarding code generation, some of the environments included in the survey are starting to use code generation mechanisms (skeleton and buggy programs) to enhance problem understanding and to allow learners to focus on the problem itself and not in the boilerplate and bureaucratic code associated.

REFERENCES

Ala-Mutka, K. M. (2007). A survey of automated assessment approaches for programming assignments. *Journal of Computer Science Education, 15*(Feb), 83–102. doi:10.1080/08993400500150747

Church, G. (2016). MOOCs versus coding bootcamps. *Class-Central*. Retrieved from https://www.class-central.com/report/moocs-versus-codingbootcamps

Coursereport. (2016). 2016 coding bootcamp market size study. In *2016 Coding Bootcamp Market Size Study*. CourseReport.

Lister, R., Adams, E., Fitzgerald, S., Fone, W., John, H., Lindholm, M., … Seppälä, O. (2004). A Multi-National Study of Reading and Tracing Skills in Novice Programmers. *ACM SIGCSE Bulletin, 36*(4), 119–150. Retrieved from http://urn.kb.se/resolve?urn=urn:nbn:se:umu:diva-15878

McCracken, M., Almstrum, V., Diaz, D., Guzdial, M., Hagan, D., Kolikant, Y., ... Wilusz, T. (2001). A multi-national, multi-institutional study of assessment of programming skills of first-year CS students. *ACM SIGCSE Bulletin, 33*(4), 180. doi:10.1145/572139.572181

MoocLab. (2015). Mooclabs league tables. *MoocLab*. Retrieved from http://www.mooclab.club/categories/league-tables.169/

O'Kelly & Gibson. (2006). RoboCode & problem-based learning: a non-prescriptive approach to teaching programming. In *Proceedings of the 11th annual SIGCSE conference on Innovation and technology in computer science education (ITICSE '06)*. ACM. DOI:10.1145/1140124.1140182

Onah, D. F. O., Sinclair, J., & Boyatt, R. (2014). Dropout rates of massive open online courses: behavioural patterns. *6th International Conference on Education and New Learning Technologies*, 5825-5834.

Robins, A., Rountree, J., & Rountree, N. (2003). Learning and Teaching Programming: A Review and Discussion. *Journal of Computer Science Education, 13*(2), 137-172. Doi:10.1076/csed.13.2.137.14200

Verdú, E., Regueras, L. M., Verdú, M. J., Leal, J. P., de Castro, J. P., & Queirós, R. (2012). A distributed system for learning programming on-line. *Computers & Education, 58*(1), 1-10. Doi:10.1016/j.compedu.2011.08.015

Xavier, J., & Coelho, A. (2011). Computer-based assessment system for e-learning applied to programming education. *Proceedings, ser. 4th International Conference of Education, Research and Innovations*, 3738–3747.

KEY TERMS AND DEFINITIONS

Application Programming Interface (API): A set of uniform programming interfaces for building software and applications.

Backend as a Service (BaaS): Cloud computing service model acting as a middleware component that allows developers to connect their applications to cloud services via API and SDK.

Game Backend as a Service (GBaaS): Is a subset of a BaaS that includes cross-platform solutions for the typical game concepts.

Gamification: Conceptual model that aims to bring game mechanics to non-game contexts.

MOOC: Massive open online courses.

Software Development Kit (SDK): A set of software development tools that allows the creation of applications for a certain operating system.

Chapter 5
Tools for the Learning of Programming Languages and Paradigms:
Integration of a Code Validator and Exercises Module Into the Moodle eLearning Platform

María A. Pérez-Juárez
University of Valladolid, Spain

Francisco J. Díaz-Pernas
University of Valladolid, Spain

Míriam Antón-Rodríguez
University of Valladolid, Spain

Mario Martínez-Zarzuela
University of Valladolid, Spain

María I. Jiménez-Gómez
University of Valladolid, Spain

David González-Ortega
University of Valladolid, Spain

ABSTRACT

The learning of programming languages and paradigms is complex and requires a lot of training. For this reason, it is very important to detect students' main problems and needs to be able to provide professors with tools that help students to overcome those problems and difficulties. One type of tool that can be used for this purpose is the code validator. This chapter explores the possibilities and impact of using different tools and strategies for learning programming languages and paradigms. To achieve this goal, the authors have conducted a comprehensive search of relevant scientific literature that has been complemented with their experience using a JavaScript code validator and exercises module integrated into the e-learning platform Moodle, with university students during a web programming course.

DOI: 10.4018/978-1-5225-7455-2.ch005

INTRODUCTION

The learning of programming languages and paradigms is quite difficult and requires a lot of additional work, especially when compared to more theoretical fields of study (Brito & Sá-Soares, 2014). According to Vega et al. (2013) students think that programming is a complicate field of study and it is quite frequent to hear about problems related to frustration and lack of motivation. Moreover, programming is hard to teach; in fact, there are professors that think that programming requires skills other than knowledge (Tan et al., 2014).

Programming students usually have a good knowledge of concepts and theory but experience problems when trying to put those into practice (Newstetter & McCracken, 2001). Research has shown that previous knowledge is very important in a learning process (Chi & Ceci, 1987; Chi et al., 1988; Glaser, 1984). For some students, unfortunately, the foreknowledge they have is wrong and they are reluctant to change those initial ideas. Along this line, Newstetter & McCracken (2001) performed a study for a better comprehension of the nature of computer programming learning. Their study showed that some students have wrong previous ideas, a fact which must be considered by lecturers. In this sense, it is very important to detect students' main problems regarding programming languages and paradigms learning, in order to be able to provide professors with tools that help students to overcome those problems and difficulties.

Moreover, in order to learn a programming language, it is necessary to be able to write code in that programming language, and not only to answer short questions. This is also the best way to determine the knowledge of students about a specific programming language (Danutama & Liem, 2013).

Besides the inherent difficulty of programming as a discipline, the focus of the problem could be in the use of inefficient and inadequate methodologies and educational tools to teach this subject. For this reason, during the last decades, experts have searched for ways to improve the academic performance of students, especially in the case of newcomer students (Moons & De Backer, 2013).

In such a complex context it is important to have a clear view of which are the main problems that students face when approaching to the theory and practice of programming languages and paradigms. The educational tools oriented to learning programming should consider those needs and provide resources and strategies to manage them.

Taking into account the difficulties related to the teaching and learning of programming languages and paradigms, this chapter explores the possibilities and impact of using different tools and strategies for the learning of programming languages and paradigms. To achieve this goal, the authors have conducted a comprehensive search of relevant scientific literature that has been complemented with their experience using a JavaScript code validator and exercises module integrated into the e-learning platform Moodle. Experience has been performed with university students during a web programming course. After describing the educational tool developed, results and final conclusions are presented.

BACKGROUND

A first key issue is the fact itself of having to use technology-based educational tools. The use of technology-based educational tools to support the process of learning programming languages and paradigms is necessary as, according to Jara et al. (2008), theoretical classes do not provide enough knowledge to students. It is true that nowadays technology is present in most schools and students reach university level having taken part in technology-based learning experiences. However, technology anxiety can assault individuals that have to use technology. In the latest years researchers had paid an increasing attention to technology anxiety and numerous studies have been published. Now the focus is not on the use of the technology itself, as younger generations are more used to use technology, but on the anxiety generated by the use of certain complex software applications. Anxiety and a negative attitude negatively affect learning and condition the use of technology (Gurcan-Namlu, 2003). For this reason, it is important that students quickly and easily adapt to use these type of software applications.

Another central issue is motivation. Students must spend a lot of time practising if they want to learn how to program and this is not possible if they are not very motivated (Law et al., 2010). According to several studies (Jenkins, 2001) (Brito & Sá-Soares, 2014), motivation is the most important factor to succeed when learning programming languages and paradigms, and a motivated student will succeed no matter other circumstances. In the same way, if a student is not motivated he will probably not succeed no matter how favourable other factors and circumstances are.

Most lecturers apply different approaches, many based on the use of technology, to support the learning process of students and to adequately motivate them. The results of different studies (Law et al., 2010) (Tuparov et al., 2012) also suggest that technology-based educational tools that are easy to use can improve motivation and efficiency in the learning process. In any case, it would be important that programming languages lecturers would be able to identify the factors that affect and motivate learning. This is especially useful to be able to help students' effectiveness (Law et al., 2010).

When teaching programming languages and paradigms it is very important to identify concepts with very precise definitions. Students must understand concepts to be able to solve programming challenges (Kazimoglu et al., 2012).

Also, in order to prepare students for programming it is important that they first know the basic concepts of algorithmic thinking. This means that students must be able to clearly define a problem, to divide it into smaller parts that are easier to solve and to determine the steps to solve the entire problem. To fulfil this objective students must be able to distinguish the essential characteristics from the unnecessary details (Denner et al., 2010). So programming requires that students understand the problem, define the solution and finally translate the solution into code by using a programming language. Different studies show that students find numerous difficulties in every step of this process (Kordaki, 2010).

There are applications especially focused on algorithmic thinking. The AlgoGames application (Douadi et al., 2012), supports beginners in the learning of algorithms. Some other authors have also proposed tools and methodologies to learn algorithms (Hundhausen & Brown, 2007; Jurado et al., 2012; Giraffa et al., 2014).

In the past few years, researchers have tried to improve the teaching of programming. To achieve this objective, they have focused on the different elements of the process. One of the aspects in which they have focused is methodologies. In fact, choosing the right methodology to teach programming is one of the main issues of the debate of teaching programming languages and paradigms (Astrachan et al., 2005; Bailie et al., 2003; Bergin et al., 2001). Another important aspect is to use an adequate programing language with beginners. Most popular programming languages for the software industry are Java or C++. However, some professors think that other languages such as Phyton are more adequate for beginners and thus more adequate for a teaching use.

A challenge is also to convert code learning into an activity that is mainly developed in groups instead of individually. With the idea of promoting teamwork in the learning process of languages and paradigms some projects have been developed like Nucleo (Sancho-Thomas et al., 2009). This project promoted that students acquired social skills and abilities for working in groups and that they adopted a more active role in the learning process. This is important as software industry projects are mainly undertaken by groups and not by individual programmers.

The use of games as learning tools has increased its importance during the last decades. Internet, the Web 2.0 or the social networks have contributed to this. Technology-based games are very popular for the younger generations, as for them technology has always existed and is integrated into their lives (Simões et al., 2013).

Educational games must be challenging for players. If there is no challenge, or if the challenge is not interesting enough, the game can be perceived by the student as boring and would be soon abandoned by him (Garcia-Peñalvo et al., 2013). One of the main objectives when designing a game for learning purposes must be to find the balance between entertainment and its added value as an educational tool (Garcia-Peñalvo et al., 2013).

Research indicates that the use of educational games during the learning process has positive effects over concentration, decision-making and problem-solving abilities, and that it also improves logical thinking, creativity and the ability to work in teams (Aguilera & Mendiz, 2003).

The use of educational games within the classroom is becoming more and more common. Games connect contents and specific abilities in a context where the student is able to try, make mistakes and finally learn from those mistakes. These educational tools can be especially useful in e-learning processes (Burgos et al., 2007).

It is also important that the educational tools and applications are accessible from mobile devices including smartphones, as nowadays most university students have one (Bento da Silva et al., 2014).

Another important stakeholder is data mining which is the process of discovering patterns in large data sets involving methods at the intersection of machine learning, statistics, and database systems. During the last years, researchers have started to use data-mining methods to improve e-learning systems (Romero et al., 2009). E-Learning systems accumulate big amounts of information which may be used to analyse students' behaviour and needs. According to Hogo (2010), data mining can be the solution to manage this huge information in order to be able to tailor the learning process to the students' needs.

It is also important to pay attention to the possibilities offered by ontologies. Ontologies can be created in every field to limit complexity and organize information into data and knowledge. As new ontologies are proposed, their use hopefully improves problem solving within that domain. It is important to develop educational tools that offer personalized and adaptive learning experiences to learners rather than just content and activities delivery. According to different authors like Rani et al (2015), ontologies can be helpful to develop personalized and adaptive e-learning tools.

Attention must also be paid to the nowadays increasing importance of competitive programming. Competitive programming is usually held over the Internet or local networks, and involves a huge number of participants trying to program according to provided specifications. Competitive programming is recognized and supported by several multinational software and Internet companies, and there are several organizations who host programming competitions on a regular basis.

In a programming competition a set of logical problems are proposed to the contestants who are required to write computer programs capable of solving each problem. Judging is based mostly upon number of problems solved and time spent for writing successful coding solutions, but may also include other factors (quality of output produced, execution time, program size, etc.)

Competitive programming has multiple benefits. One of the main benefits of competitive programming is that it promotes problem-solving and problem-solving is the key to successfully undertake nearly any task or activity. Competitive programming also increases the level of programmers' confidence in a particular language and it encourages programmers to think better and faster and to be more focused.

Finally, another tool that can play an important role in the learning of programming languages and paradigms are code validators. A code validator is a tool that can help software developers to determine if the code they wrote is correct or if their code contains errors that must be fixed. In the next sections of this chapter the authors provide a further discussion focused on code validators and describe their experience using a JavaScript code validator and exercises module integrated into the e-learning platform Moodle, with university students during a web programming course.

CODE VALIDATORS

In computing, code generation is the process by which a code generator converts some intermediate representation into a machine-code or lower-level form that can be readily executed by a machine. For example, some UML (Unified Modelling Language) CASE (Computer Assisted Software Engineering) tools are able to generate code apart from an UML Class Diagram which is a mainstay of object-oriented design that shows the classes of the system, their interrelationships (including inheritance, aggregation, and association), and the operations and attributes of the classes. Another example can be found in a compiler that is a program that in this case converts instructions into a machine-code or lower-level form so that they can be read and executed by a computer.

On the other side, a code validator is a tool that can help software developers to determine if the code they wrote contains or not errors that must be fixed. For example, a JSON validator should validate a JSON string against RFC (Request For Comments) 4627 (The application/json media type for JavaScript Object Notation) and against the JavaScript language specification. An HTML (Hypertext Markup Language) validator should validate a HTML string/file for well-formedness and compliance with w3c (World Wide Web Consortium) standards, making use of the doctype declaration to evaluate the document structure and report on, for example, missing or invalid attributes or unknown or unclosed tags. And a XML validator should validate a XML (eXtensible Markup Language) string/file against the specified XSD (XML Schema Definition) string/file or XML Schema that describes the structure of a XML document. The XML validator should check for well-formedness first, and then should validate the XML string/file against the XML Schema reporting the errors found.

Both type of tools can be very useful for both experienced programmers and learners that are making a first approach to the programming languages and paradigms. They are especially convenient in the second case because at this time a lot of errors are usually made, and these tools can be of great help to accelerate the learning process. More specifically, code validators can be one of the types of tools that can be used to teach and learn programming languages and paradigms. This type of tool can be of great help to students as they allow them to verify if their code is correct and, in case they made errors, to detect and correct those mistakes more easily and quickly. As previously discussed, programming is a skill that requires practice; and something gained with experience is that students learn better when they solve their own errors. So, providing them with a tool that makes them feel confident in programming, similar as having the professor near for helping, helps them in solving errors and understanding why it was wrong by themselves, as well as in improving not only their productivity but their motivation.

According to the authors' opinion, a good code validator must focus on different aspects. From the point of view of the student, collected during a focus group session with students, a code validator must be able to validate the code informing the student if the code is correct or incorrect. And if the code is not correct, the code validator must provide the student with information about the errors including the location and type of the errors. The code validator must also provide the student with help about the specific elements (objects, methods, etc.) of the programming language as well as with suggestions about how to correct the code, including the possibility of automatically replace a wrong code with a correct one. A final valuable element for the student is that the code validator offers statistics of the errors committed by the student. On the other side, from the point of view of the lecturer, a key aspect would be that the code validator can be customised by, for example, adding feedback for the different type of errors. Another important aspect in the case of the lecturer is the error statistics as they provide him with information about which are the issues of the programming language that are more difficult to understand for the group of students or for a specific student.

Taking both points of view into account, the authors defined the requirements that a code validator must have to be useful during the learning process. More specifically it is important that the code validator has a user-friendly interface so that it can be used without previous training. In this sense, it is also important that the code validator does not consume too many resources and that it has reasonable response times so that it offers a good user experience. Another important aspect is that the code validator is able to ensure the integrity of the data compiled and stored, especially when these data are going to be used for assessment purposes.

Students of programming languages must do a lot of training and need quick feedback during their learning processes. When the number of students is high, the professor cannot provide them with personalised and immediate feedback. And when the students have to wait a long time for the professor's advice, their learning process is slowed down. This is the reason why Danutama & Liem (2013) indicate that the use of code validators must be of great help during the learning process for programming languages students.

Other authors like Yusof et al. (2012) highlight that code validators can be useful to assess students. However, a main disadvantage is that the assessment will be mainly based on the result of the validation of the code syntax without being able to take into account other assessment criteria or other requirements specified by the lecturer.

One of the fields in which validators have traditionally been used is web programming. In this sense, an important starting point is the work developed by the w3c (W3C, 2018a) in the field of code validation, and more specifically, the code validators for HTML (W3C, 2018b) and for the Cascading Style Sheets (CSS) (W3C, 2018c). On the downside, the fact that these tools do not provide a record along time by student and by class hindered their use in the learning process, and guided us to the requirement of trying to integrate code validators into the LMS (Learning Management System) used in the teaching-learning process.

Another programming language usually used for the development of interactive web applications is the client-side scripting language JavaScript. HTML, CSS, and JavaScript are the basic three client-side technologies for web programming. Regarding JavaScript there are also some interesting tools available like Closure Compiler (Google, 2018), JSHint (JSHint.com, 2018) JSLint (JSLint.com, 2018) or ESLint (ESLint.org, 2018). However, a good pedagogical use cannot be made of these applications as they are, so the authors decided to try to provide the open source virtual e-learning platform Moodle (Moodle.org, 2018), currently used by students, with code validation facilities. This way the students perceive the code validators as tools adequately integrated in their usual virtual learning environment, unlike for example those provided by the w3c. Besides checking the code, it was decided to add some pedagogical features to help the teaching-learning process, more specifically extending the checker to include some programming recommendations and including appropriate feedback.

Moodle-Based JavaScript Code Validator and Exercises Module

The work was focused on JavaScript as it has a higher level of difficulty: while HTML is a markup language, and CSS is a style syntax, JavaScript offers different features like the possibility to work with objects or event handlers that, in the experience of several years teaching programming languages and paradigms of the authors, may cause difficulties to the students.

JavaScript is a lightweight, interpreted language that is best known as the scripting language for web pages. JavaScript runs on the client side of the web and can be used to program how the web pages behave on the occurrence of an event.

The University of Valladolid has adopted Moodle as the official e-learning platform. Moodle allows lecturers to create courses to support and improve their teaching. Students and lecturers find in Moodle a dual asynchronous path that allows them to communicate through different tools such as discussion forums. Moodle also offers a repository for learning materials so that professors can offer exercises, readings or videos for the students. Moodle is made of different modules. Moreover, new modules can be developed and integrated into Moodle. This feature has made of Moodle a very popular e-learning platform because its users can customise this e-learning platform by adding modules developed by them or by others. Of course, in order to guarantee interoperability, the new modules have to be developed following a number of requisites.

The Moodle-based JavaScript validator developed checks different syntax elements of the language, and more important offers feedback to the students which may be useful during their learning process, and the whole process takes place within the e-learning platform Moodle where the course is offered.

Some examples of the syntax checks that the JavaScript validator is able to carry out are focused on functions as the JavaScript validator searches for the open and close parentheses in the definition of the function. And it also checks that the function has a name and that it is a valid one starting with '[a-z]', '[A-Z]' o '_', and not containing blank spaces or special characters. Also, the name chosen for the function must not be itself a reserved keyword in any of the ECMAScript versions. Similar checks are done regarding the names chosen for the parameters of the function.

For example, in the case of the JavaScript definition for a function shown in Figure 1, the validator will highlight multiple mistakes including the use of the word continue for the name of the function as continue is a JavaScript reserved keyword from ECMAScript version 2, or the names chosen for the different parameters as these names include a special character (in the case of the first parameter), start with a number (in the case of the second parameter) and contain a blank space (in the case of the third parameter).

The JavaScript validator will also check if the code sentences are ended with the ';' character, although there are exceptions as in the case that the code sentence begins for example with 'function', '{ ', '}', 'if', 'elseif', 'else', 'for', 'do', 'while' – not belonging to the 'do-while' control structure –, 'switch' or 'case'.

Regarding the definition of variables, the JavaScript validator checks if the variable has been assigned a name and a value, if the value is delimited by quotation marks or if the opening and closure quotation marks used are of the same type. Moreover, the JavaScript validator performs relevant checks regarding the name given to the variable.

The JavaScript validator also focuses on the sentences for flow control like 'if', 'elseif', 'for', 'while', 'switch' or 'case' where different tailored checks are made for each case. And it is also able to identify event handlers and will warn the student in case the code contains an event handler but no value is specified for it. HTML events can be linked to HTML elements. When JavaScript is used in HTML pages, JavaScript can react on these events.

The JavaScript validator also verifies the correctness of the use of JavaScript objects. JavaScript is designed on a simple object-based paradigm. It supports prototype based object construction. Objects are created programmatically, by

Figure 1. Example of the validation of a function definition

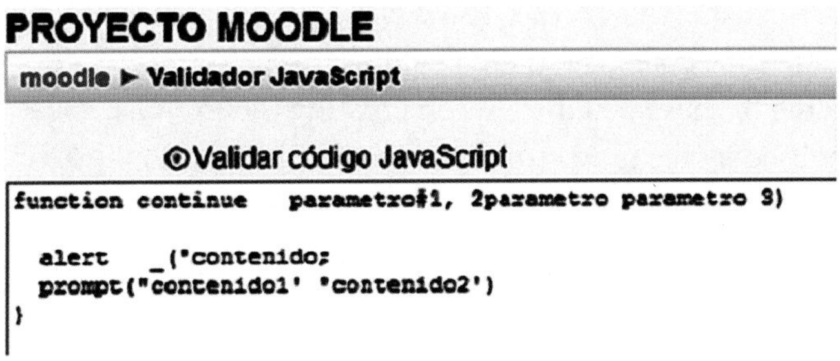

attaching methods and properties to otherwise empty objects at run time. Once an object has been constructed it can be used as a blueprint (or prototype) for creating similar objects. An object is a collection of properties, and a property is an association between a name (or key) and a value. A property's value can be a function, in which case the property is known as a method. In addition to objects that are predefined in the browser, the user can define their own objects. An object is a software bundle of related state and behaviour. Objects in JavaScript, just as in many other programming languages, are often used to model the real-world objects. The JavaScript validator checks that if any property or method is used with an object, it is one defined for that object. The JavaScript validator is able to work with both JavaScript built-in objects and with objects defined by the user.

In JavaScript, even the HTML document becomes an object (the document object) when it is loaded into a web browser. The Document Object Model (DOM) is an Application Programming Interface (API) for valid HTML. It is a platform and language-neutral interface that defines the logical structure of documents and the way a document is accessed and manipulated. With the Document Object Model, programmers can build documents, navigate their structure, and add, modify, or delete elements and content. Anything found in an HTML document can be accessed, changed, deleted, or added using the Document Object Model.

Learning how to work with objects in any programming language is a big challenge and needs a lot of training (Yusof et al., 2012). This is important as there are many programming languages that involve the use of objects and in fact software objects are the base of the Object-Oriented Programming (OOP) which is a programming language model organized around objects rather than actions and data rather than logic.

For this reason, and in order to complement the JavaScript validator and to facilitate the students the work with objects in JavaScript, a Moodle-based JavaScript exercise module has also been developed. The lecturer can create different types of exercises focused on the work with objects in JavaScript which is an essential feature of this programming language. When creating the exercises, the lecturer can determine that students receive some clues, but each clue will be accompanied by a decrease in the score. There are penalties defined by default, but the lecturer can set the value of these penalties when creating the exercise. Besides getting the feedback specified by the professor, the students can view the JavaScript object tree as help. At the end of the exercise the students will receive a scorecard revealing if their responses were correct or not. When an exercise is created by the lecturer, some information has to be provided including the name and text of the exercise and the answer of the exercise. This information regarding exercises can be modified by the lecturer at any time.

The exercises created by the lecturers can be used for the students' self-evaluation in which case at the end they will receive a score that can be viewed by the lecturer.

Students can access exercises to complete the code related to objects. If the student is not able to solve the exercise, it is possible to ask for a clue and the system will provide some information, as well as to ask to see part of the JavaScript object tree. After solving the exercise the student will get feedback from the system informing the student if the answer was correct or not.

The student can also decide to take a self-examination in which case he will be informed by the system of the penalties established by the lecturer when asking for clues at the beginning of the self-evaluation, and of the score at the end of the self-examination as shown in Figure 2. The scores obtained by the students in the self-evaluations will be accessible for the lecturers including detailed information about how many times students asked for clues or accessed the JavaScript object tree.

RESULTS AND DISCUSSION

As an open source software engineering project, the result of the present work is an application that meets all the requirements initially established. More specifically:

- It is designed as a module for the open source virtual e-learning platform Moodle and offers a friendly user interface.
- It is able to check source codes, as those typically elaborated by engineering students initiating themselves in the use of client-side web technologies.
- It is able to challenge students with exercises focused on the work with objects in JavaScript.

Figure 2. Score after a self-evaluation

Calificaciones					
EJERCICIO		RESPUESTA	PISTAS	ÁRBOL	PUNTUACIÓN
Formulario	☒	window.document.form.submit	1	0	0.00
History	☑	window.history.back	0	1	9.00
				Total:	9.00/2: **4.50**

- It provides students with tailored feedback after completing exercises.
- It allows students to undertake self-evaluations.
- It allows lecturers to access detailed information including score, about the self-evaluations undertaken by the students.

The application was tested with engineering students during an academic year. The experience took place within two different engineering study programs at the University of Valladolid as scenarios. The students were encouraged to use the JavaScript validator and exercises module and then were invited to talk about their user experience in a Moodle forum.

The great majority of the students, considered the use of these tools as very positive. They found them useful when beginning with JavaScript, as this language was quite more complex than HTML and CSS, which were the client-side technologies with which they had worked so far in the course. Students found the JavaScript validator useful to understand the theoretical basis of the programming language as it was helpful to identify common mistakes made by beginners.

Also, the great majority of the students perceived the possibility of using code validators as positive, both the ones offered by the Web Consortium and the one developed in the context of this work. And most students thought that it was better to have the code validator integrated into the virtual learning platform that gives support to the course, i.e., Moodle, rather than having to access them externally. The possibility to train with exercises was also appreciated by the students as it helped them to get experience in the work with objects in JavaScript.

However, most of the students still preferred to obtain feedback from lecturers, and the feedback from the system was appreciated in case the lecturer was not available. This is understandable because of the multiple benefits of face-to-face communication. Non-verbal cues, including body language and facial expressions, are just as crucial when communicating, as the words we say. Face-to-face communication also helps to build collaborative environments that inspire and energise students to actively participate in their learning processes. These environments foster engagement and motivation, which is important for both students and professors. The authors' intention is not to replace the face-to-face communication between students and lecturers in the context of the learning process but to offer alternatives than can enrich and improve the learning process.

Professors engaged in the performed experiences drew some conclusions regarding the behavior of the students when using the tools including the JavaScript validator and exercises module:

- Students felt encouraged to start the learning of the JavaScript programming language by themselves, reproducing and extending the examples given in class, without fear of not being able to ask for the professor's advice.
- In the laboratory, students tended to use the learning support applications less, as they preferred to ask the professor, although they often asked for issues that have arisen previously when working on their own with the applications.
- Using these kind of Moodle-based applications, students could better understand the potential of the topic studied, i.e., the client-side scripting language for web development.

This testing in a real life scenario was aimed to collect feedback data and comments in order to improve the applications tailoring it to the needs of the target users and enhancing their experience with the applications. As an open source software product, feedback from students suggested a set of further developments to provide the applications with an added value, which are the following:

Add multilingual support. Moodle works with language packages which will facilitate the translation of the application into different languages. This is important as the web development courses in which these tools were used usually have Erasmus students which may feel more confident if they have the possibility to work with the educational tools in their mother tongue languages, at least during the initial stages.

Support the checking of other programming languages other than the JavaScript client-side scripting language.

Develop a system that allows to self-complete key terms into the text editor. Even if the application was initially addressed to check a code correctness, it may be useful to incorporate the most common structure layouts used in the programming language with which it is able to work.

To integrate all the code validators in one, i.e., to count with a validation service integrated in Moodle where they could enter a code of any type, in our context HTML, CSS, or JavaScript or a mixture of those, and that the corresponding engines were called to do the necessary validation to provide the adequate feedback.

CONCLUSION

In this chapter, we have presented two educational tools focused on the client-side scripting language JavaScript to support the web development applications learning process for engineering students. The experiences were carried out during an academic course with quite positive results. Taking into consideration the results of the project, the main conclusions of the present work focusing on the pedagogic aspect, are, so far, the following:

- There are many factors that must be taken into account as they can contribute to develop personalized and adaptive e-learning tools and processes in the field of programming languages and paradigms, such as data mining, ontologies or competitive programming.
- Code validators can be very useful for learners that are making a first approach to the programming languages and paradigms field of study.
- The work of professors is very valuable and can difficulty be replaced by any ICT-based tool.
- Face-to-face communication has multiple benefits and helps to build collaborative environments that inspire and energise students to actively participate in their learning process.
- However, ICT-based tools and digital communication can enhance and enrich the experience of both students and professors during a blended learning process.
- To support a course through a single virtual learning environment is preferable than to have to access different stand-alone tools, both for professors and students.
- To count with tailored educational tools, as is the case of a JavaScript code validator and exercises module for a front-end web applications development course, is always an asset.
- The tools used in an e-learning project must be pedagogic and student-oriented.

REFERENCES

Aguilera, M. D., & Mendiz, A. (2003). Video Games and Education: Education in the Eace of a "Parallel School". *Computers in Entertainment, 1*(1), 1–10. doi:10.1145/950566.950583

Astrachan, O., Bruce, K., Koffman, K. E., Kölling, M., & Reges, S. (2005). Resolved: objects early has failed. In *Proceedings of the 36th SIGCSE technical symposium on computer science* (Vol. 37, pp. 451-452). New York: ACM. 10.1145/1047344.1047359

Bailie, F., Courtney, M., Murray, K., Schiaffino, R., & Tuohy, S. (2003). Objects first – does it work? *Journal of Computing Sciences in Colleges, 19*(2), 303–305.

Bento da Silva, J., Rochadel, W., Schardosim Simao, J. P., & Vaz da Silva Fidalgo, A. (2014). Adaptation Model of Mobile Remote Experimentation for Elementary Schools. *IEEE Revista Iberoamericana de Tecnologias del Aprendizaje, 9*(1), 28-32. Retrieved from http://ieeexplore.ieee.org/stamp/stamp.jsp?tp=&arnumber=67 19587&isnumber=6746056

Bergin, J., Eckstein, J., Wallingford, E., & Manns, M. L. (2001). Patterns for gaining different perspectives. *8th conference on Pattern Languages of Programs (PLoP 2001).*

Brito, M. A., & Sá-Soares, F. (2014). Assessment frequency in introductory computer programming disciplines. *Computers in Human Behavior, 30*, 623-628. Retrieved from http://www.sciencedirect.com/science/article/pii/S0747563213002835

Burgos, D., Tattersall, C., & Koper, R. (2007). Re-purposing existing generic games and simulations for e-learning. *Computers in Human Behavior, 23*(6), 2656-2667. Retrieved from http://www.sciencedirect.com/science/article/pii/S0747563206000963

Chi, M. T., & Ceci, S. J. (1987). Content knowledge: Its role, representation, and restructuring in memory development. In *Advances in Child Development and Behavior* (pp. 91–142). Orlando, FL: Academic Press.

Chi, M. T., Glaser, R., & Farr, M. (1988). *The nature of expertise.* Hillsdale, NJ: Lawrence Erlbaum and Associates.

Danutama, K., & Liem, I. (2013). Scalable Autograder and LMS Integration. *Procedia Technology, 11*, 388-395. Retrieved from http://www.sciencedirect.com/science/article/pii/S2212017313003617#

Denner, J., Werner, L., & Ortiz, E. (2012). Computer games created by middle school girls: Can they be used to measure understanding of computer science concepts? *Computers & Education, 58*(1), 240–249. Retrieved from http://www.sciencedirect. com/science/article/pii/S0360131511001849

Douadi, B., Tahar, B., & Hamid, S. (2012). Smart edutainment game for algorithmic thinking. *Procedia - Social and Behavioral Sciences, 31*, 454-458. Retrieved from http://www.sciencedirect.com/science/article/pii/S187704281103014X

ESLint.org. (2018). *ESLint web-site*. Retrieved from https://eslint.org/

García-Peñalvo, F. J., Johnson, M., Ribeiro-Alves, G., Minović, M., & Conde-Gonzalez, M. A. (2014). Informal learning recognition through a cloud ecosystem. *Future Generation Computer Systems, 32*, 282-294. Retrieved from http://www. sciencedirect.com/science/article/pii/S0167739X13001696

Giraffa, L. M. M., Moraes, M. C., & Uden, L. (2014). Teaching Object-Oriented Programming in First-Year Undergraduate Courses Supported By Virtual Classrooms. *Proceedings of the 2nd International Workshop on Learning Technology for Education in Cloud (Springer Proceedings in Complexity)*, 15-26. Retrieved from http://link. springer.com/chapter/10.1007/978-94-007-7308-0_2

Glaser, R. (1984). Education and thinking: The role of knowledge. *American Psychologist, 39*(2), 93-104. doi:10.1037/0003-066X.39.2.93

Glaser, R., & De Corte, E. (1992). Preface to the assessment of prior knowledge as a determinant for future learning. In F. J. R. C. Dochy (Ed.), *Assessment of prior knowledge as a determinant for future learning* (pp. 1–2). Lemma B.V./Jessica Kingsley Publishers. Retrieved from http://ericae.net/books/dochyl/

Google. (2018). *Closure compiler*. Retrieved from https://developers.google.com/ closure/compiler/

Gurcan-Namlu, A. (2003). The effect of learning strategy on computer anxiety. *Computers in Human Behavior, 19*(5), 565-578. Retrieved from http://www. sciencedirect.com/science/article/pii/S0747563203000037

Hogo, M. A. (2010). Evaluation of e-learning systems based on fuzzy clustering models and statistical tools. *Expert Systems with Applications, 10*, 6891-6903. Retrieved from http://www.sciencedirect.com/science/article/pii/S0957417410002137

Hundhausen, C. D., & Brown, J. L. (2007). What You See Is What You Code: A "live" algorithm development and visualization environment for novice learners. *Journal of Visual Languages and Computing, 18*(1), 22-47. Retrieved from http://www.sciencedirect.com/science/article/pii/S1045926X06000140

Jara, C. A., Candelas, F. A., & Torres, F. (2008). Virtual and remote laboratory for robotics e-learning. *Computer-Aided Chemical Engineering, 25*, 1193–1198. Retrieved from http://www.sciencedirect.com/science/article/pii/S1570794608802052#

Jenkins, T. (2001). The motivation of students of programming. *Proceedings of the 6th conference on innovation and technology in computer science education*, 53–56. doi: 10.1145/377435.377472

JSHint.com. (2018). *JSHint web-site*. Retrieved from http://jshint.com/

Jurado, F., Redondo, M. A., & Ortega, M. (2012). Blackboard architecture to integrate components and agents in heterogeneous distributed eLearning systems: An application for learning to program. *Journal of Systems and Software, 85*(7), 1621-1636. Retrieved from http://www.sciencedirect.com/science/article/pii/S0164121212000416

Kazimoglu, C., Kiernan, M., Bacon, L., & MacKinnon, L. (2012). Learning Programming at the Computational Thinking Level via Digital Game-Play. *Procedia Computer Science, 9*, 522-531. Retrieved from http://www.sciencedirect.com/science/article/pii/S1877050912001779

Kordaki, M. (2010). A drawing and multi-representational computer environment for beginners' learning of programming using C: Design and pilot formative evaluation. *Computers & Education, 54*(1), 69-87. Retrieved from http://www.sciencedirect.com./science/article/pii/S0360131509001845

Law, K. M. Y., Lee, V. C. S., & Yu, Y. T. (2010). Learning motivation in e-learning facilitated computer programming courses. *Computers & Education, 55*(1), 218-228. Retrieved from http://www.sciencedirect.com/science/article/pii/S0360131510000102

Moodle.org. (2018). *Moodle web-site*. Retrieved from http://moodle.org/

Moons, J., & De Backer, C. (2013). The design and pilot evaluation of an interactive learning environment for introductory programming influenced by cognitive load theory and constructivism. *Computers & Education, 60*(1), 368-384. Retrieved from http://www.sciencedirect.com/science/article/pii/S0360131512001959

Newstetter, W., & McCracken, M. (2001). Novice Conceptions of Design: Implications for the Design of Learning Environments. In *Design Knowing and Learning: Cognition in Design Education*. Elsevier Science. Retrieved from http://www.sciencedirect.com/science/article/pii/B9780080438689500048

Rani, M., Nayak, R., & Vyas, O. P. (2015). An ontology-based adaptive personalized e-learning system, assisted by software agents on cloud storage. *Knowledge-Based Systems, 90*, 33–48. doi:10.1016/j.knosys.2015.10.002

Romero, C., González, P., Ventura, S., del Jesús, M. J., & Herrera, F. (2009). Evolutionary algorithms for subgroup discovery in e-learning: A practical application using Moodle data. *Expert Systems with Applications, 36*(2), 1632-1644. Retrieved from http://www.sciencedirect.com/science/article/pii/S0957417407005933

Sancho-Thomas, P., Fuentes-Fernández, R., & Fernández-Manjón, B. (2009) Learning teamwork skills in university programming courses. *Computers & Education, 53*(2), 517-531. Retrieved from http://www.sciencedirect.com/science/article/pii/S0360131509000797

Simões, J., Díaz-Redondo, R., & Fernández-Vilas, A. (2013). A social gamification framework for a K-6 learning platform. *Computers in Human Behavior, 29*(2), 345-353. Retrieved from http://www.sciencedirect.com/science/article/pii/S0747563212001574

Tan, J., Guo, X., Zheng, W., & Zhong, M. (2014). Case-based teaching using the Laboratory Animal System for learning C/C++ programming. *Computers & Education, 77*, 39-49. Retrieved from http://www.sciencedirect.com/science/article/pii/S0360131514000888

Tuparov, G., Tuparova, D., & Tsarnakova, A. (2012). Using Interactive Simulation-Based Learning Objects in Introductory Course of Programming. *Procedia - Social and Behavioral Sciences, 46*, 2276-2280. Retrieved from http://www.sciencedirect.com/science/article/pii/S1877042812015984

Vega, C., Jiménez, C., & Villalobos, J. (2013). A scalable and incremental project-based learning approach for CS1/CS2 courses. *Education and Information Technologies, 18*(2), 309-329. Retrieved from http://link.springer.com/article/10.1007/s10639-012-9242-8#

World Wide Web Consortium (W3C). (2018a). *Web standards: technical specifications and guidelines*. Available at http://www.w3.org/

World Wide Web Consortium (W3C). (2018b). *Markup validation services.* Available at http://validator.w3.org/

World Wide Web Consortium (W3C). (2018c). *CSS validation services.* Available at http://jigsaw.w3.org/css-validator/

Yusof, N., Zin, N. A. M., & Adnan, N. S. (2012). Java Programming Assessment Tool for Assignment Module in Moodle E-learning System. *Procedia - Social and Behavioral Sciences, 56,* 767-773. Retrieved from http://www.sciencedirect.com/science/article/pii/S1877042812041766

KEY TERMS AND DEFINITIONS

Code Validation: The process of checking that the code is correct. In the case of web applications, it is the process of checking that the code is in compliance with the standards and recommendations set by the World Wide Web Consortium (W3C) for the web.

Document Object Model (DOM): An application programming interface (API) for valid HTML that defines the logical structure of documents and the way a document is accessed and manipulated.

JavaScript: A client-side scripting language commonly used in web development.

Learning Management System (LMS): A software application that allows to manage learning courses. A well-known and widely used example is Moodle.

Moodle: Acronym for modular object-oriented dynamic learning environment, a free popular learning management system used at many institutions like for example the University of Valladolid in Spain.

Programming Language: Coded language used by programmers to write instructions that a computer can understand to do what the programmer wants.

Programming Paradigm: A style of programming.

Web Application: Any software application that runs in a web browser or that is created by using a browser-supported programming language. It is stored on a remote web server and delivered over the internet to a web browser.

Chapter 6

Teaching Model-Driven Engineering in a Master's Program:
Three Editions on a PBL-Based Experience

Alexandre Bragança
Polytechnic Institute of Porto, Portugal

Isabel Azevedo
Polytechnic Institute of Porto, Portugal

Nuno Bettencourt
Polytechnic Institute of Porto, Portugal

ABSTRACT

Model-driven engineering (MDE) is an approach to software engineering that adopts models as the central artefact. Although the approach is promising in addressing major issues in software development, particularly in dealing with software complexity, and there are several success cases in the industry as well as growing interest in the research community, it seems that it has been hard to generalize its gains among software professionals. To address this issue, MDE must be taught at a higher-education level. This chapter presents a three-year experience in teaching MDE in a course of a master program in informatics engineering. The chapter provides details on how a project-based learning approach was adopted and evolved along three editions of the course. Results of a student survey are discussed and compared to those from another course. In addition, several other similar teaching experiences are analyzed.

DOI: 10.4018/978-1-5225-7455-2.ch006

INTRODUCTION

During their education, engineers learn about the relevant models in their areas and how to further apply them. One of the capabilities that students should acquire in programs that qualify for building systems, where software is a key and intense part, is "create and use models in system development" (Landwehr et al., 2017).

More intensive use of models has also been adopted for software engineering. Among them is Model-Driven Engineering (MDE), which promises several ways to address well-known problems (Somers, 2017), including software increasing complexity (Whittle, Hutchinson, & Rouncefield, 2014). Moreover, it is in line with the usual start of designing complex systems with some level of abstraction provided by models in traditional engineering disciplines.

In software product lines, substantial gains can be achieved, even for quality assurance, when the effort is put in the domain engineering instead of solely in the application engineering. In fact, MDE has been applied successfully in the industry but essentially in large corporations that can afford the inherent costs (Baker, Loh, & Weil, 2005; Burden, Heldal, & Whittle, 2014; Hossler, Born, & Saito, 2006).

However, it seems that MDE's advantages have been hard to generalize in a way that makes it available for the common developer (Haan, 2008). Also, companies that already design and use models dedicated to a particular domain may probably use MDE more than others that develop generic software (Whittle et al., 2014). Whittle et al. (2014) mentioned an organization that had to train hundreds of developers with difficulties in abstract thinking when MDE was adopted.

Multiple factors hinder organizations from embracing MDE, and its acceptance clearly requires technical changes, but also the overcoming of human attitudes when facing new techniques and the need to use new tools (Brambilla, Cabot, & Wimmer, 2012; Whittle et al., 2017). This aspect was highlighted in general some years ago (Glass, 2011) with the recognition that there is a learning curve with an initial low productivity that is acceptable when people realize the value of their adoption. In a Model-Driven Development (MDD) – which is essentially MDE focused on software development – survey, it has been found out that "in most cases, the use of the MDD in organisations depends only on the interest of people to use it" (Parviainen, Takalo, Teppola, & Tihinen, 2009) and people may only be appealed to use what they have heard about. Nevertheless, new competencies are needed, and their lack can compromise MDE appropriateness (Christensen & Ellingsen, 2016). Thus, pedagogical and training issues cannot be ignored (Goulão, Amaral, & Mernik, 2016).

In this context the authors share a three-year experience in teaching Model-Driven Engineering in a course of a master program in Informatics Engineering, a total of three editions of the course. Each one can be seen as action research (Lewin, 1946) iteration (see Figure 1) that aimed to analyse if it is possible to promote MDE subjects using a Project-Based Learning approach. This research question also reflects the desire to maintain the highest quality standards of the program, which is accredited by many international bodies. For instance, the American Board for Engineering and Technology (ABET) accreditation emphasizes the need of continuous improvement of programs. In fact, the reflection on the appropriateness of the provided learning experiences and pedagogical models has been institutionally reinforced. The continuous improvement of the course and, consequently, of the program has been the main motivation for this work. Our expectation is that the introduction of courses devoted to MDE may have the same impact on software development as Unified Modelling Language (UML) had in the past.

The rest of this chapter is organized as follows. The next section ("A Project-Based Learning Approach") details how the PBL model has been applied in the course and the continual evolution during these three editions. Results of a student survey regarding this experience are presented and discussed in the section "Feedback About the Course". An analysis of other experiences in teaching MDE is presented in the section "Other Courses on Model-Driven Engineering". The authors conclude by sharing their findings regarding how to conduct MDE teaching in order to promote a wider adoption of its advantages by future professionals in the final section.

A PROJECT-BASED LEARNING APPROACH

Boffo (2015) explore the issues related to what people are able to do and transversal capabilities, soft skills and flexible abilities. International engineering accreditation bodies such as the ABET include soft skills in their criteria under the umbrella of

Figure 1. Detailed action research iteration

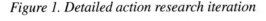
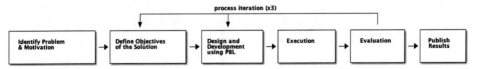

"professional skills". It is noteworthy that "a shift to outcomes-based education and accreditation" is listed among the top five ones that have occurred during the last 100 years in engineering education (Froyd, Wankat, & Smith, 2012), because of its positive effects, including the incentives to apply active learning methods.

Some ABET criteria for student outcomes in the 2019-2020 cycle even reinforce the importance of some of the non-technical skills. For instance, "an ability to function on multidisciplinary teams" is replaced with "an ability to function effectively on a team whose members together provide leadership, create a collaborative and inclusive environment, establish goals, plan tasks, and meet objectives" (ABET EAC, 2017).

However, these subjects are difficult to effectively be incorporated in academic curricula, with a clear difference between what is taught and what is translated to competences. Universities have been dealing with the need to develop non-technical skills in future software engineers, which are considered as core competencies for them (Sedelmaier & Landes, 2014).

Project-based learning (PBL) is a common instructional approach used to advance the acquisition of many skills a future software engineer will need in their professional practice (Marques, Ochoa, Bastarrica, & Gutierrez, 2018). The use of a PBL method aims at developing technical and non-technical competences in engineering students. Problem-based learning and project-based learning have some common characteristics that make them appropriate for engineering education. However, while problem-based learning focus on the solution of a problem, project-based learning concentrate in the desired product with tasks to be accomplished to that purpose (Uziak, 2016).

Both problem-based and project-based learning approaches have been used in the Informatics Engineering master's at ISEP. Currently, the program offers a curriculum organized in four specialization tracks, and one of them is Software Engineering, which was introduced in September 2015. One of the courses of this track is Domain Engineering (EDOM).

In this program, each semester has 16 weeks. The available class types (Lectures, Lab and Tutorial) have different teaching minutes assigned per week. There are two occurrences of 50 minutes for lecture classes, one occurrence of 110 minutes for its lab classes and 50 minutes for its tutorial classes (one occurrence). All classes take place after work hours.

Lectures are used to introduce or explain concepts, but also to show demonstrations related to what is being developed in lab classes. Lab lessons have hands-on classroom assignments in the first weeks and support a project development with several iterations in the final stage. Feedback about students' performance is provided in different delivery moments, facilitating the application of some pedagogical patterns, namely

Early Warning and Embrace Correction (Bergin et al., 2012). Tutorial classes are used to support the exercises, the project as well as general issues.

Each topic introduced during classroom assignments is then explored by the students during the project development. The project provides a global vision by combining the small pieces developed during the semester in a bigger project to provide enough integration of the covered topics. Thus, a minimum skill level should have been acquired when the project is launched. Students should have evidences of their work through commits in their GIT repository, which are used in the grading of exercises and project.

EDOM's major goal is to "provide students with advanced skills regarding domain engineering and some of the most recent scientific innovations and practices originating from specific approaches that are related to it: model-driven engineering, domain-specific languages (DSL) and product line engineering" (ISEP, n.d.). By the end of the course, students are able to:

- Analyse domain engineering as the top of an iceberg composed of a myriad of processes, techniques, tools and methodologies which all have reuse in software engineering as the ultimate goal;
- Analyse software product lines as a practice that promotes large scale reuse;
- Design and implement domain-specific languages and model transformations in the context of model-driven engineering;
- Manage recent approaches in the context of domain engineering and reuse: model-driven software engineering and domain-specific languages;
- Debate about options in projects related to model-driven engineering.

The detailed contents of EDOM for all editions were:

- **Domain Engineering and Practice Areas:** General concepts, reuse and abstraction, domain analysis and product line engineering.
- **Domain Modelling:** isolating the domain, the building blocks of a domain model, and the life cycle of domain objects;
- **Model-Driven Software Engineering (MDSE):** Principles and use cases, Model-Driven Architecture (MDA) and the Unified Modelling Language (UML), extensions to UML, the Object Constraint Language (OCL), and the integration of MDSE and the development process.
- **Domain-Specific Languages:** The Eclipse Modelling Framework (EMF), developing a modelling language, abstract syntax and concrete syntax, model to model transformations and out-place transformations with Atlas

Transformation Language (ATL), model to text transformations (Acceleo), code generation, and managing models.

- **Software Product Lines (SPL):** core activities (domain engineering, application engineering and product line management), SPL practice patterns, and variability models.

As mentioned, two different learning methods have been employed, as described:

- **Problem-Based Learning:** In the first weeks a problem-based learning method is used, devoted to acquisition of knowledge. The problems are to be solved in two weeks (one, in the first two editions with few exceptions), where no minimum grade is demanded.
- **Project-Based Learning:** In the final weeks the project aims to support the application of knowledge over a longer period of time. A score below 10,0 out of 20,0 is not acceptable.

These differences in time-length and in knowledge attainment or application are among the common distinctive characteristics of the two methods (Mills &Treagust, 2003).

The core recommended bibliography has been three books that cover most of the course contents, namely (Brambilla, Cabot, & Wimmer 2017), (Clements & Northrop, 2001) and (Gronback, 2009).

Since the introduction of the course two phases can be distinguished:

1st Phase: 2015-2016 and 2016-2017 academic years editions;
2nd Phase: 2017-2018 academic year edition.

Some little changes introduced in the second academic year ensured a smooth transition, without significant impact in the number of students successfully completing the course (see Table 1).

Table 1. Percentage of approvals

Academic Year Edition	Number of Students	% of Approvals, Excluding Those That Did Not Attend Classes
2015-2016	50	61
2016-2017	86	54
2017-2018	137	55*

* Preliminary number as, in accordance with the school's internal regulations, some students still have another possibility to be approved.

However, there was a significant decrease in the number of students that could not take the final exam (see Table 2) in phase 2 (2017-2018). It is still early to judge these findings and come up with possible reasons, because only one edition of the 2nd phase has passed. Nevertheless, when the two phases are discussed, some aspects are detailed that could have had an impact.

In summary the core activities related to the didactical approach adopted in the two phases are described in Table 3. The main differences are explored in the upcoming sub-sections.

It has been important the interconnection with another course, which is Software Development Organization (ODSOFT). Under the PBL approach, the proposed project has incorporated tasks for both courses with a common work assignment.

The main goal of ODSOFT is to make students "able to manage the life cycle of a software product." Therefore, the main contents of the course are deeply related to the continuous integration and delivery approach to software development. Specific topics comprise software tests, configuration management and building, versioning and deployment" (ISEP, n.d.). In ODSOFT students do manual software development with repetitive code and tasks. Not only the development is error-prone and with some degree of difficulty, but also the testing phase is extensive. In EDOM the students should achieve the same with code generation (as much as possible). There is an obvious contrast between these approaches, which is understood by the students and help them to realize the advantages of an MDE application.

All course editions included a written examination, which format has remained unchanged, as well as the covered subjects. It has had a minimum score of 8.0/20.0. The exam has been composed of groups of questions of several types, namely:

- True/False questions;
- Short answer questions;
- Essay questions.

Simple questions required an answer with justification in the first phase.

Table 2. Number of students not able to take the final exam

Academic Year Edition	Number of Students Enrolled on EDOM	Number of Students Without Course Attendance or Evaluation
2015-2016	50	14
2016-2017	86	40
2017-2018	137	7

Table 3. Main activities in all editions

Type of Activities	1st Phase	2nd Phase
Lectures	Presentations about different subjects, some demonstrations of tools and approaches.	Introduction to topics and tools, but more devoted to the exercises and the final project, with discussion of their challenges.
Exercises	Group size was 2 students and one student review the work of the colleague and proposes alternatives.	Group size was 3 students. Two students assigned for each exercise. Both students with specific assigned tasks had the need to propose alternatives for their own tasks.
Tutorial classes	Always available in the first year, and on demand in the second one.	Available on demand.
Off class support	An Hipchat forum was used to clarify doubts and propose solutions to problems mainly about exercises and tools.	A forum was used but, in another platform (Moodle).
Learning activities based on problems	One-week problems not related to the main project. The work with the lab professor is done within a two-hour lab session and the students continue their development during the rest of the week. Grading and comments available in the adopted version control platform. Group and individual deliverables.	Two-week problems as pieces to be integrated in the final project. Grading and comments orally provided after the deadline with a discussion of their options and possible alternatives. Group work with individual deliverables.
Guidance and evaluation of project intermediary state	In every class, intermediate delivery with later discussion in the classroom in a formative assessment.	In every class but with an evaluated delivery. Discussion on demand and if possible to arrange.
Presentation of final project	Many presentations, one for each course with focus on its specific parts. Group deliverables and presentations.	One presentation with discussion of everything asked for all courses. Group deliverables, and individual and group presentations.

First Phase

Main Platform for Exercises and Project

An open-source ERP system, Apache Open for Business (OFBiz), was used. The OFBiz platform is very declarative and model oriented, with many options for integrating with metamodeling tools. Even the level of specification of domain models is very interesting. Approaches such as product line of software can be easily exemplified from the platform. The project involved metamodels to generate artefacts (for example, generate the OFBiz configuration files). The possibility of some reverse engineering strand (creating models from existing artefacts) was taught but not explored.

For ODSOFT, mainly an entire automation pipeline for software development and project maintenance/ evolution was explored, with the use of configuration and build tools. Many possibilities for testing and deployment were enabled. During the exercises the students worked with some OFBiz DSLs, such as Entity DSL and Service DSL, to change or add entities and services.

For the second year, less components of OFBiz were used as a result of the many complaints related to the compilation time. Besides, the application was felt as too demanding for computers with less computational power. However, even these changes were not felt as enough and in the third edition another platform was adopted, as explained later in this chapter.

The ODSOFT exercises heavily used the OFBiz platform, but its clear use in EDOM was limited to the project.

Assessment

Students worked in groups of two during the semester in some activities/exercises and a final project (which counted for 60% of the final grade).

A Bitbucket repository was extensively used, where all artefacts produced during the assignments and project were required to be committed to the repository.

There were a set of small exercises to be executed during the first lab classes. The following rules were published:

- The student started the exercise during the lab class but might complete it after class, during the same week;
- The exercise was executed by one of the students of the group. The exercise was committed to the Bitbucket team repository with a reference to the related Bitbucket issue;
- The other student of the group needed to revise the colleague's work and report the findings as a comment recorded in the Bitbucket related issue;
- Informal feedback about the exercise occurred in the tutorial class of the following week;
- Formal feedback was given by the Lab Class teacher as a comment in the Bitbucket issue and a score for the exercise was proposed;
- Students were able to revise the exercise during one more week to be graded again (the Lab Class teacher needed to be informed);
- The plan was announced as having 6 exercises starting at the second week.

In the second edition of the course, there were mainly two changes in the assessment procedure, albeit slight:

- Students could only change the solution on two exercises at most, after knowing their grades, and not all, as previously. They needed to inform the teacher and they could modify the solution previously proposed for the exercise in one week, with later re-evaluation with use of a feedback pedagogical pattern (Grade It Again, Sam (Bergin et al., 2012));
- The plan was to have 7 exercises starting at week 2.

The rating scale was from 0 to 4, with the following semantics:

0: No submission;
1: Did not achieve the requirements of the exercise;
2: Partially achieves the requirements of the exercise;
3: Completely achieves the requirements of the exercise and justifies the options;
4: Completely achieves the requirements of the exercise, justifies the options and writes any alternatives.

However, the following remarks were provided:

- Levels 3 and 4 could only be achieved if the exercise is revised by the companion team-member;
- The lowest score of one week was to be dismissed when calculating the average of the exercises, which is considered for the calculation of their final grade.

The project consisted of a set of requirements to fulfil regarding the integration of domain engineering concerns, particularly model driven engineering methods, techniques and tools with the OFBiz software platform. Students needed to plan, apply and analyse aspects of MDE to OFBiz. The rating scale was from 0 to 4, with the following semantics:

0: No submission;
1: Did not achieve the requirements of the deadline;
2: Partially achieves the requirements of the deadline;
3: Completely achieves the requirements by the deadline and the technical report includes justifications about the options;
4: Completely achieves the requirements by the deadline, the technical report includes justifications about the options and also a detailed analysis of the alternatives.

Second Phase

In the second phase and for the first time, EDOM and ODSOFT had the same exact teachers. In the first edition just one teacher had assigned classes in both courses, a number that rose to two in the following edition, and to three in the last edition. It was easier to combine all the efforts in the grading of works, analysis of reports, final project evaluation and even in the preparation and correction of exams.

The deep knowledge about what was being done in each course was beneficial to understand students' problems and consequently in their support. Many times, the lessons of a course became classes of both with doubts that were not limited to one course or another, and often expressed by students who were not formally part of that class. At the end, the teachers reported an overwhelming sense of realization, but immense tiredness.

Another alteration in this phase was the change from Hipchat to a Moodle forum. It was dictated by the limited functionalities related to the free account of the person who owned the forum. For instance, it was impossible to see the messages after some time, and thus, at this moment, all questions and answers are no longer available. With Moodle, licensing issues are not a concern and all questions and answers are always available, which makes it easier to compare subjects, tools, exercises, or project tasks that trigger more clarification requests in the various course editions.

Main Platform for Exercises and Project

Google Web Toolkit (GWT) is a toolkit for building Asynchronous JavaScript and XML (AJAX) web applications using Java. A transpiler generates JavaScript code able to run across many different browsers. There is an integration of the compiled application frontend with other technologies such as HTML and XML. Version 2.8.2 was released in October 2017.

Its maturity, simplicity and used patterns were factors that led to its adoption. For ODSOFT, many opportunities were opened, and for EDOM the code generation for this platform was fully explored.

Enterprise platforms and applications with different development degrees have used similar possibilities. For instance, a solution that included an automatic GWT code generator (Nakoula & Houimel, 2017), a model-driven development with GWT (Ainsley, 2016) and a language for declarative code generation (Nelson, 2017) were presented in some GWT conferences. However, code generator following an MDE approach to be integrated in the GWT platform was firstly proposed in academic settings (Meliá, Gómez, Pérez, & Díaz, 2008).

A Model-driven development process was applied to a College Management System (CMS) in the third edition of the Domain Engineering course. The source code and some explanations that were complemented in person were made available at a specific repository (Bragança, Azevedo, & Bettencourt, 2018), which is based on examples from the GWT project website, specially the GWT Contacts Application (Ramsdale, 2010). This application was used as a base for the exercises and project. Starting by the domain entities and the relationships between them, represented in a Computer Independent Model (CIM) thus using transformations models, a Platform Independent Model (PIM) and a Platform Specific Model (PSM) were derived.

For ODSOFT the same ideas from previous editions were followed but now with a different platform, not OFBiz anymore. For EDOM, and for the first time, the use of the GWT platform was introduced in different exercises.

Assessment

A minor change was introduced in the final exam in this second phase. Simpler questions no longer required justification, but a penalization of wrong answers was introduced. Weighed up the pros and cons, mainly operational aspects influenced this decision.

The usual set of exercises for the first week had some changes in their formulation and assessment. Each exercise needed two components to be developed individually: (i) one base solution and (ii) one alternative solution. The alternative was defined as a solution that fulfilled the same requirements but following a different process.

Individual feedback was provided verbally for the solution of three components, i.e. base or alternative solutions for three different exercises. Thus, not all exercises were supposed to have a close collaboration of all member groups. Having a greater number of working students, these modifications may have facilitated the combination of professional obligations with the follow-up of the course and its activities, as the students were free to choose the three components to be assessed.

The rating scale for the exercises remained the same, from 0 to 4, but with different semantics:

0: Nothing relevant or no submission at all;
1: Tentative, the requirements of the exercise were not achieved;
2: Acceptable, the requirements were partially achieved;
3: Good, the requirements were completely achieved (includes incomplete analysis);
4: Very good, completely achieving the requirements of the exercise, with outstanding performance in the assessed outcomes (includes rigorous analysis).

However, levels 3 and 4 could only be achieved if the exercise included analysis with a clear justification of options and also a comparison with another solution provided by the other team-member, or another one at least delineated. This last possibility was introduced to not penalize students when a group member was not able to finish or even start the other component.

Many exercises clearly stated what was supposed to be the base and alternative solutions. For instance, for exercise four, students had to generate Java code for implementing some functional requirements by using two approaches, as follows:

- **Base Solution:** Generate a new design model from the analysis model by using an ATL transformation (UML analysis to UML design) and then generate the implementation (i.e., java code) from this new design model through an Acceleo transformation (UML design to Java code);
- **Alternative Solution:** Generate the implementation (i.e., java code) directly from the analysis model (i.e., do not generate an intermediate design model) by using an Acceleo transformation (UML to Java code).

The target was a new functionality for the College Management System, using the GWT sample application. Both solutions needed to generate code as much as possible similar to the one in the GWT CMS application and in accordance with the diagram shown in Figure 2.

For the project, the introduction of individual and group tasks was the main difference from the first phase. The assessment was divided into individual and group score and each one had a weight of 50%. In addition, two dimensions were considered for the project evaluation: requirements and analysis, each one with rating scales from 0 to 4, with the semantics adapted to suit the type of the assessment instrument, but not significantly different from what was adopted during first phase.

Figure 2. Class diagram to guide the code generation

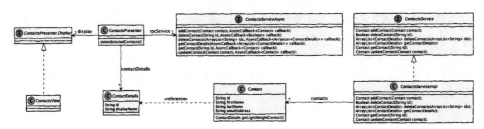

FEEDBACK ABOUT THE COURSE

In order to gather students' information relating their background, previous MDE experience and what they might have learnt during the course, a survey was outlined and filled by some attending students, at the end of each course edition.

This section details the survey questions, results and how they compare to the ones discussed by Clarke, Wu, Allen, and King (2009). While this survey has been conducted for all editions, only the 2017-2018 course edition is analysed.

Survey

For the 2017-2018 course edition, there were 137 enrolled students. Answering the survey was optional and only 35 students (about twenty-six percent) answered it. Moodle's survey tool was used, and the questions were split into the following three groups:

- **General Modelling Concepts:** This group of questions, acquires the students' global perspective about MDE's usage in their project and whether it is (or not) beneficial during a software development process. This group is shown on Table 4 and is composed by questions number 1, and 10 to 15;
- **Course:** The questions included in this group inquiry about students' overall course satisfaction *per se* and compared to other semester courses. This group is shown on Table 5 and is composed by questions number 4 to 9 and 16 to 20;
- **Students' Background:** This group helps on understanding students' background, their knowledge about other technologies and if they are student workers. This group is shown on Table 6 and is composed by questions 2 and 3.

Tables 4, 5 and 6 show survey questions, their answer types and their quantitative results. Most of the answers to questions use the Likert scale "forced choice" method, others are "Yes" or "No" answer and others accepted free form text. Questions are displayed on column "A. Question", the possible answers are displayed on column "B. Possible Answers" and the count of results for each question on EDOM's 2017-2018 edition is displayed on column "C. EDOM Results (2017 ed.)".

While 50% of students denote that this course was not in their favourite list (*c.f.* question 9), more than 80% of students agreed they understood MDE after the course

Table 4. EDOM's 2017 ed. quantitative survey results [general modelling concepts]

A. Question	B. Possible Answers	C. EDOM Results (2017 ed.)
1. What were your experiences with model-driven engineering (MDE) before this course?	I have never heard of it before.	21
	I have heard of it before but have never used it.	12
	I have already used this approach before this course.	2
10. MDE helps with your understanding of software design.	Strongly agree	5
	Agree	26
	Disagree	4
	Strongly disagree	0
11. MDE highlights the importance of creating correct models during software development.	Strongly agree	8
	Agree	24
	Disagree	3
	Strongly disagree	0
12. MDE encourages designers to understand the syntax of the modelling language.	Strongly agree	6
	Agree	26
	Disagree	3
	Strongly disagree	0
13. MDE encourages designers to understand the semantics of the modelling language.	Strongly agree	4
	Agree	27
	Disagree	4
	Strongly disagree	0
14. MDE helps with understanding how abstraction supports the creation of models for complex software products.	Strongly agree	5
	Agree	25
	Disagree	4
	Strongly disagree	1
15. MDE shows how domain-specific modelling languages may be used to rapidly develop software applications.	Strongly agree	8
	Agree	24
	Disagree	2
	Strongly disagree	1

Table 5. EDOM's 2017 ed. quantitative survey results [course]

A. Question	B. Possible Answers	C. EDOM Results (2017 ed.)
4. Have you ever created a domain-specific language before taking this course?	Yes	4
	No	31
5. Do you think you understood model-driven engineering (MDE)?	Strongly agree	2
	Agree	27
	Disagree	6
	Strongly disagree	0
6. Would you use the techniques learned in this course in practice?	Strongly agree	2
	Agree	21
	Disagree	8
	Strongly disagree	4
7. Were you satisfied with the iterative way of development used in the course?	Strongly agree	5
	Agree	20
	Disagree	8
	Strongly disagree	2
8. Rate the amount of work needed to complete the project solved in the course.	Significantly more than in other courses	9
	More than in other courses	25
	Less than in other courses	1
	Significantly less than in other courses	0
9. The course belongs to your:	Favourite subjects	3
	Rather favourite subjects	12
	Rather not favourite subjects	15
	Not favourite subjects	5
16. Have you ever used a software product line or feature models?	Yes	5
	No	30
17. What did you like about the course?	Free Form Text	22
18. What is the biggest problem you had during the course?	Free Form Text	24
19. What would you change about the course?	Free Form Text	21
20. Which of the learned techniques would you use and in what situations/projects/platforms?	Free Form Text	8

Table 6. EDOM's 2017 ed. quantitative survey results [Students' Background]

A. Question	B. Possible Answers	C. EDOM Results (2017 ed.)
2. Are you currently working in software development?	Yes	29
	No	6
3. Do you use UML in your current job?	Yes	18
	No	17

(*c.f.* question 5) and more than 65% of students agreed that the techniques provided by MDE were useful and could be used by them in the future (*c.f.* question 6).

When asked "What did you like about the course?" (*c.f.* question 17), some students wrote statements as "[It] made me feel like I was a step ahead towards the future.", "The different way of thinking in software development, allowing to think of software as models, and how to use abstractions to construct these models." and "building Domain Specific Languages denotes a far easier way of designing a complex system".

Most of the students enrolled in the survey work on software development (*c.f.* question 2) and more than half use UML at their current job (*c.f.* question 3).

Reference Values

In order to compare the obtained results with pre-existing one's, it was decided to use the results demonstrated by the authors in Clarke, Wu, Allen, and King (2009) as reference values. Despite the relatively low number of responses, almost all the students in the class used for this purpose responded to the inquiry.

The survey included some of the questions of the mentioned authors but still added some more questions related to the course itself. Because some of the reference questions have an odd number of answers and do not follow the Likert "forced choice" method used on the conducted survey, "undecided" answers were discarded from the results.

Table 7 shows a comparison between the conducted and reference surveys. Questions are displayed on column "A. Question", the possible answers are displayed on column "B. Possible Answers", the count of results and percentage for each question on EDOM's 2017-2018 edition is respectively displayed on columns "C. EDOM Results (2017 ed.)" and "E. EDOM Results (2017 ed.), the count of results and percentage for each question on the reference survey is respectively displayed

Table 7. EDOM's 2017 ed. survey results vs. reference results

A. Question	B. Possible Answers	C. EDOM Results (2017 ed.)	D. Reference Results (2009)	E. EDOM Results (2017 ed.)	F. Reference Results (2009)	G. EDOM minus Reference
1. What were your experiences with model-driven engineering (MDE) before this course?	I have never heard of it before.	21	20	60%	87%	-27%
	I have heard of it before but have never used it.	12	0	34%	0%	34%
	I have already used this approach before this course.	2	3	6%	13%	-7%
2. Are you currently working in software development?	Yes	29	12	83%	52%	31%
	No	6	11	17%	48%	-31%
3. Do you use UML in your current job?	Yes	18	5	51%	22%	30%
	No	17	18	49%	78%	-30%
10. MDE helps with your understanding of software design.	Strongly agree	5	3	14%	13%	1%
	Agree	26	12	74%	52%	22%
	Disagree	4	0	11%	0%	11%
	Strongly disagree	0	1	0%	4%	-4%
11. MDE highlights the importance of creating correct models during software development.	Strongly agree	8	8	23%	35%	-12%
	Agree	24	13	69%	57%	12%
	Disagree	3	0	9%	0%	9%
	Strongly disagree	0	0	0%	0%	0%
12. MDE encourages designers to understand the syntax of the modelling language.	Strongly agree	6	6	17%	26%	-9%
	Agree	26	14	74%	61%	13%
	Disagree	3	1	9%	4%	4%
	Strongly disagree	0	0	0%	0%	0%
13. MDE encourages designers to understand the semantics of the modelling language.	Strongly agree	4	7	11%	30%	-19%
	Agree	27	9	77%	39%	38%
	Disagree	4	0	11%	0%	11%
	Strongly disagree	0	0	0%	0%	0%
14. MDE helps with understanding how abstraction supports the creation of models for complex software products.	Strongly agree	5	2	14%	9%	6%
	Agree	25	18	71%	78%	-7%
	Disagree	4	0	11%	0%	11%
	Strongly disagree	1	0	3%	0%	3%
15. MDE shows how domain-specific modelling languages may be used to rapidly develop software applications.	Strongly agree	8	8	23%	35%	-12%
	Agree	24	13	69%	57%	12%
	Disagree	2	0	6%	0%	6%
	Strongly disagree	1	0	3%	0%	3%

on columns "D. Reference Results (2009)" and "F. Reference Results (2009). The percentage difference between the conducted and reference survey are presented on column "G. EDOM minus Reference".

Despite the fact that there are more working students on the conducted survey than on the reference survey (*c.f.* question 2), on both surveys most of the students neither have heard or used MDE previously (*c.f.* question 1). Yet, about 50% of the students in the conducted survey have used UML in their job while on the reference survey only 22% did (*c.f.* question 3).

On both surveys a vast majority of students equally recognize the importance of using MDE during software design and software development (*c.f.* questions 10, 11, 12), as well as encouraging the semantic understanding of the modelling language and its abstraction (*c.f.* question 13, 14) and agree that domain specific modelling languages can be used to rapidly develop software products (*c.f.* question 15).

Discussion

About 80% of students attending the course are working students and their primary activity is software development. Yet, when asked the question "What were your experiences with MDE before this course?", only 6% had used it before and around 33% had heard about it before but still had not actively used it in their current job. Only 11% of students had created a Domain Specific Language (DSL) before taking the course. This provides information how MDE is still not yet impregnated in software design and development and is also corroborated by the reference survey results, despite students having a different background, mostly industry working students (this survey) vs. non-working students (reference survey).

While on industry the adoption of tools like UML is still not a mainstream activity, about 50% of students use it, the adoption of MDE is still behind those numbers. The numbers related to MDE's adoption may seem low at the moment, but it can somehow be compared to the adoption of UML in the past. As described, at the moment, 50% of students state they actively use UML in their current position.

Our expectation is that the introduction of courses devoted to MDE may have the same impact on software development as UML had in the past.

OTHER COURSES ON MODEL-DRIVEN ENGINEERING

To contextualize the authors' experience in comparison to other approaches in teaching MDE this section presents an analysis of several other courses.

According to Brambilla, Cabot, and Wimmer (2018), authors of the book "Model-driven software engineering in practice" there are, at the time of this writing, 102 institutions using the book in their courses. These are courses with contents that are totally or significantly based on model-driven engineering, which is an impressive number for a field that is relatively recent to most computer science related curricula, even if ignoring other possible courses that might have adopted other books.

Furthermore, although several curricula from ACM includes specific references to modelling and modelling techniques there is no specific reference to a more holistic approach that puts models as the core concept in software development, as the MDE approach defends (Adcock et al., 2009; Force, 2013, 2015). This reflects the fact that, although MDE courses have been expanding, this is a relatively recent field in the academia and, therefore, there is limited relevant literature describing teaching experiences.

The sources for this analysis came from reputed publishing and distribution channels with description of experiences in teaching model-driven engineering. The authors did not consult with institutions, faculty members or instructors. Table 8 presents the analysed courses and their literature sources, while Table 9 details some characteristics of the analysed courses.

Academic Level

The great majority of the summarized courses is oriented towards graduate students and they are usually integrated into master programs. There are also some courses at postgraduate levels. These courses seem to be the first to be introduced and, therefore, it is natural that they are offered at a postgraduate level.

For instance, Gokhale and Gray (2005) describe 4 editions of a postgraduate MDE course oriented towards research that took place in 2004 and 2005. This course had essentially PhD students and its contents and projects were based on the research projects of the authors.

There is also a postgraduate program totally based in MDE. Cabot and Tisi (2011) describe this program as the first MDE program. The authors describe only one edition around 2007/2008.

As the MDE field matures in terms of its adoption in industry, maturity of available tools and techniques, but also as it becomes more widely known, more academic offerings at lower levels have arisen. Two significative examples in terms of number of students are the graduate MDE courses at the Vienna University of Technology and at the Technical University of Košice. For both these courses more than one hundred students are reported as attending each edition. As Brosch, Kappel, Seidl, and Wimmer (2009) state, this is really teaching MDE in the large. This is in accordance with the authors' experience with the MDE course at ISEP where editions of the course have been gradually taking more enrolment and actually there are more than one hundred students.

Apart from these larger courses, the offerings of MDE graduate courses seem to be available globally with reported experiences in Brazil (Maia, Gadelha, Borges, Muniz, Silva, & Ximenes, 2016), Turkey (Tekinerdogan, 2011), France (Combemale, Cregut, Dieumegard, Pantel, & Zalila, 2012) and the USA (Clarke, Wu, Allen, & King, 2009).

There are also some undergraduate experiences in teaching MDE. For instance, Batory and Azanza (2017) report on at least 2 editions (2011 and 2012) of an undergraduate course which includes a module on MDE. Also, Ringert, Rumpe,

Table 8. Analysed courses and their literature source

Institution	Source
Vanderbilt University (Nashville, Tennessee) and University of Alabama at Birmingham, USA	Gokhale and Gray (2005)
University of Nice Sophia – Antipolis, France	Mireille (2008)
Florida International University, USA	Clarke, Wu, Allen and King (2009)
Vienna University of Technology, Austria	Brosch, Kappel, Seidl, and Wimmer (2009)
Bilkent University, Ankara, Turkey	Tekinerdogan (2011)
Ecole des Mines, Nantes, France	Cabot and Tisi (2011)
Université de Toulouse, France	Combemale, Cregut, Dieumegard, Pantel, and Zalila (2012)
Karlsruhe University of Applied Sciences, Germany	Schmidt, Kimmig, Bittner, and Dickerhof (2014)
Technical University of Košice, Slovak Republic	Porubaen, Bacikova, Chodarev, and Nosál (2015)
Universidade Estadual do Ceará, Brasil	Maia, Gadelha, Borges, Muniz, Silva, and Ximenes (2016)
University of Texas at Austin, USA	Batory and Azanza (2017)
RWTH Aachen University, Germany	Ringert, Rumpe, Schulze, and Wortmann (2017)
Warsaw University of Technology, Poland	Derezinska (2017)

Table 9. Summary of MDE courses main characteristics

Institution	Course	Students	Editions	MDE Tools	Pedagogical Approach
University of Texas at Austin, USA	MDE module in undergraduate software design course	12(?)	3 (2011-2013)	*MDELite* - Teaching-oriented tool	Assignments
Karlsruhe University of Applied Sciences, Germany	MDSD undergraduate course	NA	8 (2006-2013)	Students build/use their own tools	Assignments and Project
RWTH Aachen University, Germany	Undergraduate and graduate MDE project class	8-14	3 (2012-2014)	MDE specific tools (e.g., MontiArcAutomation)	PBL
Warsaw University of Technology, Poland	Model transformations module in graduate software engineering course	11-27	6 (2011-2017)	EMF based tools (focus on model transformations with QVT)	Assignments
Florida International University, USA	MDE course at a graduate program	24	3 (2007-2009)	EMF based tools (e.g., GMF)	PBL
Bilkent University, Ankara, Turkey	MDE graduate course	15-20	3 (2008-2010)	EMF based tools	Assignments and Project
Universidade Estadual do Ceará, Brasil	MDE graduate course	6-13	2 (2014-2015)	EMF based tools	Assignments and Project
Technical University of Košice, Slovak Republic	MDE graduate course	137	NA	Students build/use their own tools	Task-driven case studies
Vienna University of Technology, Austria	MDE course at a master program	150	4 (2006-2009)	EMF based tools	Assignments and Project
Université de Toulouse, France	MDE graduate course (M2)	NA	NA (2007...)	EMF based tools	Assignments and Project
University of Nice Sophia – Antipolis, France	Postgraduate course on MDE	30	2 (2007-2008)	EMF based tools	PBL
Ecole des Mines, Nantes, France	MDE postgraduate diploma	6	1 (2007 or 2008)	EMF based tools	Assignments, integrating project and internship
Vanderbilt University and University of Alabama at Birmingham, USA	MDE research-oriented course	2-3(?)	4 (2004-2005)	GME based tools	Active Learning

Schulze, and Wortmann (2017) report on a software project class for undergraduate students that integrates Agile and MDE in a project. Therefore, it seems that MDE has been starting to be taught at undergraduate courses, at the moment essentially in the format of modules in software design related courses.

Pedagogical Patterns

As reports like the one from this chapter are divulgated and experiences in teaching MDE become more mature it is expected that MDE will become more widely included also at the undergraduate level.

It is interesting to check that pedagogical approaches are being experimented and discussed as MDE begins to enter the undergraduate level. For instance, Batory and Azanza (2017) propose the use of simplified tools to teach MDE. Other authors, such as Schmidt, Kimmig, Bittner, and Dickerhof (2014), propose that students learn the MDE concepts by building their own MDE tools.

It is also interesting to observe that at the undergraduate level the pedagogical approach is centred around teaching and applying MDE concepts without focusing on specific tools. This makes sense, since these courses are introductory to MDE and using complex tools or research-oriented tools would be counterproductive making students focus their effort in dealing with the complexity of the tools or solving issues related to less mature tools instead of focusing on the solution.

The majority of the courses at the undergraduate and graduate levels follow very similar pedagogical approaches. Concepts are introduced and explained in lectures. These concepts are then demonstrated using tutorials or students see how they are applied when they received partially resolved assignments or exercises. These exercises and assignments are usually focused on specific contents of MDE. For instance, they may be focused on metamodeling or model-to-model transformations or code generation but usually they do not include several MDE topics. Courses usually include a project that students must develop usually after having completed the exercises. These projects usually integrate several (if not all) the applied contents of the course and takes place in the last half of the course.

There are also several courses that apply some kind of active learning approaches to teaching MDE, specially at a more advanced level.

Mireille (2008) describes a problem-based learning approach to teaching MDE at a post-graduate level, where PhD candidates use MDE paradigms to solve real case problems. Their students have different specialities such as embedded systems or human-computer interaction. To apply this approach the course is inverted: first the project is introduced and then the lectures are used in the context of the project. Students apply the contents of the lectures during the project development. This approach is somewhere in line with authors of this chapter experience in applying problem and project-based learning.

Another active learning example is the one from the Vanderbilt University (Gokhale & Gray, 2005). In this case, the approach goes even further and there are no formal classes. The course is totally based on research projects around the GME tool. Some of the students used the project as a starting point for their master dissertation or PhD thesis.

MDE Tools

The selection of the MDE tools to use in courses is still an issue. The tools around the Eclipse Modelling Framework (EMF) seem to be the selected ones for teaching MDE although there are reports of issues relating to the adoption of EMF for teaching purposes. For instance, Batory and Azanza (2017) reported that they discontinued EMF after the first edition of their undergraduate course because of several issues in using specific EMF based tools, namely, Graphical Modelling Tooling Framework Plug-in (GMF), OCL Tools Plug-in, and EuGENia. The authors reported on general issues using these tools to build graphical editors for state diagrams. This was the main reason that lead the authors to develop a specific tool to teach MDE called MDELite. The authors based their new tool on concepts and technologies that are more familiar to their undergraduate students: Java, relational databases and Prolog.

Schmidt, Kimmig, Bittner, and Dickerhof (2014) report also on evaluating EMF for code generation on their course but opting for having students developing their own code generator. Although they do not explicitly state the reason, it seems to be more based on pedagogical options than from technical issues. Both these cases refer to undergraduate courses. The other experience in teaching MDE at the undergraduate level is reported by Ringert, Rumpe, Schulze, and Wortmann (2017) and the selected tools are also not EMF-based. In this case, the project course required the development of a Cyber-physical system using MDE specific tools, such as MontiCore, MontiArcAutomation or LeJOS LEGO. Therefore, all 3 experiences in teaching MDE in undergraduate courses do not use EMF or other mainstream MDE tool. The courses use specific pedagogical tools or teach MDE by applying its concepts using general purpose tools.

At the graduate level, EMF is the technology of choice. However, there are some exceptions. Porubaen, Bacikova, Chodarev, and Nosál (2015) in their graduate course do not use EMF. In their course, students build and use their own tools. This approach is justified by the authors because they wanted to demystify some common ideas about MDE, such as that it is not used in the industry. This approach is described as being very successful. To the authors of this chapter, this idea is promising since although there are several reports of successful industrial solutions, a significant part of them do not refer the use of EMF tools. In this way, the students become aware of the advantages of the use of MDE concepts even when not using MDE mainstream tools.

The MDE research-oriented course at the Vanderbilt University is the other example of not using EMF, but this time at a postgraduate level. In this case, the adopted tool was the Generic Modelling Environment (GME). This is very natural since the course is very research-oriented and GME is a tool based at the Vanderbilt University.

Regarding EMF and its problems, it is fair to state that the majority of issues is essentially, direct or indirectly, related to the development of graphical editors using GMF. This was reported by Batory and Azanza (2017) but also by Clarke, Wu, Allen and King (2009). Brosch, Kappel, Seidl, and Wimmer (2009) also report minor issues related to the lack of documentation of some EMF tools that they managed to surpass by producing tutorials, videos, and also using forums. The authors of this chapter also tackle this issue by using a similar approach: producing tutorials about the setup and use of the tools and having a forum to support students. So far, in these 3 editions of the course the authors have avoid the requirement of implementing graphical editors for the domain-specific languages and, therefore, have also avoid the reported problems resulting for the complexity of GMF and GMF-based tools.

Contents

The majority of the analysed courses have very similar contents. With regard to this aspect the authors find that it is very stable, for instance, when compared with the choice of tools to adopt for teaching MDE (see previous section). The main contents of the MDE courses are:

- Metamodeling and design of modelling languages;
- Model verification (usually with constraint-based languages such as OCL);
- Model-to-model transformations (with rule-based or imperative specific languages);
- Model-to-code (or model-to-text) transformations (usually with template-based languages);
- Concrete syntaxes for the modelling languages either textual or graphical.

There are, however, some small variants to this, otherwise, consensual contents. These are related to courses that focus on specific sub-areas of MDE and, therefore, seem to put more attention to specific contents of MDE. For instance, Derezinska

(2017) describes an MDE module in a graduate course on Advanced Methods for Software Engineering where the focus are model transformations that are applied essentially using the QVT language.

Another example is the one described by Schmidt, Kimmig, Bittner, and Dickerhof (2014) in an MDE course at the Karlsruhe University of Applied Sciences. In this case the focus is more on Model-Driven Software Development (MDSD) as opposed to the broader field of MDE. In this course the focus is code generation and the students develop their own code generator instead of using an existing tool. Although this specific approach should result in some constraints in the contents of the course, the authors state that they managed to cover in lectures and in exercises the following topics: templates, model, meta-model, model verification, transformation between the same, as well as between different meta-models, XML-based models and meta-models, and XMI. Therefore, it seems that even in specific approaches like this one, it is possible to cover the majority of the MDE contents. In this case the major exception was the lack of a topic on concrete syntaxes. It is the opinion of the authors of this chapter that concrete syntaxes are a very important topic but also a topic that must be carefully treated.

As described in the previous section, tools that support graphical concrete syntaxes for models are complex and usually a source of issues. It is essentially due to this fact that the authors have until this moment avoided the general use of these tools in exercises or projects to be developed by students. The topic is still lectured, and students may develop concrete graphical syntaxes if they wish to do so, but it is not a mandatory topic. This option will be regularly reviewed as tools such as EuGENia or Sirius become more mature and simpler to apply to the adopted use cases of the EDOM course.

Students' Feedback

Some of the analysed literature sources about MDE courses provide also some information about students' feedback (see also the Feedback About the Course section). Some of the key aspects referred are related to understanding metamodeling concepts and EMF tools.

Students have difficulties understanding metamodeling concepts. This is less frequent when students have previous knowledge with similar concepts like databases. To solve this issue:

- Some teachers propose that a complete example of metamodeling and code generation should be given to students at the beginning of the course;
- Other teachers propose that courses should reserve sufficient time to explain all the MDE concepts with small illustrative exercises.

Also, students complain about EMF tools. In order to reduce this issue:

- Some teachers prepare tutorials, videos or using forums, while others have developed alternative MDE tools aimed at teaching;
- Other teachers avoid the use of MDE tools and apply the concepts using general purpose tools that the students are familiar with;

According to the experience of the authors of this chapter, the major issue in EMF tools goes towards tools for concrete graphical syntaxes based on GMF that are complex and require an expert user and, therefore, should not be selected for usage by inexperienced students. The solution of the authors has been to focus on using simple and mature EMF based tools aimed only at textual concrete syntaxes.

One issue that is not very referenced by students in other MDE courses but has very significance in the MDE course at ISEP is the notion that students do not have MDE as one of their preferred courses (as presented in the Feedback About the Course section). Despite this opinion, students also state that MDE helps them improve several skills relating to software engineering. Therefore, students recognize the value of MDE, but a significant number does not like it. This student notion is similar to the one that undergraduate students have regarding analysis and design: they recognize its value, but they prefer programming. It may be expected that this notion is more significative for younger professionals and it decreases on more experienced professionals. However, in this study there is lack of data to confirm this statement.

CONCLUSION

Model-Driven Engineering promises several ways to address well-known problems in software engineering, including software increasing complexity. MDE has been applied successfully in the industry but essentially in large corporations that can afford the inherent costs and also in some specific domains. However, it seems that MDE's advantages have been hard to generalize in a way that makes it available for the common developer. Multiple factors hinder organizations from embracing MDE, and its acceptance clearly requires technical changes, but also the overcoming of human attitudes when facing new techniques and the need to use new tools. To tackle this problem, software professionals should be aware of MDE and specific training should be provided at a post-secondary level. This chapter contributes to this issue by sharing a three-year experience in teaching MDE in a course at a master's program at ISEP.

The teaching experience is based on a problem and project-based learning approach. In this approach students may develop a project in common with at least one other course.

Regarding the results of this three-year experience, the students' feedback and survey as well as inputs from other similar courses, the authors of this chapter share their findings and proposals for future approaches with respect to key issues and topics.

One issue that is regularly reported is related to problems with some MDE tools, particularly with tools based on EMF. According to the experience of the authors this issue is essentially related to GMF, an EMF based tool that is used to build graphical editors for domain-specific languages. This tool is very powerful but also very complex. Its use is not recommended as an introductory tool. The authors did not use it during these 3 editions of the MDE course. As a result, for the moment, students' projects do not require building graphical syntaxes for the domain-specific languages. For the moment the focus is on textual syntaxes. However, in future editions of the course, some more user-friendly tools for building graphical editors should be evaluated, such as Sirius. This chapter also reports that other authors tackle this issue by avoiding altogether the use of MDE specific tools and instead explore MDE concepts by applying them using general purpose tools and languages. This seems to be a promising approach that can also be used to demystify what the students usually perceive as "magic" behind the MDE tools. It is clearly an option that the authors of this chapter envision at including in future editions of the MDE course. Other practice that its recommend when adopting MDE tools (GMF or others) is to provide students with specific tutorials and online supporting forums.

Other major issue is the perception that a majority of students have regarding MDE. Students may have a perception that MDE is not used in the industry. To tackle this issue the authors have designed the MDE course around a problem and project-based learning approach.

As far as possible the authors propose that projects should also include other courses that students may be enrolled in at the same time. This chapter shares an experience where students are also attending a course on the management of the life cycle of a software product, where they apply agile project management approaches and techniques and tools such as the ones used for continuous integration. The project is common, and students learn how MDE approaches may be integrated with more common software engineering approaches such as continuous integration. Also, to tackle this issue, the authors always base the project on an adopted specific platform. OFBiz and GWT have been used. The adopted platforms have always some especial relationship with MDE. In OFBiz, several domain-specific languages are used to configure the platform, while GWT is very oriented towards code generation and it has already some examples of code generation, such as the code that IDE plugins generate for GWT RPC interfaces. Thus, this is useful to convey to students the idea that MDE techniques can be used for specific problems and that MDE is not a new paradigm that is incompatible with other approaches.

As also reported in other teaching experiences, one possible way to further promote MDE and the value of its techniques is to include its contents in undergraduate curricula. As discussed in this chapter, some experiences with course modules regarding MDE at undergraduate levels have been reported as successful, particularly regarding students' feedback. The authors of this chapter also agree with such approach. In fact, one possible way to integrate part of the MDE contents at the undergraduate level could be done, for instance, in software design courses. There, MDE concepts and techniques could be used to help students move from design to implementation, by adopting code generating approaches based on MDE. This could be done in a non-invasive way, by avoiding MDE tools and using more general-purpose tools and languages. This lighter introduction to MDE at undergraduate levels could be very fruitful in helping further demystify MDE and change the students' perception about MDE. When students moved to graduate programs, such as the one described in this chapter, their adaptation to this new software development paradigm would be easier and their perception about MDE probably would be different at the end of the course.

MDE has made its way in the industry with several very successful examples. Research in the MDE field is also very active with several related conferences and publications. However, its wider adoption by software professionals it is not a reality at this moment. This chapter aims at contributing to tackle this problem by sharing a three-year experience in teaching MDE at a graduate level. The authors hope that the shared insights inspire other teachers and faculty members and help them further promote MDE and the advantages of adopting this paradigm into existing and new courses and programs.

In the near future this work will be extended. Fluctuations in student grades are common, as students and assessment instruments vary each year. The size of these fluctuations in the last years will be verified at the end of the second course editions of the 2nd phase in order to have exactly two editions for each phase. In addition, it is also intended to have precisely two editions for the 2nd phase to check the differences in the students' responses to the survey that have been made available.

An aspect that have been neglected is the opinion of the faculty connected to the department of informatics engineering of ISEP about models as abstraction of real systems or products and their use in their teaching activities. In addition, the opinion of current and potential future employers should also be considered in order to gain a more detailed insight into the needs of the market. Thus, future work will integrate their perceptions in a process of continuous improvement.

REFERENCES

ABET EAC. (2017). *2018-2019 Criteria for Accrediting Engineering Programs.* Retrieved 7, 6, 2018, from http://www.abet.org/wp-content/uploads/2017/12/E001-18-19-EAC-Criteria-11-29-17-FINAL_updated1218.pdf

Adcock, R., Alef, E., Amato, B., Ardis, M., Bernstein, L., Boehm, B., & Willshire, M. J. (2009). *Graduate Software Engineering 2009 (GSwE2009) Curriculum Guidelines for Graduate Degree Programs in Software Engineering.* New York, NY: ACM.

Ainsley, C. (2016). Making Modelling "Fun" with GWT. GWT Con 2016, Firenze, Italy.

Baker, P., Loh, S., & Weil, F. (2005). Model-Driven engineering in a large industrial context—motorola case study. In *International Conference on Model Driven Engineering Languages and Systems.* Springer. 10.1007/11557432_36

Batory, D., & Azanza, M. (2017). Teaching model-driven engineering from a relational database perspective. *Software & Systems Modeling, 16*(2), 443–467. doi:10.100710270-015-0488-7

Bergin, J., Eckstein, J., Volter, M., Sipos, M., Wallingford, E., Marquardt, K., & Manns, M. L. (2012). *Pedagogical patterns: advice for educators.* Joseph Bergin Software Tools.

Boffo, V. (2015). *Employability for the social economy: The role of higher education. In Educational Jobs: Youth and Employability in the Social Economy.* Firenze: FUP.

Bragança, A., Azevedo, I., & Bettencourt, N. (2018). *College Management System GWT Example Application.* Available from https://bitbucket.org/mei-isep/odsoft-edom-2017-cms-students

Brambilla, M., Cabot, J., & Wimmer, M. (2012). Model-driven software engineering in practice. *Synthesis Lectures on Software Engineering, 1*(1), 1–182. doi:10.2200/S00441ED1V01Y201208SWE001

Brambilla, M., Cabot, J., & Wimmer, M. (2017). *Model driven software engineering in practice* (2nd ed.). Morgan & Claypool Publishers.

Brambilla, M., Cabot, J., & Wimmer, M. (2018). *List of institutions using the book "Model-driven software engineering in practice".* Retrieved from https://mdse-book.com/who-is-using-the-book/

Brosch, P., Kappel, G., Seidl, M., & Wimmer, M. (2009). Teaching model engineering in the large. *5th Educators' Symposium in conjunction with the 12th International Conference on Model Driven Engineering Languages and Systems (MoDELS 2009).*

Burden, H., Heldal, R., & Whittle, J. (2014). Comparing and contrasting model-driven engineering at three large companies. In *Proceedings of the 8th ACM/IEEE International Symposium on Empirical Software Engineering and Measurement.* ACM. 10.1145/2652524.2652527

Cabot, J., & Tisi, M. (2011). The mde diploma: First international postgraduate specialization in model-driven engineering. *Computer Science Education, 21*(4), 389–402. doi:10.1080/08993408.2011.630131

Christensen, B., & Ellingsen, G. (2016). Evaluating model-driven development for large-scale EHRs through the openEHR approach. *International Journal of Medical Informatics, 89,* 43–54. doi:10.1016/j.ijmedinf.2016.02.004 PMID:26980358

Clarke, P. J., Wu, Y., Allen, A. A., & King, T. M. (2009). Experiences of teaching model-driven engineering in a software design course. *Proceedings of the 5th Educators' Symposium of the MODELS Conference 2009,* 6-14.

Clements, P., & Northrop, L. (2001). *Software product lines: practices and patterns.* Addison-Wesley.

Combemale, B., Cregut, X., Dieumegard, A., Pantel, M., & Zalila, F. (2012). Teaching MDE through the Formal Verification of Process Models. *Electronic Communications of the EASST 52.*

Derezinska, A. (2017). *Experiences in Teaching Model Transformation with the QVT Language. In Software Engineering Research for the Practice* (pp. 11–24). Warsaw: Scientific Papers of the Polish Information Society Scientific Council.

Force, A. J. T. (2013). *Computer science curricula 2013: Curriculum guidelines for undergraduate degree programs in computer science.* IEEE Computer Society.

Force, A. J. T. (2015). *Curriculum Guidelines for Undergraduate Degree Programs in Software Engineering.* ACM.

Froyd, J. E., Wankat, P. C., & Smith, K. A. (2012). Five major shifts in 100 years of engineering education. *Proceedings of the IEEE, 100 (Special Centennial Issue),* 1344-1360. 10.1109/JPROC.2012.2190167

Glass, R. L. (2011). Frequently forgotten fundamental facts about software engineering. *IEEE Software*, *18*(3), 112–111. doi:10.1109/MS.2001.922739

Gokhale, A. S., & Gray, J. (2005). Advancing model driven development education via collaborative research. *Proceedings of the Educators Symposium at the 8th International Conference, MoDELS 2005*.

Goulão, M., Amaral, V., & Mernik, M. (2016). Quality in model-driven engineering: A tertiary study. *Software Quality Journal*, *24*(3), 601–633. doi:10.100711219-016-9324-8

Gronback, R. C. (2009). *Eclipse modeling project: a domain-specific language (DSL) toolkit*. Pearson Education.

Haan, J. D. (2008). *8 Reasons Why Model-Driven Approaches (Will) Fail*. Retrieved from http://www.infoq.com/articles/8-reasons-why-MDE-fails

Hossler, J., Born, M., & Saito, S. (2006). Significant Productivity Enhancement through Model Driven Techniques: A Success Story. *10th IEEE International Enterprise Distributed Object Computing Conference (EDOC'06)*, 367-373. 10.1109/EDOC.2006.53

ISEP. (n.d.). *Instituto Superior de Engenharia do Porto*. Retrieved from http://www.isep.ipp.pt/

Landwehr, C., Ludewig, J., Meersman, R., Parnas, D. L., Shoval, P., Wand, Y., ... Weyuker, E. (2017). Software Systems Engineering programmes a capability approach. *Journal of Systems and Software*, *125*, 354–364. doi:10.1016/j.jss.2016.12.016

Lewin, K. (1946). Action Research and Minority Problems. *The Journal of Social Issues*, *2*(4), 34–46. doi:10.1111/j.1540-4560.1946.tb02295.x

Maia, P., Gadelha, F., Borges, M., Muniz, L., Silva, A., & Ximenes, J. (2016). Práticas e Experiências no Ensino de Engenharia Dirigida por Modelos. *iSys-Revista Brasileira de Sistemas de Informação, 9*(2).

Marques, M., Ochoa, S. F., Bastarrica, M. C., & Gutierrez, F. J. (2018). Enhancing the Student Learning Experience in Software Engineering Project Courses. *IEEE Transactions on Education*, *61*(1), 63–73. doi:10.1109/TE.2017.2742989

Meliá, S., Gómez, J., Pérez, S., & Díaz, O. (2008). A model-driven development for GWT-based rich internet applications with OOH4RIA. In *ICWE'08 Eighth International Conference on Web Engineering*. IEEE.

Mills, J. E., & Treagust, D. F. (2003). Engineering education—Is problem-based or project-based learning the answer. *Australasian Journal of Engineering Education*, *3*(2), 2–16.

Mireille, B. (2008), Project-based teaching for model-driven engineering. *Proceedings of the 4th Educators Symposium at MoDELS 2008*.

Nakoula, Y., & Houimel, T. (2017). *Jclays, A global solution for application design and automatic GWT code generator.* GWT Con 2017, Firenze, Italy.

Nelson, J. (2017). *Xapi-lang for declarative code generation.* GWT Con 2017, Firenze, Italy.

Parviainen, P., Takalo, J., Teppola, S., & Tihinen, M. (2009). *Model-driven development processes and practices.* VTT Technical Research Centre of Finland, VTT Working Papers 114.

Porubaen, J., Bacikova, M., Chodarev, S., & Nosál, M. (2015). Teaching pragmatic model-driven software development. *Computer Science and Information Systems*, *12*(2), 683–705. doi:10.2298/CSIS140107022P

Ramsdale, C. (2010). *Building MVP apps: MVP Part I.* Available from http://www. gwtproject.org/articles/mvp-architecture.html

Ringert, J., Rumpe, B., Schulze, C., & Wortmann, A. (2017). Teaching agile model-driven engineering for cyber-physical systems. In *Software Engineering: Software Engineering Education and Training Track (ICSE-SEET), 2017 IEEE/ACM 39th International Conference on.* IEEE.

Schmidt, A., Kimmig, D., Bittner, K., & Dickerhof, M. (2014). Teaching Model-Driven Software Development: Revealing the "Great Miracle" of Code Generation to Students. *Proceedings of the Sixteenth Australasian Computing Education Conference (ACE2014), 148,* 97–104.

Sedelmaier, Y., & Landes, D. (2014). Practicing soft skills in software engineering: A project-based didactical approach. In Overcoming Challenges in Software Engineering Education: Delivering Non-Technical Knowledge and Skills (pp. 161-179). IGI Global.

Somers, J. (2017). *The Coming Software Apocalypse.* Retrieved from http://www. theatlantic.com/technology/archive/2017/09/saving-the-world-from-code/540393/

Tekinerdogan, B. (2011). Experiences in teaching a graduate course on model-driven software development. *Computer Science Education, 21*(4), 363–387. doi:10.108 0/08993408.2011.630129

Uziak, J. (2016). A Project Based Learning Approach in An Engineering Curriculum. *Global Journal of Engineering Education, 18*(2), 119–123.

Whittle, J., Hutchinson, J., & Rouncefield, M. (2014). The state of practice in model-driven engineering. *IEEE Software, 31*(3), 79–85. doi:10.1109/MS.2013.65

Whittle, J., Hutchinson, J., Rouncefield, M., Burden, H., & Heldal, R. (2017). A taxonomy of tool-related issues affecting the adoption of model-driven engineering. *Software & Systems Modeling, 16*(2), 313–331. doi:10.100710270-015-0487-8

Section 3
Domain–Specific Languages

Chapter 7
Evaluating the Refactoring Index Using Entropy Approach

Rajni Sehgal
Amity University, India

Deepti Mehrotra
Amity University, India

ABSTRACT

Software often carries the structural deficiencies that make it hard to understand, change, or test; these deficiencies are categorized as a code smell. This code smell affects the performance of software adversely, thereby increase need of maintainability. Refactoring of code helps in reducing the code smell. But refactoring is an expensive process and hence identifies which and how much code need to refactor a challenging task and is termed as refactoring index. In this chapter, entropy approach is proposed to measure the refactoring index of 20 open source software programs. Refactoring index level is given to identify the critical project which urgently required refactoring in order to improve the quality of the project.

INTRODUCTION

The quality of software depends on the quality of design and source code. Poor architectural design and implementation plan may introduce the design flaws in a program which can stop the fault-free execution of the code. According to Fowler (Fowler, M., & Beck, K. 1999). Design flaws appear at the design and code level is termed as "code smell". Code smells does not stop the functioning of the program,

DOI: 10.4018/978-1-5225-7455-2.ch007

because they are not bugs instead they slows down the development of any software. Induction of the code smell in software reduce the strength of architecture of any software, may lead to failure of software shortly. Although code smells are not bugs, detecting code smell reduce the testing and maintenance effort. Inspection is one of the static techniques of testing to detect the code smell during the verification of the code. During the software inspection, the potentially problematic areas are examined such as the program code, the design, and the software documentation. During the initial stage of development of the software, several problems due to an inefficient analysis of design can introduce the code smell in the software system.

Object-oriented software whose KLOC is large in number is difficult to maintain because of their architectural design. Quality of the source code is also degraded due to the poor architectural design. An established concept of code smells can classify shortcomings in object-oriented software architecture which is directly related to Antipattern present in the system design (Mansoor, U 2013).In an object-oriented software violation of design principles such as data abstraction, encapsulation, modularity, and hierarchy may affect the design of a class and increase the probability of induction of code smells in code. This may cause several problems in the later stage of software development. Once the code smell introduces in the code, it can only be cured by applying the suitable refactoring approach. Refactoring is improving the internal structure of the code without altering the functionality of any program. Planning a refractory strategy to enhance the quality of the code is an expensive and time-consuming process. Applying appropriate refactoring strategy is a multicriteria problem like it is dependent on the criticality of the project, and criticality of its constituent components. Taking a decision, which project requires more Refactoring and how to do the refactoring depends on the number and types of code smell present in the code. Different code smells have a different level of impact on the software system and hence estimating their relative importance need to be identified.

In this paper, a framework is proposed to evaluate how much refactoring termed as a refactoring index (R.I) is needed for given software. To identify which project requires at most priority towards the refactoring, level of refactoring is given in this paper, so that project with the highest refactoring index should be refactor first. Analytical approach entropy is applied to find out the disorder to predict the level of refactoring is necessary for the provided software. The entropy represents the countable information and has been suitably used in various domains to measure the relative importance of a variable on another variable (Hafezalkotob, et.al. 2016). This study is done on the open dataset repository Landfill where 20 software and their respective code smells are given by Palomba, F (2015)where he contributed this repository for five different code smell which is identified by 20 open source software manually. The related information of code smell is given in section 2. To measure the refactoring index SAW approach is used which is elaborated in section3. The methodology adopted in discussed in section 4. Weights are evaluated using entropy in section 5. Results evaluated is given followed by the conclusion and future directions in Section 6.

RELATED WORK

As the quality of the software may be affected in any phase of the software development, early evaluation of the software quality can improve the performance of the software. One way to improve the quality of the code is detecting code smell in the initial development life cycle. Early Identification of code smell can decrease the testing effort and enhances the quality of the software system. The various author discussed different types of code smell some of them are presented in this section. Fowler &Beck(1999) introduced the concept of code smell, According to Fowler set of metrics and their threshold value identifies the bad smell from the code. These metrics are Very helpful in finding the error-prone classes. These code smells can be recovered with refactoring. Once the software is delivered to the customer, The process of software development does not stop here; there is a continuous software requirement change from the customer, which is implemented in the maintenance phase. Implementation of this requirement in the Maintenance phase may lead to the induction of code smell in the code. Moha et al (2010) finds out that code smells are design flaws which create a problem during the maintenance of the software. In their study, they proposed a new algorithm for automatic detection of code smell Singh & Chopra (2013) presented the drawbacks of various code smells when they introduced in the code Tufano et al.(2015) have taken 200 open source project and found out them the not only introduction of the code smell, but the frequency of occurrence of code smell also affects the quality of the code. Andrade(2013)discussed the (i) frequently occurring architectural code smell(ii) the impact of these code smells on software life cycle(iii) Impact on the software quality with the lifespan of a code smell in the code. Peters & Zaidman, (2012) depict that lifespan of the code smell in the code has a high contribution towards the quality of the software.

Li & Shatnaw(2007) showed that there is a close relationship between class error probability with bad smell by taking error log of an open source software, i.e., Bug Zilla. This study finds out that there is a close relationship between bad smell and error in the class of object-oriented system. Van Emden & Moonen (2002) presents an approach to detect the code smell automatically by the code smell browser jCOSMO. Fontana, et.al.(2012)Reviews the aspect of various tools which can detect the code smell from source code automatically. Hamid et. al(2013) has done the comparative study on the code smell detection tools, they have discussed various tools for finding the code smell like JDeodorant, in Code, etc. Dhillon & Sidhu(2012) states that design change in the object-oriented system is continuous which can create code smell in code which decays the quality of code. Mantyla, et al. (2003) Study the code smells to find out the quality of code, According to them, all code smells is not co-related.

This section presents the various techniques to detected code smells by different authors. Lieberman(1997)depict that code clones always increase the size of the code, In this study, the relationship between cloning and defect proneness is analyzed by taking four different case studies. Guptaet al. (2016) Find out the Interrelationship among these code smells using total interpretive structural modeling (TISM), they have classified this code smells into four clusters based on their driving power and dependence power. Kapila,& Singh(2014) states that code smells depict the complex class, which should be simplified to make good quality code. In this study, the Bayesian inference is applied to predict the bad smell in the source code. Pietrzak & Walter (2006) proposed a multi-criteria model, which is holistic for detection of code smell. This model is combining the various source information like(a) Programmer's intuition and experience(b)Metrics values(c) Analysis of a source code syntax tree (d) History of the changes made in code(e) Dynamic behavior of the code(f) Existence of other smells. Greiler, et. al (2013)Mines Git and SVN repositories by using the tool like test Evo hound for the test fixture smells. Mansoor et.al.(2013)depict that code smells are design flaws which make the maintenance of the system difficult, multi-objective programming is applied to combine the Metrics for the detection of the code smell from the code. Carneiroet. al. (2010) has identified the code smell on five different version of software code. Palomba et al. (2013)detected five different code smells namely Divergent Change, Shotgun Surgery, Parallel Inheritance, Blob, and Feature Envy after examining the change history information mined from the versioning system. Jaafaret. al.(2014)analyzed the mutation of Anti-pattern by taking the 27 releases of three open source software systems.

Quality of the software system is a significant concern for the software industry. The literature discussed in this section reveals that the quality of any software system is degraded with the presence of code smell in the code. Refactoring is the only solution to resolve the problem of code smell. Industry people need to prioritize the refactoring effort as refactoring is an expensive process. In next section, a new metrics to find out the refactoring index is proposed.

FRAMEWORK FOR PROPOSED METRICS

To find out the Refactoring Index a framework is proposed Figure1..Refactoring Index is an indicator that is used to determine the level of refactoring required in the given software. Refactoring requirement depends on the number of code smell and type of code smell present in the code. Thus finding refactoring need for a code (R.I) is a multicriteria problem. The higher value of R.I. means the number of code smell present in the code is severs and more refactoring effort is required and vice versa (Table 1). To find out the refactoring index, a data set from the Landfill repository has been taken (Palomba, F 2015), and Shannon's Entropy method is applied to find out the relative weight of the code smell present in the code (Shannon, C. E. 2001). Finally, Simple Additive Weighted (SAW) Equation (1) method is applied which is a sum of products of code smell present (s_{ij}) in the given software and the relative importance of the code smell (w_j) to find out the refactoring Index.

$$R.I = \sum_{j=1}^{n} w_j * s_{ij} \text{ where } i = 1 \ldots m, j = 1 \ldots n \tag{1}$$

where R.I represents the Refactoring Index

w_j represents the weight which reflect the relative critically of code smell for given software

s_{ij} is the Normalized value of the code smell of different projects which is taken from landfill repository.

Table 1 describes the need of refactoring according to the range of refactoring index (R.I). Below Figure 1 describes the frame work to find out the refactoring index (R.I). In this study five different code smell is taken namely(i) Divergent Change (D.C) (ii) Shotgun Surgery (iii) Parallel Inheritance (P.I) (iv) Blob (B.B) (v) Feature Envy (F.E) which is part of data set of taken from landfill (Palomba, F 2015). Weights of each code smells are measured individually, finally each weight of the code smell is multiply with its corresponding code smell to find out the need of refactoring need.

Table 1. Range of refactoring index

S. No	Range of Refactoring		Requirement of refactoring
1.	0-1	Very Low	There is no requirement of refactoring for a given project
2.	1-3	low	There is a requirement of refactoring but it is not very urgent.
3.	3-5	medium	There is requirement of refactoring but need, importance can be given to critical project.
4.	5-7	high	Requirement of refactoring is urgent for the project
5.	7-10	Very high	Project with the very high range of refactoring index should be refactor first in order to improve the quality of the code.

Entropy Based Refactoring Index Evaluation (EBRIE) Algorithm

The occurrence of code smell in the software required refactoring of the code. Refactoring is to change the external behavior of any system without affecting the internal design of any software system. In this given study, five types of the code smells are identified from open data set namely Divergent change(DC), Shotgun surgery(SS), Parallel Inheritance(PI), Blob(BL), Feature Envy(FE)(Palomba, F 2015). To find out the Refactoring Index entropy-based algorithm is:

Figure 1. Proposed Framework

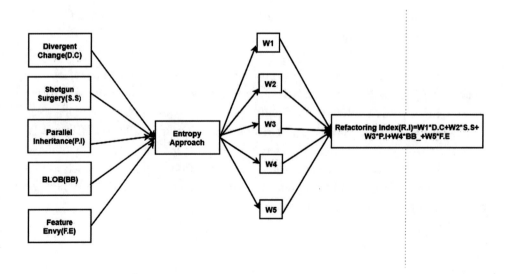

Step 1: Determine the code smell present in the given software. Researchers employ a various tool like JDeodorant, inCode, and DÉCOR to find the code smell in the code (Hamid, A., 2013).

Step 2: Normalized the value of identified code smell. The different data measurement unit is converted into the Compactable unit through normalization. Vector normalization, linear scale transformation (MIN-MAX), linear scale transformation (MAX), and linear scale conversion (sum Method) are some standard normalization approach (Mantyla, M et al. 2003). The values in given paper are normalized using Linear Scale Conversion method Eq. (2)

$$w_j = \frac{x_{ij}}{\sum_{j=1}^{n} x_{ij}} \quad j=1...n \tag{2}$$

Step 3: Compute the entropy: In this paper, Shannon entropy is used which is given in Eq. (3)

$$E_j = -j \sum_{i=1}^{n} s_{ij} * \ln\left(s_{ij}\right), j = 1, 2, 3, n \tag{3}$$

j is the entropy constant which is $j = \dfrac{1}{\ln\left(n\right)}$

Step 4: To find the criticality of code smell in the code Weights are calculated using Eq.(4) where $\sum_{j=1}^{n} w_j = 1$

Step 5: Evaluate the Refactoring Index using Simple Additive Weighted (SAW) Eq.(1)

METHODOLOGY

For this study 20 different projects considered. The dataset is collected from open dataset repository of code smell called LANDFILL, which is a Web-based platform designed sharing code smell datasets (Palomba, F 2015). The five popular code smell considered for the study are Divergent change (DC), Shotgun surgery(SS), Parallel Inheritance(PI), Blob(BL), Feature Envy(FE). Different refactoring approaches are adopted for handling the code smell. Each code smell and their respective refactoring approach is discussed below

Divergent Change

In software industry to develop software a structural methodology is adapted to adopt the dynamic changes in the software requirement. Frequent changes in the code result in the occurrence of code smell in the code. The one particular reason for the occurrence of divergent shift code smell in the code is when a piece of code is altered for different reasons. This type of code smell can be handled by using class refactoring opportunity called Extract class. The aim of this class is to create smaller classes so that changes can be isolated.

Shotgun Surgery

The reason for the occurrence of this code smell in the code is opposite to the different change code smell. This smell occurs in the code when a single task performed by a program is distributed among different classes of the program and if there is a modification in the task, there is a need to change in different class. Move Method or Field refactoring approach can handle this smell.

Parallel Inheritance

When a subclass of one class is made, it becomes mandatory to create the subclass of another class. This is a particular case of code smell when there is a change in the object of class simultaneously there is a change in the object of the other class. The best way to remove this code smell from the code is refactoring by extract subclass method which is based on redistributing responsibilities among the classes.

Blob (God Class)

When a particular class with vast attributes, and hulking operations and it is overburden with many responsibilities with data class, then the smell occurred in the code is called the blob or God Class smell. This code smell is only removed with a particular refactoring technique which is called exact class approach.

Feature Envy

When the method of class access the data of another class than its own class, then the smell occur in the code is called the feature envy code smell. Solution to this code smell is that shift that particular method to another class only. This can be achieved by move method.

As all five different codes smell is considered for all 20 entire projects. To identify which of project needs maximum refactoring, the cumulative effect all code smell is considered. The relative importance of code smell is determined using entropy approach.

Above mentioned all code smells can be measured manually or using the automated tool. To measure these code smells manually we need to measure the each and every design metrics associated with a particular code smell. There are numerous tool available to measure the code smells from the code like incode, jdeordent, Decor tool as it is mentioned in Table 2.

ENTROPY METHOD FOR WEIGHT CALCULATION

Entropy is a popular method introduced by C. E Shannon which is popularly used in thermodynamics to measure the disorder of the system (Shannon, C. E. 2001). This is an probability based approach which emphasis on the measurement of randomness of information of the system. This approach is applied in numerous domains like pattern detection, Natural language processing, statistical inference (Zhang, H. P. 2015; Liu, W., & Cui, J. 2008) but it plays very important role in the study of introduction of code smell with code change(Gupta, A 2018). In software industry requirements from the customer are not fixed that leads to frequent code change which may introduce the code smell in the code, these frequent changes can be easily measured by entropy (Palomba, F 2017). Introduction of code smell in the code due to frequent code change may also affect the sustainability, reliability and quality of the code, entropy measure the effect of these code changes on the quality of code rather counting the number of changes happened to the code. The entropy method calculates the weights of the code smells by maintaining the balance in

Table 2. Code smell measurement Techniques

Code Smell	Manual Code Smell Measurement Through Design Metrics	Code Smell Detection Using Automatic Tool
Divergent Change	Divergent change code smell can be calculated by evaluating the Dependency Oriented Complexity Metric for an Artifact Affected by $$\text{Ripples(DOCMA)} = \frac{\sum_{i=1}^{n} DCPP_{ij}}{(n-1)}$$ (Reddy, K 2009) Where DCPP= Design change propagation probabilities.	infusion, JDeodorant(eclipse plugin)
Shotgun Surgery	([CM] is in top20%) AND ([CM]>10)AND ([chC]>5) Where CM= Changing Methods ChC= Changing Classes (Li, W 2012)	infusion
Parallel Inheritance	DIT >3‖NSC > 4 Where= Depth of Inheritance Tree NCS= Number of children (Cespo et al. 2005)	infusion, JDeodorant(eclipse plugin)
Blob(God class)	*God class = WMC ≥ VERY _ HIGH ^ ATFD > FEW ^ TCC < 1 / 3* Where WMC= Weighted Method Count TCC= Tight Class Cohesion ATFD= Access to Foreign Data VERY_HIGH=47 FEW=5 (Fontana F. 2012)	infusion, JDeodorant(eclipse plugin)
Feature Envy	Feature Envy= $$FDP \leq FEW \,{}^{\wedge} ATFD > FEW \,{}^{\wedge} LAA < \frac{1}{3}$$ Where ATFD=Access to Foreign Data LAA=Locality of attribute access FDP= Foreign Data Providers. (Fontana F. 2012)	Infusion, JDeodorant(eclipse plugin)

between the code smell. In order to calculate the weights of different code smell a data from the landfill repository has been taken (Palomba, F 2015) and weights of each code smell is determined (Table 3).

Below given are the steps of evaluation of weights

1. The value of the code smells of 20 projects are normalized by using the equation (2). Normalized values of code smell are shown in Table 4.
2. Entropy is evaluated using the equation(3).Values of entropy for different code smell is given in Table 5.

Table 3. Code smell for 20 projects

Projects	Sij=				
	Code Smell				Feature Envy
	Divergent Change	Shotgun Surgery	Parallel Inheritance	Blob	
Apache Ant	0	0	7	8	8
Apache Tomcat	5	1	9	5	3
jEdit	4	1	3	5	10
Android API (framework-opt-telephony)	0	0	0	13	0
Android API (frameworks-base	3	1	3	8	17
Android API (frameworks-support)	1	1	0	5	0
Android API (sdk)	1	0	9	10	3
Android API (tool-base)	0	0	0	0	0
Apache Commons Lang	1	0	6	3	1
Apache Cassandra	3	0	3	2	28
Apache Commons Code	0	0	0	1	0
Apache Derby	0	0	0	9	0
Eclipse Core	1	1	8	4	3
Apache James Mime	1	0	0	0	9
Google Guava	0	0	0	1	2
Aardvark	0	1	0	1	0
And Engine	0	0	0	0	1
Apache Commons	1	0	1	2	1
Apache Commons Logging	2	0	2	2	0
Mongo	1	0	0	3	0

Table 4. Normalized value of code smell

S. No	Divergent Change	Shotgun Surgery	Parallel Inheritance	Blob	Feature Envy
			$S_{ij} =$		
1.	0.000	0.000	0.137	0.090	0.093
2	0.208	0.166	0.176	0.060	0.034
3	0.166	0.166	0.058	0.060	0.116
4	0.000	0.000	0.000	0.158	0.000
5	0.125	0.166	0.058	0.090	0.197
6	0.041	0.166	0.000	0.060	0.000
7	0.041	0.000	0.176	0.121	0.034
8	0.000	0.000	0.000	0.000	0.000
9	0.041	0.000	0.117	0.036	0.011
10	0.125	0.000	0.058	0.024	0.325
11	0.000	0.000	0.000	0.012	0.000
12	0.000	0.000	0.000	0.109	0.000
13	0.041	0.166	0.156	0.048	0.034
14	0.041	0.000	0.000	0.000	0.104
15	0.000	0.000	0.000	0.012	0.023
16	0.000	0.166	0.000	0.012	0.000
17	0.000	0.000	0.000	0.000	0.011
18	0.041	0.000	0.010	0.024	0.011
19	0.083	0.000	0.039	0.024	0.000
20	0.041	0.000	0.000	0.036	0.000

Table 5. Value of Entropy for code Smell

S. No	Code Smell	Entropy
1.	Divergent change	0.760
2.	Shotgun Surgery	0.598
3.	parallel Inheritance	0.711
4.	Blob	0.860
5.	Feature Envy	0.663

3. Calculations of entropy weights using equation4 is given in Table 6.
4. Refactoring index can be calculated by multiplying the entropy weights and normalized values of code smell

$$R.I = \sum_{j=1}^{n} w_j * S_{ij} \tag{5}$$

where i…m.

RESULTS

The proposed refactoring index is given in Eq. (5) is used to evaluate the Refactoring requirement to improve the code smell in a software system. Refactoring Index is calculated by multiplying entropy weights and number of code smell present in the software is given as

Refactoring Index (R.I) = 0.170*D.C+0.285*S.S+0.205*P. I+0.098*BB+0.239*F.E

Where D.C=Divergent changes, S.S=Shotgun Surgery, P.I= Parallel Inheritance, BB=Blob, F.E=Feature Envy. Table 7 shows the refactoring index for different project.

Among the given set of software ApacheCassandraneeds maximum refactoring and Android API (tool-base) do not need refactoring.

Table 6. Weights of code smell

S. No	Code Smell	Weights
1.	Divergent change	0.170
2.	Shotgun Surgery	0.285
3.	parallel Inheritance	0.205
4.	Blob	0.098
5.	Feature Envy	0.239

Table 7. Refactoring Index for different projects

S. No	Projects	Refactoring Index
1.	Apache Cassandra	8.032
2.	Android API (frameworks-base	6.276
3.	jEdit	4.473
4.	Apache Tomcat	4.198
5.	Apache Ant	4.145
6.	Android API (sdk)	3.726
7.	Eclipse Core	3.213
8.	Apache James Mime	2.326
9.	Apache Commons Lang	1.938
10.	Android API (framework-opt-telephony)	1.286
11.	Android API (frameworks-support)	0.950
12.	Apache Commons Logging	0.948
13.	Apache Derby	0.890
14.	Apache Commons	0.812
15.	Google Guava	0.578
16.	Mongo	0.466
17.	Aardvark	0.384
18.	And Engine	0.239
19.	Apache Commons Code	0.098
20.	Android API (tool-base)	0.000

CONCLUSION

The code smell distribution modeling in software is fascinating area and has drawn a wide attention of researchers and software. Machine learning and other techniques are used for understanding the behavior of code smell. These methods are effective when there is an extensive collection of observations are available. Collecting and analyzing this observation is a complex and time-consuming task. With a small dataset, available variance entropy concept can be suitably used for design a model or metrics for describing the system.

Although the word entropy was originally used in thermodynamics, its concepts have been widely in the various field of software engineering, as it is suitably used for describing the distribution of variables on which system depends. In this Study, a new metrics refactoring index is introduced to prioritize the code smell and find the software that needs maximum refactoring. In this study Refactoring index is calculated for an entire project whereas entropy method can be used for component based system where code smells can be detected from an individual components and components are prioritize according to refactoring need.

REFERENCES

Andrade, H. (2013). *Identifying Architectural Bad Smells in Software Product Lines*. Academic Press.

Carneiro, G. D. F., Silva, M., Mara, L., Figueiredo, E., Sant'Anna, C., Garcia, A., & Mendonca, M. (2010). Identifying code smells with multiple concern views. In *Software Engineering (SBES), 2010 Brazilian Symposium on* (pp. 128-137). IEEE.

Crespo, Y., Lopez, C., Marticorena, R., & Manso, E. (2005). Language independent metrics support towards refactoring inference. *9th ECOOP Workshop on QAOOSE 05*.

Dhillon, P. K., & Sidhu, G. (2012). Can Software Faults be Analyzed using Bad Code Smells? An Empirical Study. *International Journal of Scientific and Research Publications*, *2*(10), 1–7.

Fontana, F. A., Braione, P., & Zanoni, M. (2012). Automatic detection of bad smells in code: An experimental assessment. *Journal of Object Technology*, *11*(2), 5–1.

Fowler, M., & Beck, K. (1999). *Refactoring: improving the design of existing code*. Addison-Wesley Professional.

Greiler, M., Zaidman, A., Deursen, A. V., & Storey, M. A. (2013). Strategies for avoiding text fixture smells during software evolution. In *Proceedings of the 10th Working Conference on Mining Software Repositories* (pp. 387-396). IEEE Press. 10.1109/MSR.2013.6624053

Gupta, A., Suri, B., Kumar, V., Misra, S., Blažauskas, T., & Damaševičius, R. (2018). Software Code Smell Prediction Model Using Shannon, Rényi and Tsallis Entropies. *Entropy (Basel, Switzerland)*, *20*(5), 372. doi:10.3390/e20050372

Gupta, V., Kapur, P. K., & Kumar, D. (2016). Modelling and measuring code smells in enterprise applications using TISM and two-way assessment. *International Journal of System Assurance Engineering and Management*, *7*(3), 332–340. doi:10.100713198-016-0460-0

Hafezalkotob, A., & Hafezalkotob, A. (2016). Extended MULTIMOORA method based on Shannon entropy weight for materials selection. *Journal of Industrial Engineering International*, *12*(1), 1–13. doi:10.100740092-015-0123-9

Hamid, A., Ilyas, M., Hummayun, M., & Nawaz, A. (2013). A comparative study on code smell detection tools. *International Journal of Advanced Science and Technology*, *60*, 25–32. doi:10.14257/ijast.2013.60.03

Jaafar, F., Khomh, F., Guéhéneuc, Y. G., & Zulkernine, M. (2014). Anti-pattern Mutations and Fault-proneness. In *Quality Software (QSIC), 2014 14th International Conference on* (pp. 246-255). IEEE. 10.1109/QSIC.2014.45

Kapila, H., & Singh, S. (2014). Bayesian Inference to Predict Smelly classes Probability in Open source software. *International Journal of Current Engineering and Technology, 4*(3), 1724–1728.

Li, W., & Shatnawi, R. (2007). An empirical study of the bad smells and class error probability in the post-release object-oriented system evolution. *Journal of Systems and Software, 80*(7), 1120–1128. doi:10.1016/j.jss.2006.10.018

Lieberman, R. (1997). What is that Smell? *College & Undergraduate Libraries, 4*(2), 51–53. doi:10.1300/J106v04n02_08

Liu, W., & Cui, J. (2008). Entropy coefficient method to evaluate the level of sustainable development of China's sports. *International Journal of Sports Science and Engineering, 2*(2), 72–78.

Mansoor, U., Kessentini, M., Bechikh, S., & Deb, K. (2013). *Code-smells detection using good and bad software design examples.* Technical report.

Mantyla, M., Vanhanen, J., & Lassenius, C. (2003). A taxonomy and an initial empirical study of bad smells in code. In *Software Maintenance, 2003.ICSM 2003. Proceedings. International Conference on* (pp. 381-384). IEEE.

Moha, N., Guéhéneuc, Y. G., Le Meur, A. F., Duchien, L., & Tiberghien, A. (2010). From a domain analysis to the specification and detection of code and design smells. *Formal Aspects of Computing, 22*(3-4), 345–361. doi:10.100700165-009-0115-x

Palomba, F., Bavota, G., Di Penta, M., Oliveto, R., De Lucia, A., & Poshyvanyk, D. (2013). Detecting bad smells in source code using change history information. In *Proceedings of the 28th IEEE/ACM International Conference on Automated Software Engineering* (pp. 268-278). IEEE Press. 10.1109/ASE.2013.6693086

Palomba, F., Di Nucci, D., Tufano, M., Bavota, G., Oliveto, R., Poshyvanyk, D., & De Lucia, A. (2015). Landfill: An open dataset of code smells with public evaluation. In *Mining Software Repositories (MSR), 2015 IEEE/ACM 12th Working Conference on* (pp. 482-485). IEEE.

Palomba, F., Zanoni, M., Fontana, F. A., De Lucia, A., & Oliveto, R. (2017). Toward a smell-aware bug prediction model. *IEEE Transactions on Software Engineering,* 1. doi:10.1109/TSE.2017.2770122

Peters, R., & Zaidman, A. (2012). Evaluating the lifespan of code smells using software repository mining. In *Software Maintenance and Reengineering (CSMR), 2012 16th European Conference on* (pp. 411-416). IEEE.

Pietrzak, B., & Walter, B. (2006). Leveraging code smell detection with inter-smell relations. In *International Conference on Extreme Programming and Agile Processes in Software Engineering* (pp. 75-84). Springer. 10.1007/11774129_8

Reddy, K. R., & Rao, A. A. (2009). Dependency oriented complexity metrics to detect rippling related design defects. *Software Engineering Notes*, *34*(4), 1–7. doi:10.1145/1543405.1543421

Shannon, C. E. (2001). A mathematical theory of communication. *Mobile Computing and Communications Review*, *5*(1), 3–55. doi:10.1145/584091.584093

Singh, G., & Chopra, V. (2013). A study of bad smells in code. *Int J SciEmergTechnol Latest Trends*, *7*(91), 16–20.

Tufano, M., Palomba, F., Bavota, G., Oliveto, R., Di Penta, M., De Lucia, A., & Poshyvanyk, D. (2015). When and why your code starts to smell bad. In *Software Engineering (ICSE), 2015 IEEE/ACM 37th IEEE International Conference on* (Vol. 1, pp. 403-414). IEEE.

Van Emden, E., & Moonen, L. (2002). Java quality assurance by detecting code smells. In *Reverse Engineering, 2002. Proceedings. Ninth Working Conference on* (pp. 97-106). IEEE.

Zhang, H. P. (2015). Application on the entropy method for determination of weight of evaluating index in fuzzy mathematics for wine quality assessment. *Advance Journal of Food Science and Technology*, *7*(3), 195–198. doi:10.19026/ajfst.7.1293

Chapter 8
Operator Overloading as a DSL Parsing Mechanism

Alberto Simões
Polytechnic Institute of Cávado and Ave, Portugal

Rui Miguel da Costa Meira
Polytechnic Institute of Cávado and Ave, Portugal

ABSTRACT

This chapter describes an approach for the implementation of embedded domain-specific languages by using operator overloads and the creation of abstract syntax trees in run-time. Using the host language parser, an AST is created stating the structure of the DSL expression that is later analyzed, simplified, and optimized before the evaluation step. For the illustration of this process, the chapter proposes a domain-specific language for a basic linear algebra system dealing with matrices algebra and its optimization.

INTRODUCTION

Domain Specific Languages (DSL) are, undoubtedly, a great approach for the acceleration of processes (Kosar et al, 2015). These processes can be at different level: either for a specific purpose, completely outside of the scope of the programming paradigm (e.g. a specific language for describing a taxonomy of a thesaurus) or to help in the development process (e.g. the well-known flex and bison languages, designed to help in the development of compilers). While the first require a syntax specifically designed for that purpose, as the end users are not necessarily programmers, the

DOI: 10.4018/978-1-5225-7455-2.ch008

second usually take a hybrid approach, where some details are described in a new syntax, but a lot of the syntax is from the target language.

Usually DSL are classified as proper languages, when they are developed as a standard new language, where parsing follows the traditional approach (lexical and syntactic analysis, abstract syntax tree creation, tree manipulation and code generation or evaluation) or as an embedded language.

For this second situation, some DSL implement code generation, creating code in the target language that will be compiled and integrated with other host language files, or allowing its evaluation on run time (mainly for interpreted or other languages with reflection or meta-programming support (Bracha & Ungar, 2015)).

As parsing mechanism, this second case uses language constructs to define a dialect of the host language or, in some other situations, a hybrid parsing approach where some high order function transforms parts of the DSL syntax in the host language syntax (see (Simões & Almeida, 2010) for such a DSL implementation).

In this chapter we present another way for the development of embedded DSL through the use of operator overloading. While operator overloading is a common functionality on recent object-oriented languages, like C++, Java, C#, Python or Perl, the way these operators are used is, in most situations, the simple replacement of the default operator behavior (for example, the sum of two numeric values) with a similar one (for example, the sum of two vectors).

There are other situations where these operator overloads can create an abstract syntax tree (AST) instead of trying to evaluate the operator semantic. Thus, this behavior would be very similar to what a traditional parser would do when analysing the language. The main different is that it will be done in run time.

Note that this is not a new approach, as the way some libraries work show that similar approaches are used. An example is the way TensorFlow (Abadi et al, 2016) is able to compute what they call a computation graph, and later infer this computation derivative automatically. Therefore, this chapter does not claims a new methodology, but rather the clear definition of the structure of such a DSL implementation. Another example is MXNet (Chen et al, 2015) library. While the authors refer the usage of embedding a DSL in a host language, no references are made. Authors describe their systems results rather the way their implementation was done.

A few other references (Corliss & Griewank, 1993; Phipps & Pawlowski, 2012) were found, where the idea of operator overloading is discussed in order to enable differentiation and integration of expressions. But no details on DSL embedding are given.

MOTIVATION

The motivation for the approach here described is the construction of a basic Perl framework to act like TensorFlow, for simple neural networks, and easy to understand and edit by the community. While the module is under work and at a reasonable distance from being really useful, its development arose some problems that lead to the architecture here described.

The implementation of a neural network deals mainly with Basic Linear Algebra (BLA) operations. Given the requirement of fast implementations, these operations were obtained through a Basic Linear Algebra Subprograms (BLAS) library. The more relevant methods were defined: matrix sum and subtraction, element-wise operators (sum, multiplication, exponentiation, etc), matrices inner product, matrix transposition, matrix inverse, sigmoid and tanh, and some other operations.

To allow the users to easily write algebraic expressions with matrices, common operators were overloaded. The four arithmetic operators were overloaded for element-wise operators or matrix-matrix operator (if making sense) just by looking to the operator arguments' types. The special 'x' repetition operator existing in Perl was overloaded for the matrix inner product. Other than operators, some functions were defined for transposition, inverse, sigmoid, tanh, softmax and other relevant operations.

As these operators are guaranteed by the BLAS library, the first overload mechanism was to directly call the respective BLAS function for each required operation.

While working, this approach had some drawbacks:

- It was not possible to take advantage of specific optimizations present in the library. As an example, Lapack (Anderson et al, 1999) BLAS implementation allows the inner product between two matrices to be done with optional transpositions for any of the matrix arguments. If the evaluation is done at each operator or function call, when the expression A x B^T is parsed, first B would be transposed, and only then the inner product would be performed. Nevertheless, it is possible to do everything at once with BLAS.

- For neural networks and deep learning, some operations need to be done over and over again, with the same expression, replacing only one of the arguments. If every operation is performed as soon as it is parsed by Perl, they will be evaluated every time, even if a subexpression is not changed and its value can be reused.

- In the future, if there is the interest of computing derivatives automatically (this is not yet a priority in our work) we will need to store the computation graph (basically, an AST for the expression) to be able to obtain its derivative automatically.

These problems and goals were the main reason for applying the approach we describe in the next sections. As our development continues, the choice seems adequate and working as expected.

ARCHITECTURE

The common approach for the implementation of a programming language compiler or interpreter is comprised by the lexical and syntactic analysis part, the creation of an abstract syntax tree (AST), a possible step on optimization that rewrites the AST, and the AST traversal for code generation or execution.

In our proposed approach all these steps exist as well. The main difference is that the lexical and syntactic analysis is performed by the original host language parser (in this case, hitchhiking with the Perl parser). This means that the syntax of the defined DSL should be somehow a subset of the host language. While this can be a limitation, if the host language is properly chosen, it might not be a real problem. Figure 1 shows this architecture as a diagram.

In the next step, an abstract syntax tree should be created. This is performed by a set of methods, one for each overloaded operator or function, that returns an AST node. For a Object Oriented language these methods are very simple, gathering the objects returned by each operand, and saving a reference to them in the tree node. These are the methods that will be called by the overloaded operators, instead of the

Figure 1. Proposed architecture

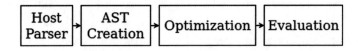

common evaluation methods. Thus, the result of parsing an expression is a variable holding a tree of objects.

Follows the optimization step, adapting the AST accordingly with the language needs. Usually it can be implemented as a simply tree traversal, that change its structure where required. The main challenge is to understand when this step should be performed, and guarantee that, if performed once in a subtree, it is not performed again (in order to guarantee execution performance).

The final step is the evaluation or code generation. It is responsible for a final traversal of the tree. For interpreted languages, the traversal will evaluate through a depth-first tree traversal. First evaluating the leafs of the tree, and then applying each operator to the already evaluated children. Whenever possible, the implementation should take care of guaranteeing that the evaluation for a subtree is cached and not performed each time the expression value is needed (as long as its argument values are unchanged).

The next sections will describe each one of these three steps: the AST construction, the Optimization of the AST, and its Evaluation. While the explained ideas are not language dependent, the examples will be shown using Perl syntax, for the motivating DSL: a simple Basic Linear Algebra (BLA) expression evaluator.

AST CREATION

As the goal is to implement BLA expressions, AST leafs are scalar objects: matrices, numeric values, and placeholders (used for the user to replace a specific value in the computation graph). Internal nodes are standard objects. While Perl is not typed, and therefore, uses untyped variables, it is possible to query scalar values in order to know if they are basic types (as numeric values or strings) or objects, and for these detect their type (if they are matrices or internal nodes).

For the creation of matrices leafs (we consider a vector as a matrix where one dimension is 1) a call for the matrix constructor is needed. There are different constructors, for matrices of zero values, matrices where all values are the number 1, matrices of random values, identity matrices, or specific values matrices. All these constructors have a shorthand method name, that is exported to the host language function table, and declared with the exact amount of parameters needed. This allows their usage with (or without) the need of syntactic sugar:

```
$zeros = Zeros 10, 20;
$ones = Ones 1, 50;
$random = Random 20, 20;
$identity = Identity 10;
$custom = M [[10, 20, 30], [40, 50, 60]];
```

Note that Perl allows that, for methods defined prior their usage with a specific signature, to discard the usual parenthesis used in function call. Thus, the only syntactic sugar required by the host language are the dollar signs in the variable names, and the semicolon at the end of each command. For other leaf types, like integer or real values, they are used in their host language format.

To create the AST nodes, as already mentioned, our approach uses operator overloading, and function creation or redefinition. Given the flexibility of Perl basic object system, the AST internal tree nodes are generic dictionaries, where each key is a field, and values are those fields values. This allows different nodes to have different structures without the need to define different classes.

For simple algebra operators (sum, subtraction, division and multiplication) the AST creation is a simple call to the constructor for a tree node structure, where the operator and arguments are supplied accordingly. As an example, follows the implementation for the method that is used to overload the sum operator:

```
sub sum ($left, $right) {
      return AST_Node(operator =>  'sum', args => [$left,
$right]);
}
```

Note that operator precedence table is shared with the precedence table of the host language operators. Thus, when overloading a specific binary operator, the host language is responsible for supplying the left and right operands to the overloading function. The overload for the 'x' operator is similar, as it is also a binary operator (although not much languages have it available).

For functions, like the computation of the transposed matrix, inverse, softmax, sigmoid, etc., the tree constructor is called from the called method. As an example, the T function is defined as:

```
sub T ($matrix) {
    return AST_Node(operator => 'transpose', args => [ $matrix
]);
}
```

While the user is calling a method to compute the transposed matrix, what is done really, is to store its AST, and do the required computation only when needed. Again, Perl allows the resulting DSL to recognize the following syntax:

```
$c = $a x T $b;
```

Indeed, this syntax is still close to the host language syntax. But it is clean and, to be used as an embedded DSL, acceptable, as it is both versatile enough, and similar with the host language.

For other functions, like trigonometric functions or the exponential or logarithmic functions, that already exist in the host language, a little more work is needed, as it does not make sense to create a function with a different name to be used in the DSL. Specially as it would result in different function names for numeric values (the built-in functions) and for matrices (our defined functions).

The solution was possible given Perl reflection and meta-programming. A reference to the original functions is fetched from the symbol table and stored with a different name. The new function is defined with the name of the built-in method, but returning the AST node for that operation. Later, in the evaluation function, the original method is called when the argument is a numeric value, and the matrices method call when dealing with a matrix.

OPTIMIZATION AND SIMPLIFICATION

The optimization or simplification step tries to find similar or related operations that can be performed more efficiently as a single one, than when executed independently. Examples are the inner product between two matrices, where one or both of them are transposed. BLAS implementations allow these different situations to be handled by the same method. Another situation is the sequence of similar operations where the temporary matrices created by each operator evaluation method can be reduced. These two examples are detailed below.

This task can be defined as a tree rewriting process, that detects tree patterns that can be simplified or optimized, and replaces them with the respective optimized version.

The approach implemented for our DSL is based on a depth-first traversal, starting to optimize leafs, their parents, and up the tree to the root node. This way each node optimization can query their children that are already optimized or simplified. Also, given that a subtree can be shared between two or more tree expressions, the optimization process adds a flag to each tree node stating the status of that subtree optimization.

Also relevant is to refer that this optimization does not need to be performed at the end. It can be done at the same time as the AST tree is being built. Everytime a new node is added, the direct subtree can be analysed and the group of nodes simplified when possible.

Follows two specific examples of optimizations implemented in our BLA language:

1. First, the inner product where one of the matrices is transposed: $M_1 \times M_2^T$

While the transposition can be done first, and then the inner product, this process can be made faster as the usual implementation of the inner product allows the usage of the same code when one or the two matrices are transposed, as there is only a change of the order of the two nested cycles (for columns and rows). Figure 2 presents at the left the original expression, and at the right the optimized version, where the transposing information was synthesized by the main operator: $M_1 \times^T M_2$.

Figure 2. Example of optimization for dot product

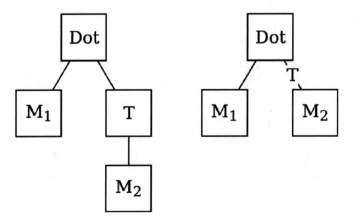

2. Second, a sequence of the same algebraic operator: $M_1 + M_2 + \dots + M_n$

This expression AST is created like the example at the left of Figure 3. This means that, for a sequence of k matrices, k-1 nodes are created. When each of these nodes are evaluated, a new temporary matrix is created to store the sum result. Thus, a total of k-1 temporary matrices are needed. The optimization step can transform this tree into a single node AST, as presented at the right in Figure 3. This solution will create a new temporary matrix with the sum of the two first matrices, and them accumulate in that temporary matrix the value for the remaining sums. While the operation is repeated the same k-1 times, the lack of a temporary matrix is enough to make the process both faster and less memory consuming.

EVALUATION

While the evaluation of an AST is not a problem, the main issue is to understand when this evaluation can be performed. This can highly depend on the host language and its functionalities regarding operator overloading and meta-programming availability.

The main problem is that the evaluation can not be done at the same time as the tree is constructed. For example, when adding a new node (say, a transposition operator), there is no information about its parent node type, and therefore, there is no enough information regarding if that node should be evaluated (and the transposed

Figure 3. Example of optimization for a sequence of n-1 sums

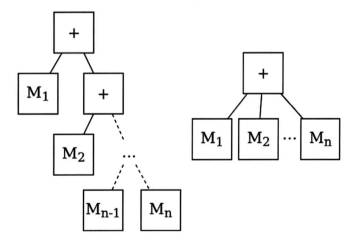

matrix computed) or if it should be kept intact, so that, later, its parent can take advantage of it, and optimize the complete evaluation.

Thus, the evaluation should be performed when there is the need to query the final value of the expression. For a matrix, when it is being printed, compared, or a specific element value is retrieved. For a computation that yields a numeric value, when that value is needed to be compared, or printed.

For Perl there are a few tricks that help this process. First, Perl includes two pseudo-operators that can be overloaded, namely 0+ and "". These operators refer, respectively, to a method to convert a variable into a value number, and to a method that converts the stored data into a string. These two methods are available to Perl as it does not distinguish data types, and whenever it needs to perform a computation with a value, it uses the 0+ overload to obtain the numeric value; and uses the "" overload whenever it needs to print that value. Thus, with these two specific operators we can infer that evaluation should take place whenever they are called.

Unfortunately there are other problems. Given a matrix is stored as an object, some methods (like the accessor for a value stored in a specific position of the matrix) require that the expression is evaluated, so that the matrix is available, and that specific position can be queried. One option could be adding code to each of these methods, in order to evaluate the expression before running its behavior. But this process is not easily scalable.

Fortunately, Perl allows the programmer to intersect calls to an object when there is not a method available with the referred name. For example, if a method "xpto" is called in an object that does not implement it, before complaining, perl calls a AUTOLOAD method, that can load dynamically methods from external libraries.

Our implementation uses this functionality. When an unknown method is called for an expression, the expression object can infer that the method should not be called on the expression itself (as it is not defined for that kind of objects), but on the result of its evaluation. With this in mind, the evaluation method is called once, the evaluation value cached, and the method called on the evaluation result (typically a matrix). While this works perfectly, there is some kind of indirection that is not possible to implement in all OO languages.

CONCLUSION

Using operator overload, as well as defining new functions or redefining functions from a host language is a simple way to embed some type of domain specific languages in a host language. While the majority of the host language structure is kept, it is possible to redefine the operators to make them act correctly for the specific arguments they receive.

While operator overloading is a common thing, most users do this as an evaluation step, meaning that the overload for a specific operator executes immediately the operation on their parameters. This approach works perfectly for basic languages, but is not versatile when there can be some kind of optimization or simplification of compound operations.

To help on this process, we describe how the operator overload and new defined methods can be used to create an abstract syntax tree (instead of direct evaluation) that can be then simplified or optimized as needed. Finally, whenever the real result of the expression is needed, the computation graph can be evaluated.

This is not a new approach, and is being used on some libraries. Nevertheless, our main contribution is the systematic description of the process as reference for other language designers who need similar functionalities for their projects.

One of the main advantages of this process is that, given operators and functions operate at the object level, one host language might embed more than one of these domain specific languages, given their overloads will not collide. This is a real advantage, as most embedding approaches usually require a parsing step which might interfere with the parsing step for a different embedded language.

REFERENCES

Abadi, M., Barham, P., Chen, J., Chen, Z., Davis, A., Dean, J., . . . Kudlur, M. (2016, November). Tensorflow: a system for large-scale machine learning. In OSDI (Vol. 16, pp. 265-283). Academic Press.

Anderson, E., Bai, Z., Bischof, C., Blackford, L. S., Demmel, J., Dongarra, J., & Sorensen, D. (1999). *LAPACK Users' guide*. Society for Industrial and Applied Mathematics. doi:10.1137/1.9780898719604

Bracha, G., & Ungar, D. (2015). OOPSLA 2004: mirrors: design principles for meta-level facilities of object-oriented programming languages. *ACM SIGPLAN Notices*, *50*(8), 35–48. doi:10.1145/2854695.2854699

Chen, T., Li, M., Li, Y., Lin, M., Wang, N., Wang, M., . . . Zhang, Z. (2015). *MXNet: A Flexible and Efficient Machine Learning Library for Heterogeneous Distributed Systems*. Retrieved from http://arxiv.org/abs/1512.01274

Corliss, G. F., & Griewank, A. (1993). Operator overloading as an enabling technology for automatic differentiation (ANL/MCS/CP--79481). Academic Press.

Kosar, T., Bohra, S., & Mernik, M. (2015). Domain-Specific Languages: A Systematic Mapping Study. *Information and Software Technology*, *71*. doi:10.1016/j.infsof.2015.11.001

Phipps, E., & Pawlowski, R. (2012). Efficient Expression Templates for Operator Overloading-Based Automatic Differentiation. In Recent Advances in Algorithmic Differentiation (pp. 309-319). Academic Press.

Simões, A., & Almeida, J. J. (2010). Processing XML: a rewriting system approach. In XATA 2010 --- 8ª Conferência Nacional em XML. Aplicações e Tecnologias Associadas.

Chapter 9
RESTful Web Services Development With a Model– Driven Engineering Approach

Rafael Corveira da Cruz Gonçalves
Polytechnic Institute of Porto, Portugal

Isabel Azevedo
Polytechnic Institute of Porto, Portugal

ABSTRACT

A RESTful web service implementation requires following the constrains inherent to REST architectural style, which, being a non-trivial task, often leads to solutions that do not fulfill those requirements properly. Model-driven techniques have been proposed to improve the development of complex applications. In model-driven software development, software is not implemented manually based on informal descriptions but partially or completely generated from formal models derived from metamodels. A model-driven approach, materialized in a domain specific language that integrates the OpenAPI specification, an emerging standard for describing REST services, allows developers to use a design first approach in the web service development process, focusing in the definition of resources and their relationships, leaving the repetitive code production process to the automation provided by model-driven engineering techniques. The code generation process covers the entire web-service flow from the description and exposure of the endpoints to the definition of database tables.

DOI: 10.4018/978-1-5225-7455-2.ch009

INTRODUCTION

During the last few years, offering software in the form of web services has gained popularity due to the evolution of cloud architectures and the impact of the Internet of Things (IoT) on the number of connections that can take place.

Ever since its introduction by Fielding (Fielding, 2000), the REpresentational State Transfer (REST) architectural style has been increasingly preferred by developers for its simplicity and scalability (Haupt, Leymann, Scherer, & Vukojevic-Haupt, 2017). REST comprises a set of rules and practices and allows simple comprehensible Application Programming Interfaces (APIs), clear representations, and scalable services (Dimitrieski et al., 2017).

In an attempt at defining a set of standards to describe APIs, and to aid developers in the creation of the interfaces, the OpenAPI Initiative (OAI) was formed by "a consortium of forward-looking industry experts who recognize the immense value of standardizing on how REST APIs are described. As an open governance structure under the Linux Foundation, the OAI is focused on creating, evolving and promoting a vendor neutral description format" (The Linux Foundation, 2017a).

The OpenAPI Specification requires the description of the capabilities of each service without mandating a specific development process, such as design-first or code-first, but does facilitate either technique by establishing clear interactions with a REST API (The Linux Foundation, 2017b).

Meanwhile, from an automated software engineering perspective, Model Driven Engineering (MDE) is gaining popularity (Zolotas, Diamantopoulos, Chatzidimitriou, & Symeonidis, 2017), and it can be useful for the development of REST APIs. A great amount of time is required because developers must address several issues, such as software architecture, error handling, security, access rules, among others, to ensure a suitable design and the desired usability (Schreibmann & Braun, 2014). To implement this solution according to all the best practices is time consuming and it is an expensive part of every software project.

The specification of the structural and behavioral aspects of an application using model-driven principles can be used for code generation (Schreibmann & Braun, 2015).

With the standardization of REST APIs description, provided by the OAI, an MDE approach for the development of a domain specific language (DSL) to generate full API applications can be a helpful and powerful resource for the developers (Scheidgen, Efftinge, & Marticke, 2016). Although there have been several initiatives devoted to the modeling and formal description of REST applications, most of them do not support or even force RESTful compliance (Ed-Douibi, Izquierdo, Gómez,

Tisi, & Cabot, 2015; El-khoury, Gurdur, & Nyberg, 2016), i.e. conformity to the REST architectural style.

The domain of REST APIs development conducts to solutions with repetitive or very similar code between the different interfaces. This is the realm where Model-Driven Development can be useful, abstracting this characteristic, using models as the primary artifact of the development process.

The objective of this research and overall work is to come up with a solid, feasible and efficient engineering solution, based on MDE techniques, specifically DSLs, to take as inputs the structural and the behavioral aspects of the business domain, and then generate the associated RESTful web services, while being compliant with the most recent version of the Open API Specification (OAS).

Therefore, some questions can be derived from the earlier paragraphs, summarizing the main objectives that this work intends to achieve:

1. What are the compromises to specify a language agnostic meta-model to represent and define the OpenAPI specification?
2. Is it possible to define a DSL from the previous model to aid in the web services development process?
3. From the DSL and applying model-to-text transformations, ready-to-deploy RESTful web services can be generated?

The rest of this chapter is organized as follows. The next section ("Background") discuss the main concepts related to the focus of this work, providing an overview of their relationships, and how they work together in a web service development context. The work carried out and the results achieved are detailed presented and discussed in the section "Domain Specific Language based on the OpenAPI Specification". The section "Future Research Directions" mentions some possibilities to extend the actual solution. The last section summarizes the achievements of an approach that integrates the OpenAPI specification in a model-driven engineering process of web services development.

BACKGROUND

Service-Oriented Architecture (SOA) has established itself as the main architectural pattern for web applications development. Services constitute the basic constructs that support rapid, low-cost and easy composition of distributed applications, allowing the integration and interaction in/between heterogeneous environments (Huhns &

Singh, 2005). This interoperability is not original but was addressed before with the use of Common Object Request Broker Architecture (CORBA) as a distributed component framework, but also with Open System Interconnection (OSI) and Remote Procedure Call (RPC), among others.

In SOA, a service is "a logical representation of a repeatable business activity that has a specified outcome" (SOA Work Group, 2016). This definition follows the same direction as (W3C, 2004), that defines a service as "a web interface that supports interoperable operations between different software applications using a standard messaging protocol". These definitions focus on the abstraction of the service concept, which is needed when thinking of a model representing a business process, since it usually encapsulates some complex logic, whose implementation should not be addressed by the client.

Web services, the most popular implementation of SOA, have some fundamental characteristics: they offer robustness and agility to business enterprises, allowing them to perform their business processes efficiently by supporting software reuse, application-to-application interoperability, design flexibility, and a loosely coupled architecture.

When the web services implementation is based on the REST software architectural style they are denominated as "RESTful web services". The conformity with REST allows the web services to avoid the performance degradation resulting from the use of SOAP (Simple Object Access Protocol) and XML (Tihomirovs & Grabis, 2016), (Haupt, Karastoyanova, Leymann, & Schroth, 2014), (Pavan, Sanjay, & Zornitza, 2012).

Services designed through the RESTful approach expose their functionality as Web resources, where each resource is addressed with a unique Uniform Resource Identifier (URI): a user can directly access a specific resource by the associated URI or traverse the offered functionality through a hierarchical structure.

The modeling process of RESTful applications includes structural and behavioral parts (Schreier, 2011). The structural modeling describes the resource types, their attributes, and relations, as well as their interface and representations, while the latter offers the possibility to describe the behavior with state machines. Thereafter, these models are interpreted by a developer with the purpose of gathering the necessary information to build the application. The solution, in this context, usually leads to the implementation of the classic Create, Read, Update and Delete (CRUD) operations over the defined resources and their relationships, always considering the underlying purpose of obtaining a REST compliant application.

Following the constrains inherent to the REST architectural style imposes constraints that are not trivial to fulfill properly (Haupt et al., 2014) as the potential of the REST architectural style is not entirely explored. Moreover, the similarity between the written code for the CRUD operations for all resources makes the development process tedious and error prone.

Model-driven techniques have been proposed to improve the development of complex applications (Stahl, Völter, Bettin, Haase, & Helsen, 2006). In model-driven software development (MDSD), software is generated from formal models. This approach in general leads to better code quality, fewer errors, increased reuse of best practices, better maintainability through "standardized" code, and increased portability through the separation of platform independent models (PIM) and platform specific models (PSM). Given the several issues the developers have to address to ensure a suitable design and the desired usability, an MDE based approach would vastly improve the developer's productivity, while also increasing the code quality (Schreibmann & Braun, 2014).

As said before the introduction of an MDE approach to develop RESTful web services needs the definition of a formal description/model of the application to be developed. While there is not an accepted standard for describing REST Services, an emerging specification standard, the OpenAPI Specification within the Open API Initiative, backed up by some industry giants, like Google, Microsoft, IBM, PayPal, etc., is gaining relevance as the main "programming language-agnostic interface description for REST APIs, which allows both humans and computers to discover and understand the capabilities of a service without requiring access to source code."(The Linux Foundation, 2017b).

The conjunction between the OAS, as a standard to describe the web services, with a model-driven approach based on a meta-model whose implementation takes into consideration the REST constrains, would lead to a development solution that can improve the quality and productivity of the software development process, allowing the developers to focus on the business core rules. The meta-model gives a generic mechanism to create formal specifications based on the OAS. Afterward, the conceptual models created can be used for generating machine readable specifications or the integration code by the corresponding transformation rules. Additionally, the OAS standard allows the mitigation of another frequent problem in RESTful web services development sphere: the proper documentation of the web service. The origin of OAS, previously known as Swagger, allows an easy integration within a web platform where all the involved stakeholders can access the authorized information related to the web services, and even test them against either a real back-end infrastructure or a mocked one.

Writing RESTful web services is a time-consuming matter and there is no guarantee that the outcome will be REST-conform. Also, when many web services are to be implemented the challenges raised usually lead to redundant program code that covers the same functionality over multiple and different layers of the software architecture. This often leads to mistakes as a developer introduces unintentional errors to the repetitive code constructs. Furthermore, the configuration of web services architecture is not a trivial task and it requires a complex and redundant work to be performed (Dimitrieski et al., 2017).

RESTful Web Services

REST is an acronym for REpresentational State Transfer and it is an "architectural style for distributed hypermedia systems" (Fielding, 2000). REST is not considered to be an architecture, but it is described as a "set of constraints applied to elements within the architecture" (Giessler, Gebhart, Sarancin, Steinegger, & Abeck, 2015). Fielding describes the constraints in his dissertation as:

- Client-Server.
- Stateless.
- Cache.
- Interface/Uniform contract.
- Layered system.
- Code-on-demand.

The "Interface/Uniform contract" establishes itself as the central feature that distinguishes REST architectural style from other network-based styles is its emphasis on a uniform interface between components (client, server). To obtain a uniform interface, REST defines four interface requirements:

1. Identification of resources.
2. Manipulation of resources through representations.
3. Self-descriptive messages and.
4. Hypermedia as the application state mechanism.

Web services are currently the most common way to exchange data among information systems. Web services comprehend some fundamental characteristics: they are self-contained, modular and dynamic (Vasudevan, 2017). SOAP and REST are the most usual implementation of web services, where each of these approaches has its own advantages and disadvantages. Its fundamental to choose the right type of web services, otherwise it can lead to certain problems in data exchange or impose some restrictions.

The constrains identified by Fielding (API Evangelist, 2015), if fulfilled by a web service implementation and behavior, compose the essential requirements to define the service as RESTful. The only exception is "Code-on-Demand", since it is an optional constraint and has not to be implemented by a web service.

Model-Driven Engineering

Using models to raise the level of abstraction and automate the development process of building software is the core process of Model-Driven Engineering paradigm. To cope with complexity, abstraction is a fundamental technique, whereas automation is an effective method to increase productivity and quality (Ed-douibi, Izquierdo, Gómez, Tisi, & Cabot, 2016).

In model-driven software development, the first-class elements are models, which are all structured by a meta-model. Concisely, models are defined according to the semantics of a meta-model, which is a model for specifying models.

Model-driven engineering methodologies have been applied as a solution for better reaction to business trends and aims to increase efficiency as well as bring more agility to the development life-cycle of cloud and distributed systems ("EMF-REST Documentation," 2015)

Domain Specific Languages (DSLs)

Many computer languages are domain specific rather than general purpose languages(GPLs). DSLs trade generality for expressiveness in a limited domain. By providing notations and constructs tailored toward a particular application domain, they offer substantial gains in expressiveness and ease of use compared with GPLs for the domain in question, with corresponding gains in productivity and reduced maintenance costs.

The following is a grammar for arithmetic expressions using only addition:

```
Expression::= number | number "+" expression
number::= [1-9][0-9]*
```

For simple arithmetic, 1+2+3 is according to grammar, while 1+2+ is not. The vocabulary of this language is: expression, number and addition. The semantics of this simple language is: the first and second operands of an expression are added.

The vocabulary of a DSL is taken from its domain. The syntax should be created to fit the domain, and preferably also the conventions within the domain.

A particular case of a DSL is a Domain-Specific Modeling Language (DSML), which is a DSL aimed at modeling.

Xtext and Xtend

Xtext was the elected framework to implement the DSL. It covers all aspects of a complete language infrastructure, starting from the parser, code generator, or interpreter, up to a complete Eclipse IDE integration with all the typical IDE features. A standalone specific version, called Eclipse DSL, that natively supports this framework is available, currently at version "Oxygen 2". Xtext generates a default grammar example, that can be seen in the following code snippet.

```
grammar org.example.entities.Entities with org.eclipse.xtext.
common.Terminals
generate entities "http://www.example.org/entities/Entities"
Model:
greetings+=Greeting*;
Greeting:
        'Hello' name = ID '!';
```

The code generation process was achieved through Xtend a fully featured general purpose Java-like language that is completely interoperable with Java. Xtend has a more concise syntax than Java and provides powerful features such as type inference, extension methods, dispatch methods, and lambda expressions, not to mention multiline template expressions, which are useful when writing code generators.

Since Xtend is completely interoperable with Java, all the Java libraries can be reused. Moreover, all the Eclipse JDT (Java Development Tools) will work with Xtend seamlessly.

```
package org.example.xtend.examples
class XtendHelloWorld {
def static void main(String[] args) {
println("Hello World")
}
}
```

The similarities with Java are evident, though the removal of syntactic noise is already obvious by the fact that terminating semicolons (;) are optional in Xtend. All method declarations start with either def or override. Methods are public by default.

OpenAPI Specification

RESTful APIs being described in multiple and heterogeneous ways, complicated their understanding by potential consumers and incremented the amount of implementation logic needed to interact with different services. To solve these problems and standardize the process of defining RESTful APIs, some proposals emerged.

The OpenAPI Specification, originally known as the Swagger Specification, was born when SmartBear, the company that maintained the Swagger specification and associated tools, announced that it was helping create a new organization, under the sponsorship of the Linux Foundation, called the Open API Initiative. A variety of companies, including Google, IBM and Microsoft are founding members. SmartBear donated the Swagger specification to the new group. RAML and API Blueprint were also under consideration by the group. On 1 January 2016, the Swagger specification was renamed the OpenAPI Specification.

Basically, an OpenAPI Specification file describes an API, including (among others):

1. General information about the API.
2. Available paths (/resources).
3. Available operations on each path (get/resources).
4. Input/output for each operation.

The OpenAPI Specification is a formal specification for description of RESTful APIs in JavaScript Object Notation (JSON) or YAML Ain't Markup Language (YAML), two formats focused on data serialization and accessible to humans and machines. At the time of writing the most recent version is 3.0.1.

Figure 1 shows the main components of OpenAPI 3.0 specification.

The new version of the OpenAPI Specification differs from its predecessor by a clearer structure. At the top level, the structure has been cleaned up, with the result that the new version is incompatible with the existing one (but migration is possible automatically).

Table 1 describes the most relevant objects that integrate an OAS file:

Figure 1. OpenAPI 3.0 main components
Source: based on API Evangelist, 2017

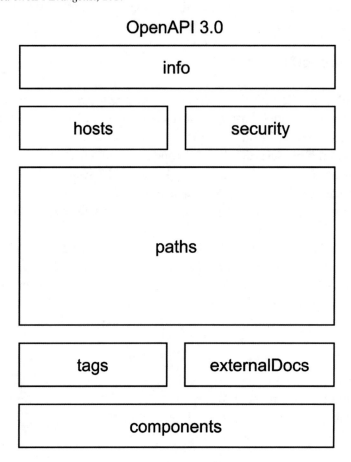

Table 1. OpenAPI 3.0 structure

Object	Description
info	Contains basic information about the API, including the title, a description, version, link to the license, link to the terms of service, and contact information.
servers	Specification of the base path used in the API requests. The base path is the part of the URL that appears before the endpoint.
security	Defines a security scheme that can be used by the operations.
paths	Holds the relative paths to the individual endpoints and their operations.
tags	A list of tags used by the specification with additional metadata.
externalDocs	Allows referencing an external resource for extended documentation.
components	Holds a set of reusable objects for different aspects of the OAS.

Other Specifications

- **WSDL:** The Wed Service Description Language (WSDL) defines a system for describing services, based on XML. This XML Schema describes the format of the methods to be called, parameters to be passed, operations, encoding schemes, etc. Its main objective is to describe the interfaces presented and to point out the location of its Web Services, available in a network location, which allows the client to access it reliably.

- **API Blueprint:** It is a description language oriented to the documentation of Web APIs, basically consisting of a set of assumptions made through Markdown syntax. Documentation for the service in question is produced by writing a Markdown document, in which the Web service or only part of it is described, with API creators being responsible for choosing which parts they want to document. The documentation produced must comply with a given structure, since each section has a different meaning and position in the document, considering the basic structure of the specification. However, it is not mandatory for the document in question to have all sections, all of which are optional, although in the case they exist, they must comply with the structure defined by API Blueprint.

- **RAML:** Is a YAML-based language and defines a media type "application / raml + yaml" for the description and documentation of REST APIs in a way that is easily read and interpreted by both humans and computers. Thus, it allows that, in addition to anyone being able to understand the service specification, it is also possible to be interpreted by API code generators, and by the services themselves to create the user documentation or even client code. This specification also introduces a concept of resource types and their characteristics that allows the characterization of a REST API in a simpler way, minimizing the repetitions necessary for its documentation.

LITERATURE REVIEW

Aiding REST web services development through MDE techniques is not a new idea and some existing solutions have already addressed this kind of approach, which are described in this section. Their main features are also compared to support a solution perspective, focusing on the appropriate technologies and the DSL design. Finally, an evaluation procedure to assess the solution suitability is described.

This section briefly summarizes currently available tools which are relevant to REST web services implementation and code generation.

APImatic

It is a "code-generation-as-a-service" (APIMatic, 2018) platform. It is an automatic SDK generator for REST APIs that tries to cover all aspects concerning REST, from the API definition on the backend, to generation of SDKs to the frontend. With APImatic the developer must interactively define resources and their attributes using a web-interface. An API providing CRUD operations on these resources and SDKs to be used in different clients is then generated.

APImatic allows developers to import Swagger or WADL descriptions of an API to their platform, streamlining the creation of web services and easing the migration from existing projects. The code generation can also be configured through a simple interface where the developer can decide some generic behaviors and implementation details.

RAML Framework

This framework comprises a pack of tools to define, create, test, and publish RESTful APIs. RAML uses YAML as markup language and is based on the idea of defining resources and their representations as JSON schemas. The created schema is used as an input in the code generator tool, RAML for JAX-RS (Java API for RESTful Web Services - set of APIs to create web services following the REST architecture), scaffolding a JAVA + JAX-RS application based on the RAML API definition. At the time of this work, the code generator only supports JAX-RS (Java API for RESTful Web Services), a Java programming language API spec.

Swagger CodeGen

Inserted in the Swagger ecosystem, the Swagger CodeGen generates API client libraries (SDK generation), server stubs and documentation automatically given an OpenAPI Specification.

Swagger CodeGen comes with 25+ server stub generators for different server-side frameworks such as PHP Symfony, C# Nancy, Java Spring, Python Flask, etc. The auto-generated server-side code allows back-end developers to easily implement a RESTful backend given an OpenAPI/Swagger 2.0 specification file. The CodeGen project provides a command-line interface (CLI), which is a framework for plugins supporting output to various technologies.

REST United

REST United features an easy-to-use interface that allows users to build automatically generated API client libraries (SDK generation) with customizable documentation and code samples. It uses a customized version of Swagger CodeGen project (Torchiano, Tomassetti, Ricca, Tiso, & Reggio, 2013). REST United offers an easy-to-use wizard to generate SDKs for a REST API in 5 steps.

Restlet Framework

Restlet Framework is a Java based framework to develop REST APIs in the same programming language. It complies with REST API specifications, supports standard security and authentication methods, and, with the built-web server, provides an environment suitable for both server and client Web applications.

Restlet Studio uses Swagger CodeGen for Objective-C but has its own CodeGen engine for Android and Java (Sharma & Chug, 2015).

AutoRest

The AutoRest tool generates client libraries for accessing RESTful web services. Input to AutoRest is a spec that describes the REST API using the OpenAPI Specification format. It uses a configuration file to control the code generation process. AutoRest can generate client-side code from the Swagger specification files. The generator supports C#, Java, Node, Python and Ruby programming languages.

EMF REST

EMF REST is a framework build on the top of the Eclipse/Java/EMF development stack and it transforms an ecore model into a functional REST API. This is a solution for developers familiar with EMF and ecore models. It also provides a JavaScript library for the generated API, so the developer can include this library and use it as a middle-man in the communication between the server and the client. It is meant to be a solution useful for prototyping and validation purposes (Hutchinson, Whittle, & Rouncefield, 2014). EMF-REST automatically creates a RESTful API conforming to the JAX-RS specification that can be automatically deployed in an application server. Generation of REST services in the server based on the Java JAX-RS specification.

Comparative Analysis

Table 2, from a high-level analysis of the previous identified frameworks, presents a comparative assessment of the most significant features.

It can be concluded that, overall, the available solutions present the same drawbacks:

- Poor hypermedia support.
- Poor code quality metrics.
- Poor support of OAS (version 3.0).
- No database related scripts generation.
- No integration and unit tests support.

Table 2. Code generation tools comparison

	Apimatic	RAML	Swagger-codegen	REST United	Restlet Framework	AutoRest	EMF REST
Authentication code	Yes	No	Yes	Yes	Yes	Yes	Yes
Hypermedia support	No	No	No	No	Yes	No	No
Most common supported specifications	API Blueprint, WADL, WSDL, RAML, OAS	RAML	Swagger, OAS	RAML, Swagger, 3Scale, I/O Docs Blueprint	Swagger, OAS, RAML	OAS	-
Code quality	Code comments, Coding standards for some languages	-	-	-	Code comments	Code comments	-
Language support	Java, C#, iOS, Android, PHP, Ruby, Python, Golang, Angularjs, Nodejs	Java	30 languages, including: Ada, C#, C++, Clojure, Erlang, Java, Kotlin, PHP, etc.	Android, C#, ActionScript, Java, Objective-C, PHP, Python, Ruby, Scala	Android, Java, Objective-C, AngularJS, Node.js	C#, Go, Java, Node.js, TypeScript, Python, Ruby, PHP	Java

DOMAIN SPECIFIC LANGUAGE BASED ON THE OpenAPI SPECIFICATION

The idea behind this approach is to specify an abstract model, which envelops the problem space and allows the developer to solve it. The model is defined in a domain specific language, which defines a syntax and a semantic for the domain. In case of the presented framework, the DSL is tailored to the OpenAPI specification and is constructed from a meta-model.

In the classic development process of a REST API, the developer must implement multiple classes - usually one per resource - each with similar source code. Every minor API design change could lead to multiple hours of work. The model-driven approach allows to automate this task by changing only the lightweight model. The new model supplies the developer with a new version of his API. In addition to the higher code quality the rate of reuse is extremely high as, for a new customer, the developers only specify a new model and adapt the generated outcome to the specific requirements.

Main Challenges

The main challenge in this approach is how to capture the behavior, and implementation details of a typical web service, and how these can be derived from the respective specification in the OpenAPI format. This last one requires by itself a specific parser to interpret the multiple components that structure the specification.

Figure 2, based on Cosentino, Tisi, & Izquierdo, 2015, gives an overview of the architectural approach followed in the web service MDE development process.

Figure 2. Architectural overview of the approach followed

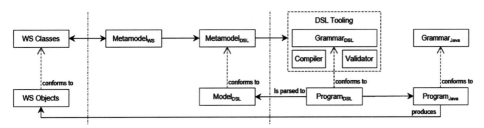

Figure 2 spans through three technical spaces: the first one in which web service objects conforms to the set of defined web service classes and establishes itself as the foundation to develop the code-generation output; the second one where the meta-models associated with the web service and the developed DSL (OpenAPI based) are defined; and the last one where the grammar for the previous defined DSL, and the related code generation process is established, in conjunction with the base Java grammar foundations.

The focus of this work is the third technical space, where, through DSL tooling, a grammar based on the OpenAPI specification is implemented, and a Java code-generation process is defined and outputs a functional web service structure.

Domain Modeling Language

A modeling language raising the level of abstraction allows the reuse of models and keeps platform-specific artifacts at a separated tier in the development workflow. A modeling language based on the OpenAPI specification, with the ability to set aside technical concerns and still be able to tackle a problem in a specific platform is the main purpose of this work.

Nguyen, Qafmolla, & Richta, 2014 defines a set of features that are essential to the DSL design in model-driven development of web services:

- **Effectiveness:** The language needs to be able to deliver a usable output without having to re-tailor based on specific use case, while being easy to read and to understand. This means that the language can bring up good solutions on the specific domain it was designed for and focus on solving the associated range of problems. It also needs to guarantee the non-ambiguity feature of language expressions and capability to describe the problem from a higher.
- **Automation and Agility:** As the modeling language can raise the level of abstraction away from programming code by directly using domain concepts, an important aspect is the ability to generate final artifacts from these high-level specifications. This automatic transformation must fit the requirements of the specific domain. Agility is essential to ensure that models can adapt to changes efficiently.
- **Support Integration:** The DSL needs to be able to integrate with other parts of the development process. This means that the language is used for editing, debugging, compiling and transformation. It should also be able to be integrated together with other languages and platforms without a significant effort.

OpenAPI Meta-Model

Figure 3 depicts a meta-model that uses Unified Modeling Language (UML) as meta meta-model for providing a better understanding of the multiple OpenAPI components and allows the inclusion of UML specific features into the modeling phase.

The meta-model aids in finding an appropriate model by exploring the boundaries and the core of the domain. It is derived from the concepts and properties described in the OpenAPI specification document and using UML and its artifacts allows a better understanding of the relationships between the multiple OpenAPI objects, providing an unambiguous and broad range of the assumed specification interpretation.

The showed concepts can be divided in three main parts (Nguyen et al., 2014):

- **Behavioral Elements:** In this category, the "Paths", "OperationObject" and "ResponsesObject" objects assume the most relevant role in defining and interpreting the overall API behavior, mainly the exposed services and how it is supposed to answer to external calls.
- **Structural Elements:** The main component that define how each OpenAPI object is built, describing the data types and available data structures, is the "Schema" object, which is used in multiple objects, allowing to define structures based on the JSON Schema Specification, with some OpenAPI specific features.

Figure 3. OpenAPI meta-model

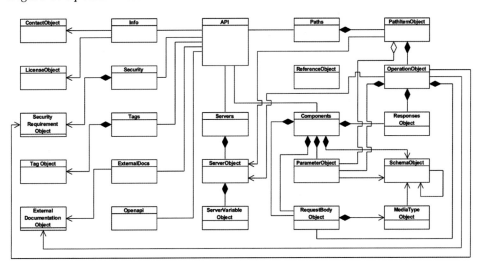

- **Serialization/Deserialization Elements:** In this group are included the elements that support the serialization and deserialization of OpenAPI models in JSON or YAML formats, namely the "Paths", "OperationObject" and "SchemaObject" concepts.

Given the formerly described meta-model and associated categories, a DSL was developed allowing the definition of a web service, following the OpenAPI specification, while building the foundation to a code-generation process.

DSL Specification

The main challenge while developing the OpenAPI based DSL was maintaining the structure of the original document, the OpenAPI specification, while avoiding the introduction of ambiguities in the grammar.

A document conforming to the OpenAPI specification is itself a JSON object, that can be represented either in JSON or YAML format: while the YAML format has a friendlier structure for a human reader by resorting to indentation to delimit the different components of the specification, the JSON version eases the interpretation of this limits programmatically, with use of specific characters - curly brackets. This factor, and the existence of multiple tools that allow the conversion between the two formats, defined that the developed DSL would interpret the JSON format only.

```
OpenAPIObject:
    '{'
        (documentOpenAPIVersion=OpenAPIVersionField)
        (infoField=InfoField)
        (serversField=ServersField)?
        (pathsField=PathsField)
        (componentsField=ComponentsField)?
        (securityField=SecurityField)?
        (tagsField=TagsField)?
    '}';
OpenAPIVersionField:
    ('"openapi"':'openApi=STRING',');
InfoField:
    ('"info"':'info=InfoObject);
InfoObject:
    '{'
        ('"title"':'title=STRING',')
        ('"description"':'description=STRING',')?
```

```
('"termsOfService":'termsOfService=STRING',')?
('"contact":'contact=ContactObject)?
('"license":'license=LicenseObject)?
('"version":'version=STRING)?
'},';
```

The previous code snipped provides a glimpse of how the grammar is implemented, and how it interprets a OpenAPI specification document: the main structure of the specification is parsed by the "OpenAPIObject", where the seven major components (see Figure 1) that constitute the OpenAPI specification document are clearly demarcated; each one of the components delegate the parsing of their content in inner objects with the required logic.

The following code-snippet is responsible for parsing the "PathsObject" and "PathItemObject" and provides one additional example of how the objects are defined in the Xtext grammar.

```
PathsObject:
    Url ':'
    '{'
        pathsObject+=PathItemObject+
    ('}' | '},');
PathItemObject:
    (httpMethod+=HttpMethod ':''{'operation+=OperationObject
('}'|'},'))+
    ('"$ref":' '{'ref=PathItemObject '}' ',')?
    ('"summary":'summary=STRING',')?
    ('"description":'description=STRING',')?
    ('"servers":'('['servers+=ServerObject']'|
servers+=ServerObject)',')?
    '"parameters":' '['parameters+=ParameterObject']'
HttpMethod:
    {HttpMethod} httpMethod=STRING;
Url:
    {Url} url=STRING;
```

In the context of this objects, two parser rules, "HttpMethod" and "Url", can be identified and at first sight any string value can be assigned to them. However, semantically, the "HttpMethod" can only be assigned with a limited number of values (get, put, post, delete, options, head, patch and trace), and the "Url" value must agree with a specific format (e.g., /user/{id}/address).

The grammar should validate the values that can be assigned to this parser rules. This was achieved through the implementation of validators, like in the next code snippet.

```
class OasDslValidator extends AbstractOasDslValidator {
    private static val INVALID_HTTP_METHOD =
"invalidHttpMethod"
    private val validHttpMethods = "get|put|post|delete|options
|head|patch|trace"

    def checkValidHttpMethod(HttpMethod httpMethod) {
        if (!httpMethod.getHttpMethod().
matches(validHttpMethods)) {
        error('Invalid HTTP method!',
            OasDslPackage.Literals.HTTP_METHOD__HTTP_METHOD,
            OasDslValidator.INVALID_HTTP_METHOD)
        };
    }
}
```

This approach allows to establish a first layer of validations when using the DSL to define an OpenAPI specification document, aiding the code generation process, by releasing it from this additional processing requirement. Writing wrong resource specification without following the rules mentioned above, and others implemented to conform with the OpenAPI, will result in a project run-time error which will not generate the code in the target project.

Model

The model is written with the developed DSL, and, as intended, has an identical structure to the OpenAPI specification in its JSON version:

```
{
  "openapi": "3.0.0",
  "info": {
      (...)
  },
  "servers": [
    {
      "url": "https://development.gigantic-server.com/v1",
```

```
          "description": "Development server"
      }
  ],
  "paths": {
    "/path/": {
      "get": {
        "tags": [
          "Tag 1",
          "Tag 2"
        ],
        "summary": "summary example",
        "description": "description example",
        "externalDocs": "external documentation example",
        "operationId": "operation Id",
        "parameters": [
            {
                "name": "parameter1",
                "in": "query",
                "description": "description example",
                "required": true,
                "deprecated": false,
                "allowEmptyValue": false,
                "allowReserved": false
            }
        ],
        "responses": {
          "200": {
            (...)
          },
          "default": {
            (...)
          }
        },
        "deprecated": true
      },
      (...)
    }
  }
}
```

The outcome of the defined model are resource classes, mapped through multiple layers (see Figure 4), and interfaces with essential HTTP method implementations included.

Code-Generation

This section focuses on the coding generation process through the interpretation of models build from the DSL specification described previously. The software generator gets an OpenAPI model as input and creates all necessary artifacts for a complete backend that contains the web service, the business logic, and the source code of the persistence layer.

Figure 4 gives an overview of most of the components that are generated in this process, while providing additional information regarding the web service architecture adopted for the implementation.

A four-layer architecture was considered:

- **Gateway Layer:** It exposes the web services endpoints and delegates the received requests to the subsequent layer:
    - ◦ **ResourceWs:** It is an interface with the exposed web service endpoint.
    - ◦ **ResourceWsImpl:** It is an implementation of the resource web service interface.
- **Presentation Layer:** This intermediate layer between the presentation layer and the layer with the business logic that delegates the requests from the first to the second:
    - ◦ **ResourceWorkflow:** It is a class responsible for controlling the flow of the service, calling the managers of the lower layer, after mapping the ResourseApi entities to ResourceEntity entities.
    - ◦ **ResourceApiMapper:** It maps ResourceApi to ResourceEntity entities and vice-versa (business layer).
    - ◦ **ResourceApi:** This entity represents the JSON or XML entities accepted in the services.
- **Business Layer:** In this layer the business models are defined, with all associated operations:
    - ◦ The ResourceManager manages the operations in the business context.
    - ◦ The ResourceEntityMaper maps ResourceEntity to ResourceDbo (database layer) and vice-versa.
    - ◦ The ResourceEntity is a business entity.

Figure 4. Layered architecture

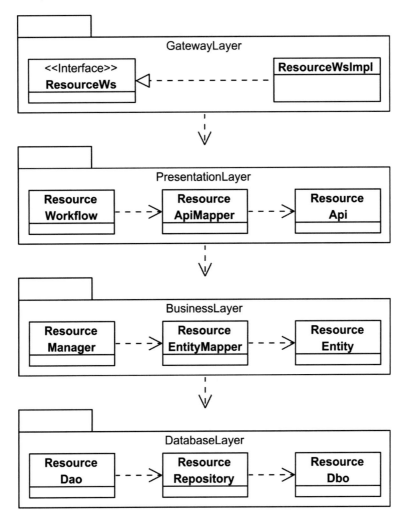

- **Database Layer:** It is responsible for managing the database:
  - **ResourceDao:** Data access object that encapsulates the database operations (save, update delete and retrieve) over the database objects;
  - **ResourceRepository:** Encapsulates and manages the access to the database;
  - **ResourceDbo:** Entity representative of the database table.

Each one of the previous described components is generated associated it the respective resource in the code generated process, detailed in the next section.

As platform for the web service Java was chosen as the programming language and Maven as the building tool. The Java specification requests (JSR) 339 define a framework to implement RESTful APIs in Java. The reference implementation is Jersey (Gulabani, 2014) which is used in combination with other open source libraries and frameworks for processing XML and JSON.

UML Mapping to OpenAPI

To provide a better understanding on how the web service code is generated from the developed DSL and consequent model, an UML-OpenAPI base mapping approach is defined, where the involved rules are exposed in table format and are structured built on the UML artifacts defined in Figure 4.

The main components that must be identified and extracted from the specification are the resources that compose the substance of the web service, and the endpoints that needed to be exposed in each one.

Following the OpenAPI structure, and analyzing the existing objects, it can be observed that two of them provide the required info to identify the mentioned resources and services:

- **Paths object:**

```
paths:
  /pet:
    get:
      description:
      operationId:
      parameters:
      responses:
      (...)
    post:
      (...)
```

The Path element contains a relative path to an individual endpoint and the operations for the HTTP methods. The description of an operation (operation element) includes an identifier operationId, the MIME types the operation can consume/produce, and the supported transfer protocols for the operation (schema attribute). An operation includes also the possible responses returned from executing the operation (responses reference).

- **Components object:**

```
        components:
schemas:
responses:
parameters:
requestBody:
(...)
```

The components object behaves like an appendix where the re-usable details are provided. If multiple parts of the specification have the same schema, each of these references can be pointed to the same object in the components object, and in so doing you single source the content.

The following tables expose the most relevant mappings between the OpenAPI objects and the UML artifacts.

Table 3 reflects how the entities are mapped from the OpenAPI components object to UML classes, materializing the web service resources, and allowing the code implementation.

Figure 5 and the associated code snippet is an example of the mapping result between the schemas attribute, in the components OpenAPI object, and the UML classes is shown.

```
UML class-OpenAPI component artifact mappingUML class
OpenApi component artifact
components:
  schemas:
```

Table 3. Code generation: mapping between classes and OpenAPI components artifact

UML/Code Artifact		OpenAPI Components Artifact
Entity	name	schemas field → key in Map[string, schema object I reference object]
	attributes	schemas field → schema object → properties field
	generalization class	schemas field → schema object → allOf (and the combining schemas)
Entity attributes	name	schemas field → schema object → properties field → name
	type	schemas field → schema object → properties field → type
	multiplicity	schemas field → schema object → properties field → type array

```
Pet:
  type: "object"
  required:
    - "name"
  properties:
    id:
      type: "integer"
    category:
      $ref: "#/definitions/Category"
    name:
      type: "string"
    photoUrls:
      type: "array"
      items:
        type: "string"
    tags:
      type: "array"
      items:
        $ref: "#/definitions/Tag"
    status:
      type: "string"
      enum:
        - "available"
        - "pending"
Category:
  type: "object"
  properties:
    id:
      type: "integer"
      format: "int64"
    name:
      type: "string"
Tag:
  type: "object"
  properties:
    id:
      type: "integer"
    name:
      type: "string"
```

This mapping allows the definition of the web service main resources (Pet), its attributes and its relationships with other sub resources (Category and Pet). Even though the "required" attribute, inside the Pet schema, has no relevance in the GET service, when creating a new Pet - in the POST service - this constitutes an initial validation in the web service, where these attributes must be present in the body of the request associated. In the following code-snippet the generated validation is presented.

```
public abstract class PetBaseValidation implements
EntityValidator<PetEntity> {
  public final boolean validate(PetEntity entity) throws
PetException {
    if (entity == null) {
      throw new PetException(PetErrorMessage.NULL_RESOURCE);
    }
    if (entity.getName() != null) {
      throw new PetException(PetErrorMessage.MISSING_REQ_PARAM,
"name");
    }
    if (entity.getId() != null) {
      throw new PetException(PetErrorMessage.MISSING_REQ_PARAM,
"id");
    }
    return customValidations(entity);
  }
  protected abstract boolean customValidations(PetEntity
entity) throws PetException;
}
```

The OpenAPI specification has a specific object - Paths object - where the available services are exposed, identifying the most relevant attributes:

- endpoint.
- HTTP method.
- parameters respective location.
- possible responses.

Table 4 displays the web service mapping from the paths object is presented, identifying the correspondence between the specification and the code artifact.

Table 4. Code generation: mapping between web service classes and OpenAPI paths object

UML/Code Artifact		OpenAPI Paths Object
WebService	path	paths object → field pattern
	HTTP verb	paths object → path item object → http method
	parameters	paths object → path item object → operation object → parameters
	request body	paths object → path item object → operation object → request body
	responses	paths object → path item object → operation object → responses
	content type	paths object → path item object → operation object → responses → content type
	security	paths object → path item object → operation object → security

In the sequence, a concrete example is shown, mapping the GET service by id, that returns the required resource:*Web service class implementation*

```
(...)
@GET @Path("{petId}")
public class PetWs {
  private PetWorkflow petWorkflow;

  @GET
  @Produces({MediaType.APPLICATION_JSON})
  public Response retrievePet(
                    @PathParam("id") long id){

    PetApi petApi = null;
    Response finalResponse = null;
    try {
      petApi = getUserWorkflow()
                    .retrievePet(id);

    response = new Response<>(
                    petApi,
                    Status.OK);
    } catch (Exception exception) {
      response = new Error<>(
                    "unexpected error",
                    Status.BAD_REQUEST);
```

```
        }
        return Response
                .status(response.getStatus())
                .entity(response)
                .build();
}
(…)
OpenApi component artifact
(…)
paths:
  /pet/{petId}:
    get:
        summary: Info for a specific pet
        operationId: showPetById
        tags:
          - pets
        parameters:
          - name: petId
            in: path
            required: true
            description: The id of the pet to
                         retrieve
            schema:
              type: string
        responses:
          '200':
            description: Expected response to a
                         valid request
            content:
              application/json:
                schema:
                  $ref:"#/components/schemas/Pet"
          default:
            description: unexpected error
            content:
              application/json:
                schema:
                  $ref:"#/components/schemas/Error"
(…)
```

The exposed endpoint is easily identified and is followed by the related HTTP verb. Then, the required parameters are exposed, the location in the request ("query", "header", "path" or "cookie") and the mandatory character of the parameter. Succeeding, the possible responses are detailed, with the reference pointing to the component object detailing the response schema, or even the schema itself.

These two mapping procedures are the most relevant ones in the web service building process, allowing the definition of the resources, and the endpoints to be exposed. From this two mapping processes, mainly the resources identification process, other code artifacts are inferred:

- Database entities and SQL scripts.
- API entities.
- Associated mappers.

Information about the server or servers that support the API function, with the URL that incorporates the available endpoints is detailed in the server object, allowing the definition of these structural parameters in the implementation.

Furthermore, the OpenAPI specification provides information regarding other components that can compose a web service, but whose scope is not the focus of this work:

- **Security Requirement:** Allows the specification of which security mechanisms can be used across the API.
- **External Documentation:** Reference to external documentation regarding the web service.

The next section gives some insights on the technical side of the code-generation process, supported by the Xtend framework.

Xtend

Defined the mapping process that makes the transformation of the OAS in code artifacts possible, the code generation was implemented through Xtend. Being a Java based framework, it allows the easy iteration of the OAS model, and, resorting to predefined code templates, generate valid software classes and data structures.

The following code snippet illustrates the generation of the database entities, where, from the resource identification, multiple fields are inferred and structured in a valid Java class.

```
class DatabaseLayerEntityGenerator {
    @Inject extension DatabaseLayerGeneratorHelper
    (…)
    def generateClass(Resource resource) '''
        /**
        * The persistent class for the «resource.
generateDatabaseTableName» database table.
        */
        @Entity
        @XmlRootElement
        @Cacheable(false)
        @Table(name = "«resource.generateDatabaseTableName»")
        @AdditionalCriteria("this.deleted = 0")
        @NamedQuery(name = "«resource.
generateDatabaseTableName».findAll",
                    query = "SELECT u FROM «resource.
generateDatabaseEntityName» u")
        public class «resource.generateDatabaseEntityName»
implements Serializable {
            private static final long serialVersionUID = 1L;
            «generateAttributes(resource)»
            «generateAttributesGettersAndSetters(resource)»
                }
        '''
    (…)
}
```

This constitutes a simple example on how Xtend was used to enrich the code generation process, integrating the available Java functionalities to parse the model defined through the DSL with templating techniques. The template definition is intimately connected to the layered architecture presented in Figure 4, since it establishes the web service structure, defining the required software packages, while also providing an overview of what classes are required for the services and resources definitions.

FUTURE RESEARCH DIRECTIONS

The OAS meta-model presented, that establishes itself as the base for the DSL development, can be improved by detailing additional relationships, that will also ensure a better coverage of the OAS multiple objects.

At the grammar specification definition, and in order to improve the overall usability of the domain specific language when developing OpenAPI models, changes should be made to allow the unordered definition of the OpenAPI specification objects. While the use of unordered groups arises ambiguity questions in the grammar definition and consequently results in larger decisions trees for the parser, the possibility of defining the OpenAPI specification without needing to comply to a specific order in the objects definition, will vastly increase the DSL usability.

Another improvement that can be easily achieved is related to the inclusion of security layers using the OpenAPI Security Requirement Object (SmartBear, 2018) for the definition of the prescribed security schemas. Given that several security solutions are well standardized, defining a template for the most common ones would result in a robust addition to the overall DSL and code-generation process, allowing the definition of a security layer in the web service access, from the Open API specification. However, these and other aspects are planned to be more widely addressed by applying Model Driven Security (MDS) (Basin, Clavel, & Egea, 2011; Basin, Doser, & Lodderstedt, 2005, 2006) guidelines and technologies. MDS is a specialization of model-driven development that uses security design models to drive the built of secure applications.

Related to a recent subject, the European General Data Protection Regulation, 2016/679/EU (European Union (EU), 2016) that enforces the protection of user's private data, the code-generation process could also ensure that sensitive data would be properly used. At the time the OpenAPI specification does not possess any attribute that allows the easy identification of data that needs to be encrypted, which means that while no official solution is provided, the inclusion of a custom attribute can be used for this and only purpose.

Focusing on the code generation process and to improve the integration of this MDE process in development environments, a strategy for the generation of specific code sections, while preserving the others already implemented, would vastly improve the usability of the DSL.

Finally, the generated web services code should be subjected to a detailed performance evaluation and a quality code metrics survey, in order to identify enhancement areas in need of a re-engineering process to improve the overall web service technical quality.

CONCLUSION

Concluding Remarks

Given the initially proposed objectives, it was presented a custom meta-model - Figure 3 - illustrative of the OpenAPI specification, from which a domain specific modeling language was developed. This model is a simplification of the main concepts that integrate the OAS, giving a high-level interpretation of the relationships between them, while supporting the DSL development. This meta-model answers the first presented question, on what were the main compromises in the specification of a language agnostic model to represent the OAS, since it deliberately leaves out some OAS concepts.

The two remaining questions/objectives are intrinsically related and were successfully achieved: a DSL was built over the meta-model previously defined, providing a platform that aids developers in the design process of web services, qualified with some intellisense capabilities, giving suggestions on the possible elements for each OpenAPI object, while ensuring fully specification compliance. From this DSL a code-generation process was defined, whose main objective was to generate a full web service implementation, compliant with the RESTful constrains.

Referring to the points mentioned in the literature review, concretely the identified drawbacks of the exposed commercial solutions, the templating process ensures that each service has basic hypermedia support; integration tests that ensure the functionality is the expected one; the adequate use of design patterns promoting the code reuse; and, while the implemented solution is JPA based, it also generates SQL scripts to create the database tables related to each identified resource

All these processes were developed based on a Java stack, using Xtend and a Java reference implementation, to guide the code-generation process. Xtext was the elected framework to implement the grammar of the domain specific language.

Overall, the approach presented bridges the knowledge gap between the business rules and the technical implementation of the web services, providing, through a common platform easily understandable by both sides (the OAS), a way to expose the business concepts, and how they relate to each other.

Overall Coverage

This chapter presents an approach that integrates the OpenAPI specification in a model-driven engineering process of web services development. A domain specific language based on the specification was built, allowing the easy implementation of models that comply with it, while generating a Java implementation of web services using code-generating techniques.

Before presenting the technical development details of the implementation, broad definitions of the main concepts that integrate this work are provided, given some technical context regarding the foundations that motivated the presented solution.

The main challenges that are proposed to be overcome are explained, while some functional reasoning regarding the domain specific language in a development context is provided.

The most expressive applications that exist commercially were presented, synthesizing the main functionalities of each one, and how they compare against each other's, pointing the overall strengths and weaknesses. Throughout this section a vision of the solution that was expected to implement was presented.

The subsequent sections were dedicated to explaining the used procedure to implement the envisioned solution, describing the overall followed approach and then exploring the mapping process between the OpenAPI objects and the UML/ code artifacts that compose the web service implementations.

Finally, an assessment of the initial objectives that this work was proposed to achieve is made, after tracing some future research directions.

REFERENCES

API Evangelist. (2015). *Comparison of Automatic API Code Generation Tools For Swagger.* Retrieved January 28, 2018, from https://apievangelist.com/2015/06/06/comparison-of-automatic-api-code-generation-tools-for-swagger/

API Evangelist. (2017). *What Will It Take To Evolve OpenAPI Tooling to Version 3.0.* Retrieved May 13, 2018, from https://apievangelist.com/2017/03/16/what-will-it-take-to-evolve-openapi-tooling-to-version-30/

APIMatic. (2018). *APIMatic - Developer Experience Platform for APIs.* Retrieved May 30, 2018, from https://apimatic.io/

Basin, D., Clavel, M., & Egea, M. (2011). A decade of model-driven security. In *Proceedings of the 16th ACM symposium on Access control models and technologies - SACMAT '11* (pp. 1–10). Academic Press. 10.1145/1998441.1998443

Basin, D., Doser, J., & Lodderstedt, T. (2005). Model driven security. In *Engineering theories of software intensive systems* (pp. 353–398). Dordrecht: Springer. doi:10.1007/1-4020-3532-2_12

Basin, D., Doser, J., & Lodderstedt, T. (2006). Model driven security: From UML models to access control infrastructures. *ACM Transactions on Software, 15*(1), 39–91. doi:10.1145/1125808.1125810

Cosentino, V., Tisi, M., & Izquierdo, J. L. C. (2015). *A Model-Driven Approach to Generate External DSLs from Object-Oriented APIs.* Academic Press. doi:10.1007/978-3-662-46078-8_35

Dimitrieski, V., Terz, B., Dimitrieski, V., Kordić, S., Milosavljević, G., & Luković, I. (2017). *MicroBuilder : A Model-Driven Tool for the Specification of REST Microservice Architectures.* Academic Press.

Ed-Douibi, H., Izquierdo, J. L. C., Gómez, A., Tisi, M., & Cabot, J. (2015). *EMF-REST Generation of RESTful APIs from Models.* CoRR, abs/1504.0, 39–43. doi:10.1145/2851613.2851782

Ed-douibi, H., Izquierdo, J. L. C., Gómez, A., Tisi, M., & Cabot, J. (2016). Emf-Rest. *Proceedings of the 31st Annual ACM Symposium on Applied Computing - SAC '16, 2*(3), 1446–1453. 10.1145/2851613.2851782

El-khoury, J., Gurdur, D., & Nyberg, M. (2016). *A Model-Driven Engineering Approach to Software Tool Interoperability based on Linked Data.* Academic Press.

EMF-REST Documentation. (2015). Retrieved January 28, 2018, from https://som-research.uoc.edu/tools/emf-rest/documentation.html

European Union (EU). (2016). Regulation 2016/679 of the European parliament and the Council of the European Union. *Official Journal of the European Communities, 59*, 1–88.

Fielding, R. T. (2000). Architectural Styles and the Design of Network-based Software Architectures. *Building, 54*, 162.

Giessler, P., Gebhart, M., Sarancin, D., Steinegger, R., & Abeck, S. (2015). Best Practices for the Design of RESTful Web Services. In *ICSEA 2015 : The Tenth International Conference on Software Engineering Advances* (pp. 392–397). Barcelona, Spain: Academic Press.

Gulabani, S. (2014). *Developing RESTful Web Services with Jersey 2. 0.* Birmingham: Packt Publishing Ltd.

Haupt, F., Karastoyanova, D., Leymann, F., & Schroth, B. (2014). A model-driven approach for REST compliant services. *Proceedings - 2014 IEEE International Conference on Web Services, ICWS 2014*, 129–136. 10.1109/ICWS.2014.30

Haupt, F., Leymann, F., Scherer, A., & Vukojevic-Haupt, K. (2017). A Framework for the Structural Analysis of REST APIs. In *Proceedings of the 1st IEEE International Conference on Software Architecture, ICSA 2017* (pp. 55–58). Gothenburg: IEEE Computer Society. 10.1109/ICSA.2017.40

Huhns, M., & Singh, M. P. (2005). Service-Oriented Computing: Key Concepts and Principles. *Proceedings - Fifth International Conference on Commercial-off-the-Shelf (COTS)-Based Software Systems, 13*(1), 1–7. 10.1016/j.compind.2009.07.006

Hutchinson, J., Whittle, J., & Rouncefield, M. (2014). Model-driven engineering practices in industry: Social, organizational and managerial factors that lead to success or failure. *Science of Computer Programming, 89*(Part B), 144–161. doi:10.1016/j.scico.2013.03.017

Nguyen, V.-C., Qafmolla, X., & Richta, K. (2014). Domain Specific Language Approach on Model-driven Development of Web Services. *Acta Polytechnica Hungarica, 11*(8), 121–138. Retrieved from http://www.uni-obuda.hu/journal/Nguyen_Qafmolla_Richta_54.pdf

Pavan, K. P., Sanjay, A., & Zornitza, P. (2012). Comparing Performance of Web Service Interaction Styles : SOAP vs. REST. *Proceedings of the Conference on Information Systems Applied Research*, 1–24.

Scheidgen, M., Efftinge, S., & Marticke, F. (2016). Metamodeling vs metaprogramming: A case study on developing client libraries for REST APIs. Lecture Notes in Computer Science, 9764, 205–216. doi:10.1007/978-3-319-42061-5_13

Schreibmann, V., & Braun, P. (2014). Design and Implementation of a Model-Driven Approach for Restful APIs. *5th IEEE Germany Student Conference*. Retrieved from http://www.ieee-student-conference.de/fileadmin/papers/2014/ieeegsc2014_submission_8.pdf

Schreibmann, V., & Braun, P. (2015). Model-driven Development of RESTful APIs. *Proceedings of the 11th International Conference on Web Information Systems and Technologies*, 5–14. 10.5220/0005411200050014

Schreier, S. (2011). Modeling RESTful applications. *Proceedings of the Second International Workshop on RESTful Design - WS-REST '11*, 15. 10.1145/1967428.1967434

Sharma, H., & Chug, A. (2015). Dynamic metrics are superior than static metrics in maintainability prediction: An empirical case study. *2015 4th International Conference on Reliability, Infocom Technologies and Optimization: Trends and Future Directions, ICRITO 2015*, 2–7. 10.1109/ICRITO.2015.7359354

SmartBear. (2018). *OpenAPI Specification | Swagger*. Retrieved May 31, 2018, from https://swagger.io/specification/

SOA Work Group. (2016). *Service-Oriented Architecture*. Retrieved January 18, 2018, from http://www.opengroup.org/soa/source-book/soa/index.htm

Stahl, T., Völter, M., Bettin, J., Haase, A., & Helsen, S. (2006). *Model-Driven Software Development: Technology, Engineering, Management*. Wiley.

The Linux Foundation. (2017a). *Open API Initiative*. Retrieved October 21, 2017, from https://www.openapis.org/

The Linux Foundation. (2017b). *The OpenAPI Specification*. Retrieved October 22, 2017, from https://github.com/OAI/OpenAPI-Specification

Tihomirovs, J., & Grabis, J. (2016). Comparison of SOAP and REST Based Web Services Using Software Evaluation Metrics. *Information Technology and Management Science*, *19*(1), 92–97. doi:10.1515/itms-2016-0017

Torchiano, M., Tomassetti, F., Ricca, F., Tiso, A., & Reggio, G. (2013). Relevance, benefits, and problems of software modelling and model driven techniques - A survey in the Italian industry. *Journal of Systems and Software*, *86*(8), 2110–2126. doi:10.1016/j.jss.2013.03.084

Vasudevan, K. (2017). *The Importance of Standardized API Design*. Retrieved January 29, 2018, from https://swaggerhub.com/blog/api-design/the-importance-of-standardized-api-design/

W3C. (2004). *Web Services Architecture*. Retrieved January 9, 2018, from https://www.w3.org/TR/ws-arch/

Zolotas, C., Diamantopoulos, T., Chatzidimitriou, K. C., & Symeonidis, A. L. (2017). From requirements to source code: A Model-Driven Engineering approach for RESTful web services. *Automated Software Engineering*, *24*(4), 791–838. doi:10.100710515-016-0206-x

Compilation of References

Abadi, M., Barham, P., Chen, J., Chen, Z., Davis, A., Dean, J., . . . Kudlur, M. (2016, November). Tensorflow: a system for large-scale machine learning. In OSDI (Vol. 16, pp. 265-283). Academic Press.

Abelló Gamazo, A., Ayala Martínez, C. P., Farré Tost, C., Gómez Seoane, C., Oriol Hilari, M., & Romero Moral, Ó. (2017). A Data-driven approach to improve the process of data-intensive API creation and evolution. In *International Conference on Advanced Information Systems Engineering (CAiSE 2017)* (pp. 1-8). Essen, Germany: CEUR-WS.org.

ABET EAC. (2017). *2018-2019 Criteria for Accrediting Engineering Programs.* Retrieved 7, 6, 2018, from http://www.abet.org/wp-content/uploads/2017/12/E001-18-19-EAC-Criteria-11-29-17-FINAL_updated1218.pdf

Adcock, R., Alef, E., Amato, B., Ardis, M., Bernstein, L., Boehm, B., & Willshire, M. J. (2009). *Graduate Software Engineering 2009 (GSwE2009) Curriculum Guidelines for Graduate Degree Programs in Software Engineering.* New York, NY: ACM.

Aguilera, M. D., & Mendiz, A. (2003). Video Games and Education: Education in the Eace of a "Parallel School". *Computers in Entertainment*, *1*(1), 1–10. doi:10.1145/950566.950583

Ainsley, C. (2016). Making Modelling "Fun" with GWT. GWT Con 2016, Firenze, Italy.

Ala-Mutka, K. M. (2007). A survey of automated assessment approaches for programming assignments. *Journal of Computer Science Education*, *15*(Feb), 83–102. doi:10.1080/08993400500150747

Alemerian K. A., (2013). *Evaluation of Software Testing Coverage Tools: An Empirical Study.* Academic Press.

Ali, J. (2016). *Mastering php design patterns. Mastering PHP Design Patterns.* Packt Publishing Limited.

Amannejad, Y. a. (2014). A Search-Based Approach for Cost-Effective Software Test Automation Decision Support and an Industrial Case Study. In *Software Testing, Verification and Validation Workshops (ICSTW), 2014 IEEE Seventh International Conference on* (pp. 302-311). Cleveland, OH: IEEE.

Anand, K. (2014). *Automatic Test Case Generation Using Modified Condition/ Decision Coverage Testing* (Master's thesis). National Institute of Technology, Rourkela, India.

Anderson, E., Bai, Z., Bischof, C., Blackford, L. S., Demmel, J., Dongarra, J., & Sorensen, D. (1999). *LAPACK Users' guide.* Society for Industrial and Applied Mathematics. doi:10.1137/1.9780898719604

Andrade, H. (2013). *Identifying Architectural Bad Smells in Software Product Lines.* Academic Press.

API Evangelist. (2015). *Comparison of Automatic API Code Generation Tools For Swagger.* Retrieved January 28, 2018, from https://apievangelist.com/2015/06/06/ comparison-of-automatic-api-code-generation-tools-for-swagger/

API Evangelist. (2017). *What Will It Take To Evolve OpenAPI Tooling to Version 3.0.* Retrieved May 13, 2018, from https://apievangelist.com/2017/03/16/what-will-it-take-to-evolve-openapi-tooling-to-version-30/

Apiary. (2017). *API Blueprint.* Retrieved from GitHub: https://github.com/apiaryio/ api-blueprint

APIMatic. (2018). *APIMatic - Developer Experience Platform for APIs.* Retrieved May 30, 2018, from https://apimatic.io/

Astrachan, O., Bruce, K., Koffman, K. E., Kölling, M., & Reges, S. (2005). Resolved: objects early has failed. In *Proceedings of the 36th SIGCSE technical symposium on computer science* (Vol. 37, pp. 451-452). New York: ACM. 10.1145/1047344.1047359

Bailie, F., Courtney, M., Murray, K., Schiaffino, R., & Tuohy, S. (2003). Objects first – does it work? *Journal of Computing Sciences in Colleges, 19*(2), 303–305.

Baker, P., Loh, S., & Weil, F. (2005). Model-Driven engineering in a large industrial context—motorola case study. In *International Conference on Model Driven Engineering Languages and Systems.* Springer. 10.1007/11557432_36

Basin, D., Clavel, M., & Egea, M. (2011). A decade of model-driven security. In *Proceedings of the 16th ACM symposium on Access control models and technologies - SACMAT '11* (pp. 1–10). Academic Press. 10.1145/1998441.1998443

Basin, D., Doser, J., & Lodderstedt, T. (2005). Model driven security. In *Engineering theories of software intensive systems* (pp. 353–398). Dordrecht: Springer. doi:10.1007/1-4020-3532-2_12

Basin, D., Doser, J., & Lodderstedt, T. (2006). Model driven security: From UML models to access control infrastructures. *ACM Transactions on Software, 15*(1), 39–91. doi:10.1145/1125808.1125810

Batory, D., & Azanza, M. (2017). Teaching model-driven engineering from a relational database perspective. *Software & Systems Modeling, 16*(2), 443–467. doi:10.100710270-015-0488-7

Bento da Silva, J., Rochadel, W., Schardosim Simao, J. P., & Vaz da Silva Fidalgo, A. (2014). Adaptation Model of Mobile Remote Experimentation for Elementary Schools. *IEEE Revista Iberoamericana de Tecnologias del Aprendizaje, 9*(1), 28-32. Retrieved from http://ieeexplore.ieee.org/stamp/stamp.jsp?tp=&arnumber=67 19587&isnumber=6746056

Bergin, J., Eckstein, J., Volter, M., Sipos, M., Wallingford, E., Marquardt, K., & Manns, M. L. (2012). *Pedagogical patterns: advice for educators*. Joseph Bergin Software Tools.

Bergin, J., Eckstein, J., Wallingford, E., & Manns, M. L. (2001). Patterns for gaining different perspectives. *8th conference on Pattern Languages of Programs (PLoP 2001)*.

Bhatt, D. (2017). A Survey of Effective and Efficient Software Testing Technique and Analysis. *Iconic Research and Engineering Journals (IREJOURNALS)*.

Boffo, V. (2015). *Employability for the social economy: The role of higher education. In Educational Jobs: Youth and Employability in the Social Economy*. Firenze: FUP.

Bowes, D. a. (2017). How good are my tests? In *Emerging Trends in Software Metrics (WETSoM), 2017 IEEE/ACM 8th Workshop on* (pp. 9-14). Buenos Aires: IEEE.

Bracha, G., & Ungar, D. (2015). OOPSLA 2004: mirrors: design principles for meta-level facilities of object-oriented programming languages. *ACM SIGPLAN Notices, 50*(8), 35–48. doi:10.1145/2854695.2854699

Bragança, A., Azevedo, I., & Bettencourt, N. (2018). *College Management System GWT Example Application.* Available from https://bitbucket.org/mei-isep/odsoft-edom-2017-cms-students

Brambilla, M., Cabot, J., & Wimmer, M. (2018). *List of institutions using the book "Model-driven software engineering in practice".* Retrieved from https://mdse-book.com/who-is-using-the-book/

Brambilla, M., Cabot, J., & Wimmer, M. (2012). Model-driven software engineering in practice. *Synthesis Lectures on Software Engineering, 1*(1), 1–182. doi:10.2200/S00441ED1V01Y201208SWE001

Brambilla, M., Cabot, J., & Wimmer, M. (2017). *Model driven software engineering in practice* (2nd ed.). Morgan & Claypool Publishers.

Brauer, J., Dahlweid, M., & Peleska, J. (2015). *Tool-Supported Structural Coverage Analysis for DO-178C Compliant Software.* Academic Press.

Brito, M. A., & Sá-Soares, F. (2014). Assessment frequency in introductory computer programming disciplines. *Computers in Human Behavior, 30*, 623-628. Retrieved from http://www.sciencedirect.com/science/article/pii/S0747563213002835

Brosch, P., Kappel, G., Seidl, M., & Wimmer, M. (2009). Teaching model engineering in the large. *5th Educators' Symposium in conjunction with the 12th International Conference on Model Driven Engineering Languages and Systems (MoDELS 2009).*

Burden, H., Heldal, R., & Whittle, J. (2014). Comparing and contrasting model-driven engineering at three large companies. In *Proceedings of the 8th ACM/IEEE International Symposium on Empirical Software Engineering and Measurement.* ACM. 10.1145/2652524.2652527

Burgos, D., Tattersall, C., & Koper, R. (2007). Re-purposing existing generic games and simulations for e-learning. *Computers in Human Behavior, 23*(6), 2656-2667. Retrieved from http://www.sciencedirect.com/science/article/pii/S0747563206000963

Cabot, J., & Tisi, M. (2011). The mde diploma: First international postgraduate specialization in model-driven engineering. *Computer Science Education, 21*(4), 389–402. doi:10.1080/08993408.2011.630131

Campbell, A. G. (2018, September 10). *Cognitive Complexity, A new way of measuring understandability.* Retrieved October 18, 2018, from https://www.sonarsource.com/docs/CognitiveComplexity.pdf

Carneiro, G. D. F., Silva, M., Mara, L., Figueiredo, E., Sant'Anna, C., Garcia, A., & Mendonca, M. (2010). Identifying code smells with multiple concern views. In *Software Engineering (SBES), 2010 Brazilian Symposium on* (pp. 128-137). IEEE.

Charles, O. (1997). *Application of test hypotheses to a definition of coverage* (Ph.D. thesis). Henri Poincare University - Nancy 1, Nancy, France.

Chen, T., Li, M., Li, Y., Lin, M., Wang, N., Wang, M., . . . Zhang, Z. (2015). *MXNet: A Flexible and Efficient Machine Learning Library for Heterogeneous Distributed Systems.* Retrieved from http://arxiv.org/abs/1512.01274

Chi, M. T., & Ceci, S. J. (1987). Content knowledge: Its role, representation, and restructuring in memory development. In *Advances in Child Development and Behavior* (pp. 91–142). Orlando, FL: Academic Press.

Chi, M. T., Glaser, R., & Farr, M. (1988). *The nature of expertise.* Hillsdale, NJ: Lawrence Erlbaum and Associates.

Christensen, B., & Ellingsen, G. (2016). Evaluating model-driven development for large-scale EHRs through the openEHR approach. *International Journal of Medical Informatics*, *89*, 43–54. doi:10.1016/j.ijmedinf.2016.02.004 PMID:26980358

Church, G. (2016). MOOCs versus coding bootcamps. *Class-Central.* Retrieved from https://www.class-central.com/report/moocs-versus-codingbootcamps

Clarke, P. J., Wu, Y., Allen, A. A., & King, T. M. (2009). Experiences of teaching model-driven engineering in a software design course. *Proceedings of the 5th Educators' Symposium of the MODELS Conference 2009*, 6-14.

Clements, P., & Northrop, L. (2001). *Software product lines: practices and patterns.* Addison-Wesley.

Combemale, B., Cregut, X., Dieumegard, A., Pantel, M., & Zalila, F. (2012). Teaching MDE through the Formal Verification of Process Models. *Electronic Communications of the EASST 52.*

Corliss, G. F., & Griewank, A. (1993). Operator overloading as an enabling technology for automatic differentiation (ANL/MCS/CP--79481). Academic Press.

Cosentino, V., Tisi, M., & Izquierdo, J. L. C. (2015). *A Model-Driven Approach to Generate External DSLs from Object-Oriented APIs.* Academic Press. doi:10.1007/978-3-662-46078-8_35

Costa, B. a. (2014). Evaluating a Representational State Transfer (REST) Architecture: What is the Impact of REST in My Architecture? In *Software Architecture (WICSA), 2014 IEEE/IFIP Conference on* (pp. 105-114). Sydney: IEEE.

Coursereport. (2016). 2016 coding bootcamp market size study. In *2016 Coding Bootcamp Market Size Study*. CourseReport.

Crespo, Y., Lopez, C., Marticorena, R., & Manso, E. (2005). Language independent metrics support towards refactoring inference. *9th ECOOP Workshop on QAOOSE 05*.

Dadheech, K., Choudhary, A., & Bhatia, G. (2018). De-Militarized Zone: A Next Level to Network Security. *2018 Second International Conference on Inventive Communication and Computational Technologies (ICICCT)*. 10.1109/ICICCT.2018.8473328

Danutama, K., & Liem, I. (2013). Scalable Autograder and LMS Integration. *Procedia Technology, 11*, 388-395. Retrieved from http://www.sciencedirect.com/science/article/pii/S2212017313003617#

De, B. (2017). API Management. In B. De (Ed.), *API Management* (pp. 15–28). Berkeley, CA: Apress. doi:10.1007/978-1-4842-1305-6_2

Denner, J., Werner, L., & Ortiz, E. (2012). Computer games created by middle school girls: Can they be used to measure understanding of computer science concepts? *Computers & Education, 58*(1), 240–249. Retrieved from http://www.sciencedirect.com/science/article/pii/S0360131511001849

Derezinska, A. (2017). *Experiences in Teaching Model Transformation with the QVT Language. In Software Engineering Research for the Practice* (pp. 11–24). Warsaw: Scientific Papers of the Polish Information Society Scientific Council.

Dhillon, P. K., & Sidhu, G. (2012). Can Software Faults be Analyzed using Bad Code Smells? An Empirical Study. *International Journal of Scientific and Research Publications, 2*(10), 1–7.

Dimitrieski, V., Terz, B., Dimitrieski, V., Kordić, S., Milosavljević, G., & Luković, I. (2017). *MicroBuilder : A Model-Driven Tool for the Specification of REST Microservice Architectures*. Academic Press.

DOT/FAA/AR-06/54. (2007). *Software Verification Tools Assessment Study*. Air Traffic Organization Operations Planning Office of Aviation Research and Development.

Douadi, B., Tahar, B., & Hamid, S. (2012). Smart edutainment game for algorithmic thinking. *Procedia - Social and Behavioral Sciences, 31*, 454-458. Retrieved from http://www.sciencedirect.com/science/article/pii/S187704281103014X

Ed-Douibi, H., Izquierdo, J. L. C., Gómez, A., Tisi, M., & Cabot, J. (2015). *EMF-REST Generation of RESTful APIs from Models.* CoRR, abs/1504.0, 39–43. doi:10.1145/2851613.2851782

El-khoury, J., Gurdur, D., & Nyberg, M. (2016). *A Model-Driven Engineering Approach to Software Tool Interoperability based on Linked Data.* Academic Press.

EMF-REST Documentation. (2015). Retrieved January 28, 2018, from https://som-research.uoc.edu/tools/emf-rest/documentation.html

ErnstFriedman, J. (2017). *Open API Initiative Announces Release of the OpenAPI Spec v3 Implementer's Draft.* Retrieved from Open API Initiative: https://www.openapis.org/blog/2017/03/01/openapi-spec-3-implementers-draft-released

ESLint.org. (2018). *ESLint web-site.* Retrieved from https://eslint.org/

European Union (EU). (2016). Regulation 2016/679 of the European parliament and the Council of the European Union. *Official Journal of the European Communities, 59*, 1–88.

Fielding, R. T. (2000). *Architectural Styles and the Design of Network-based Software Architectures* (Doctoral dissertation). University of California, Irvine, CA.

Fielding, R. T. (2000). Architectural Styles and the Design of Network-based Software Architectures. *Building, 54*, 162.

Finsterwalder, M. (2001). Automating acceptance tests for GUI applications in an extreme programming environment. *Proceedings of the 2nd International Conference on eXtreme Programming and Flexible Processes in Software Engineering*, 114-117.

Fontana, F. A., Braione, P., & Zanoni, M. (2012). Automatic detection of bad smells in code: An experimental assessment. *Journal of Object Technology, 11*(2), 5–1.

Force, A. J. T. (2013). *Computer science curricula 2013: Curriculum guidelines for undergraduate degree programs in computer science.* IEEE Computer Society.

Force, A. J. T. (2015). *Curriculum Guidelines for Undergraduate Degree Programs in Software Engineering.* ACM.

Fowler, M., & Beck, K. (1999). *Refactoring: improving the design of existing code.* Addison-Wesley Professional.

Froyd, J. E., Wankat, P. C., & Smith, K. A. (2012). Five major shifts in 100 years of engineering education. *Proceedings of the IEEE, 100 (Special Centennial Issue)*, 1344-1360. 10.1109/JPROC.2012.2190167

García-Peñalvo, F. J., Johnson, M., Ribeiro-Alves, G., Minović, M., & Conde-Gonzalez, M. A. (2014). Informal learning recognition through a cloud ecosystem. *Future Generation Computer Systems, 32*, 282-294. Retrieved from http://www.sciencedirect.com/science/article/pii/S0167739X13001696

Garlan, D. a. (1993). An Introduction to Software Architecture. In *Advances in Software Engineering and Knowledge Engineering* (pp. 1–39). World Scientific. doi:10.1142/9789812798039_0001

Garousi, V., & Felderer, M. (2016). Developing, verifying and maintaining high-quality automated test scripts. *IEEE Software, 33*(3), 68–75. doi:10.1109/MS.2016.30

Giessler, P., Gebhart, M., Sarancin, D., Steinegger, R., & Abeck, S. (2015). Best Practices for the Design of RESTful Web Services. In *ICSEA 2015 : The Tenth International Conference on Software Engineering Advances* (pp. 392–397). Barcelona, Spain: Academic Press.

Gifford, W. (1996). Structural Coverage. *Analytical Methods*, 15.

Giraffa, L. M. M., Moraes, M. C., & Uden, L. (2014). Teaching Object-Oriented Programming in First-Year Undergraduate Courses Supported By Virtual Classrooms. *Proceedings of the 2nd International Workshop on Learning Technology for Education in Cloud (Springer Proceedings in Complexity)*, 15-26. Retrieved from http://link.springer.com/chapter/10.1007/978-94-007-7308-0_2

Glaser, R. (1984). Education and thinking: The role of knowledge. *American Psychologist, 39*(2), 93-104. doi:10.1037/0003-066X.39.2.93

Glaser, R., & De Corte, E. (1992). Preface to the assessment of prior knowledge as a determinant for future learning. In F. J. R. C. Dochy (Ed.), *Assessment of prior knowledge as a determinant for future learning* (pp. 1–2). Lemma B.V./Jessica Kingsley Publishers. Retrieved from http://ericae.net/books/dochyl/

Glass, R. L. (2011). Frequently forgotten fundamental facts about software engineering. *IEEE Software, 18*(3), 112–111. doi:10.1109/MS.2001.922739

Gokhale, A. S., & Gray, J. (2005). Advancing model driven development education via collaborative research. *Proceedings of the Educators Symposium at the 8th International Conference, MoDELS 2005.*

Google. (2018). *Closure compiler*. Retrieved from https://developers.google.com/closure/compiler/

Goulão, M., Amaral, V., & Mernik, M. (2016). Quality in model-driven engineering: A tertiary study. *Software Quality Journal*, *24*(3), 601–633. doi:10.100711219-016-9324-8

Greiler, M., Zaidman, A., Deursen, A. V., & Storey, M. A. (2013). Strategies for avoiding text fixture smells during software evolution. In *Proceedings of the 10th Working Conference on Mining Software Repositories* (pp. 387-396). IEEE Press. 10.1109/MSR.2013.6624053

Gronback, R. C. (2009). *Eclipse modeling project: a domain-specific language (DSL) toolkit*. Pearson Education.

Gulabani, S. (2014). *Developing RESTful Web Services with Jersey 2. 0.* Birmingham: Packt Publishing Ltd.

Gupta, A., Suri, B., Kumar, V., Misra, S., Blažauskas, T., & Damaševičius, R. (2018). Software Code Smell Prediction Model Using Shannon, Rényi and Tsallis Entropies. *Entropy (Basel, Switzerland)*, *20*(5), 372. doi:10.3390/e20050372

Gupta, V., Kapur, P. K., & Kumar, D. (2016). Modelling and measuring code smells in enterprise applications using TISM and two-way assessment. *International Journal of System Assurance Engineering and Management*, *7*(3), 332–340. doi:10.100713198-016-0460-0

Gurcan-Namlu, A. (2003). The effect of learning strategy on computer anxiety. *Computers in Human Behavior, 19*(5), 565-578. Retrieved from http://www.sciencedirect.com/science/article/pii/S0747563203000037

Haan, J. D. (2008). *8 Reasons Why Model-Driven Approaches (Will) Fail*. Retrieved from http://www.infoq.com/articles/8-reasons-why-MDE-fails

Hafezalkotob, A., & Hafezalkotob, A. (2016). Extended MULTIMOORA method based on Shannon entropy weight for materials selection. *Journal of Industrial Engineering International*, *12*(1), 1–13. doi:10.100740092-015-0123-9

Hamid, A., Ilyas, M., Hummayun, M., & Nawaz, A. (2013). A comparative study on code smell detection tools. *International Journal of Advanced Science and Technology, 60*, 25–32. doi:10.14257/ijast.2013.60.03

Haupt, F., Karastoyanova, D., Leymann, F., & Schroth, B. (2014). A model-driven approach for REST compliant services. *Proceedings - 2014 IEEE International Conference on Web Services, ICWS 2014*, 129–136. 10.1109/ICWS.2014.30

Haupt, F., Leymann, F., Scherer, A., & Vukojevic-Haupt, K. (2017). A Framework for the Structural Analysis of REST APIs. In *Proceedings of the 1st IEEE International Conference on Software Architecture, ICSA 2017* (pp. 55–58). Gothenburg: IEEE Computer Society. 10.1109/ICSA.2017.40

Hogo, M. A. (2010). Evaluation of e-learning systems based on fuzzy clustering models and statistical tools. *Expert Systems with Applications, 10*, 6891-6903. Retrieved from http://www.sciencedirect.com/science/article/pii/S0957417410002137

Hossler, J., Born, M., & Saito, S. (2006). Significant Productivity Enhancement through Model Driven Techniques: A Success Story. *10th IEEE International Enterprise Distributed Object Computing Conference (EDOC'06)*, 367-373. 10.1109/EDOC.2006.53

Hotomski, S. a. (2018). Keeping Evolving Requirements and Acceptance Tests Aligned with Automatically Generated Guidance. In *International Working Conference on Requirements Engineering: Foundation for Software Quality* (pp. 247-264). Springer. 10.1007/978-3-319-77243-1_15

Huhns, M., & Singh, M. P. (2005). Service-Oriented Computing: Key Concepts and Principles. *Proceedings - Fifth International Conference on Commercial-off-the-Shelf (COTS)-Based Software Systems, 13*(1), 1–7. 10.1016/j.compind.2009.07.006

Hundhausen, C. D., & Brown, J. L. (2007). What You See Is What You Code: A "live" algorithm development and visualization environment for novice learners. *Journal of Visual Languages and Computing, 18*(1), 22-47. Retrieved from http://www.sciencedirect.com/science/article/pii/S1045926X06000140

Hutchinson, J., Whittle, J., & Rouncefield, M. (2014). Model-driven engineering practices in industry: Social, organizational and managerial factors that lead to success or failure. *Science of Computer Programming, 89*(Part B), 144–161. doi:10.1016/j.scico.2013.03.017

ISEP. (n.d.). *Instituto Superior de Engenharia do Porto*. Retrieved from http://www. isep.ipp.pt/

Jaafar, F., Khomh, F., Guéhéneuc, Y. G., & Zulkernine, M. (2014). Anti-pattern Mutations and Fault-proneness. In *Quality Software (QSIC), 2014 14th International Conference on* (pp. 246-255). IEEE. 10.1109/QSIC.2014.45

Jara, C. A., Candelas, F. A., & Torres, F. (2008). Virtual and remote laboratory for robotics e-learning. *Computer-Aided Chemical Engineering, 25*, 1193–1198. Retrieved from http://www.sciencedirect.com/science/article/pii/S1570794608802052#

Jenkins, T. (2001). The motivation of students of programming. *Proceedings of the 6th conference on innovation and technology in computer science education*, 53–56. doi: 10.1145/377435.377472

JSHint.com. (2018). *JSHint web-site*. Retrieved from http://jshint.com/

Jurado, F., Redondo, M. A., & Ortega, M. (2012). Blackboard architecture to integrate components and agents in heterogeneous distributed eLearning systems: An application for learning to program. *Journal of Systems and Software, 85*(7), 1621-1636. Retrieved from http://www.sciencedirect.com/science/article/pii/S0164121212000416

Kapila, H., & Singh, S. (2014). Bayesian Inference to Predict Smelly classes Probability in Open source software. *International Journal of Current Engineering and Technology, 4*(3), 1724–1728.

Kazimoglu, C., Kiernan, M., Bacon, L., & MacKinnon, L. (2012). Learning Programming at the Computational Thinking Level via Digital Game-Play. *Procedia Computer Science, 9*, 522-531. Retrieved from http://www.sciencedirect.com/science/article/pii/S1877050912001779

Key benefits of Structural Coverage Analysis for DO-178B Systems. (n.d.). Retrieved from https://www.rapitasystems.com/blog/4_key_benefits_structural_coverage_DO-178B_systems

Kochhar, P. S., Bissyande, T. F., Lo, D., & Jiang, L. (2013). Adoption of Software Testing in Open Source Projects--A Preliminary Study on 50,000 Projects. *2013 17th European Conference on Software Maintenance and Reengineering*. doi:10.1109/csmr.2013.48

Kordaki, M. (2010). A drawing and multi-representational computer environment for beginners' learning of programming using C: Design and pilot formative evaluation. *Computers & Education, 54*(1), 69-87. Retrieved from http://www.sciencedirect.com./science/article/pii/S0360131509001845

Kosar, T., Bohra, S., & Mernik, M. (2015). Domain-Specific Languages: A Systematic Mapping Study. *Information and Software Technology, 71*. doi:10.1016/j.infsof.2015.11.001

Kruchten, P., Nord, R. L., & Ozkaya, I. (2012). Technical Debt: From Metaphor to Theory and Practice. *IEEE Software, 29*(6), 18–21. doi:10.1109/MS.2012.167

Landwehr, C., Ludewig, J., Meersman, R., Parnas, D. L., Shoval, P., Wand, Y., ... Weyuker, E. (2017). Software Systems Engineering programmes a capability approach. *Journal of Systems and Software, 125*, 354–364. doi:10.1016/j.jss.2016.12.016

Law, K. M. Y., Lee, V. C. S., & Yu, Y. T. (2010). Learning motivation in e-learning facilitated computer programming courses. *Computers & Education, 55*(1), 218-228. Retrieved from http://www.sciencedirect.com/science/article/pii/S0360131510000102

Lewin, K. (1946). Action Research and Minority Problems. *The Journal of Social Issues, 2*(4), 34–46. doi:10.1111/j.1540-4560.1946.tb02295.x

Li, N. (2014). *Evaluation of Modified Condition/Decision Coverage in Testing a Web Server* (Research thesis).

Lieberman, R. (1997). What is that Smell? *College & Undergraduate Libraries, 4*(2), 51–53. doi:10.1300/J106v04n02_08

Limoncelli, T. A. (2018). Documentation is Automation. *Communications of the ACM, 61*(6), 48–53. doi:10.1145/3190572

Lister, R., Adams, E., Fitzgerald, S., Fone, W., John, H., Lindholm, M., … Seppälä, O. (2004). A Multi-National Study of Reading and Tracing Skills in Novice Programmers. *ACM SIGCSE Bulletin, 36*(4), 119–150. Retrieved from http://urn.kb.se/resolve?urn=urn:nbn:se:umu:diva-15878

Liu, W., & Cui, J. (2008). Entropy coefficient method to evaluate the level of sustainable development of China's sports. *International Journal of Sports Science and Engineering, 2*(2), 72–78.

Li, W., & Shatnawi, R. (2007). An empirical study of the bad smells and class error probability in the post-release object-oriented system evolution. *Journal of Systems and Software, 80*(7), 1120–1128. doi:10.1016/j.jss.2006.10.018

Maia, P., Gadelha, F., Borges, M., Muniz, L., Silva, A., & Ximenes, J. (2016). Práticas e Experiências no Ensino de Engenharia Dirigida por Modelos. *iSys-Revista Brasileira de Sistemas de Informação, 9*(2).

Mansoor, U., Kessentini, M., Bechikh, S., & Deb, K. (2013). *Code-smells detection using good and bad software design examples.* Technical report.

Mantyla, M., Vanhanen, J., & Lassenius, C. (2003). A taxonomy and an initial empirical study of bad smells in code. In *Software Maintenance, 2003.ICSM 2003. Proceedings. International Conference on* (pp. 381-384). IEEE.

Marques, M., Ochoa, S. F., Bastarrica, M. C., & Gutierrez, F. J. (2018). Enhancing the Student Learning Experience in Software Engineering Project Courses. *IEEE Transactions on Education, 61*(1), 63–73. doi:10.1109/TE.2017.2742989

Massé, M. (2011). *REST API Design Rulebook: Designing Consistent RESTful Web Service Interfaces.* O'Reilly Media, Inc.

McConnell, S. (2016). *Code complete.* Redmond, WA: Microsoft Press.

McCracken, M., Almstrum, V., Diaz, D., Guzdial, M., Hagan, D., Kolikant, Y., ... Wilusz, T. (2001). A multi-national, multi-institutional study of assessment of programming skills of first-year CS students. *ACM SIGCSE Bulletin, 33*(4), 180. doi:10.1145/572139.572181

Meliá, S., Gómez, J., Pérez, S., & Díaz, O. (2008). A model-driven development for GWT-based rich internet applications with OOH4RIA. In *ICWE'08 Eighth International Conference on Web Engineering.* IEEE.

Meng, M. a. (2017). Application Programming Interface Documentation: What Do Software Developers Want? *Journal of Technical Writing and Communication.*

Mills, J. E., & Treagust, D. F. (2003). Engineering education—Is problem-based or project-based learning the answer. *Australasian Journal of Engineering Education, 3*(2), 2–16.

Mireille, B. (2008), Project-based teaching for model-driven engineering. *Proceedings of the 4th Educators Symposium at MoDELS 2008.*

Mohammed, N. M., Niazi, M., Alshayeb, M., & Mahmood, S. (2017). Exploring software security approaches in software development lifecycle: A systematic mapping study. *Computer Standards & Interfaces, 50,* 107–115. doi:10.1016/j.csi.2016.10.001

Moha, N., Guéhéneuc, Y. G., Le Meur, A. F., Duchien, L., & Tiberghien, A. (2010). From a domain analysis to the specification and detection of code and design smells. *Formal Aspects of Computing, 22*(3-4), 345–361. doi:10.100700165-009-0115-x

Montandon, J. E. (2013). Documenting apis with examples: Lessons learned with the apiminer platform. In *Reverse Engineering (WCRE), 2013 20th Working Conference on* (pp. 401-408). Koblenz: IEEE.

MoocLab. (2015). Mooclabs league tables. *MoocLab.* Retrieved from http://www.mooclab.club/categories/league-tables.169/

Moodle.org. (2018). *Moodle web-site.* Retrieved from http://moodle.org/

Moons, J., & De Backer, C. (2013). The design and pilot evaluation of an interactive learning environment for introductory programming influenced by cognitive load theory and constructivism. *Computers & Education, 60*(1), 368-384. Retrieved from http://www.sciencedirect.com/science/article/pii/S0360131512001959

Mulloy, B. (2013). *Web API design.* Academic Press.

Nakoula, Y., & Houimel, T. (2017). *Jclays, A global solution for application design and automatic GWT code generator.* GWT Con 2017, Firenze, Italy.

Namin, S., & Kakarla, S. (2011). The use of mutation in testing experiments and its sensitivity to external threats. *ISSTA,* 342–352.

Nasehi, S. M. (2012). What makes a good code example? A study of programming Q&A in StackOverflow. In *Software Maintenance (ICSM), 2012 28th IEEE International Conference on* (pp. 23-34). Trento: IEEE.

Nelson, J. (2017). *Xapi-lang for declarative code generation.* GWT Con 2017, Firenze, Italy.

Newstetter, W., & McCracken, M. (2001). Novice Conceptions of Design: Implications for the Design of Learning Environments. In *Design Knowing and Learning: Cognition in Design Education.* Elsevier Science. Retrieved from http://www.sciencedirect.com/science/article/pii/B9780080438689500048

Nguyen, V.-C., Qafmolla, X., & Richta, K. (2014). Domain Specific Language Approach on Model-driven Development of Web Services. *Acta Polytechnica Hungarica*, *11*(8), 121–138. Retrieved from http://www.uni-obuda.hu/journal/Nguyen_Qafmolla_Richta_54.pdf

O'Kelly & Gibson. (2006). RoboCode & problem-based learning: a non-prescriptive approach to teaching programming. In *Proceedings of the 11th annual SIGCSE conference on Innovation and technology in computer science education (ITICSE '06)*. ACM. DOI:10.1145/1140124.1140182

Onah, D. F. O., Sinclair, J., & Boyatt, R. (2014). Dropout rates of massive open online courses: behavioural patterns. *6th International Conference on Education and New Learning Technologies*, 5825-5834.

Open API Initiative. (2017). *OpenAPI Specification*. Retrieved from GitHub: https://github.com/OAI/OpenAPI-Specification/blob/master/versions/3.0.1.md

Open API Initiative. (2018). *OpenAPI Specification*. Retrieved from GitHub: https://github.com/OAI/OpenAPI-Specification

Ostrand, T. (2002). White-Box Testing. In J. J. Marciniak (Ed.), Encyclopedia of Software Engineering. Academic Press. doi:10.1002/0471028959.sof378

Pachauri, A., & Srivastava, G. (2012). Program Test Data Generation for Branch Coverage with Genetic Algorithm: Comparative Evaluation of a Maximization and Minimization Approch, *ITCS, SIP, JSE-2012. CS & IT*, *4*, 443–454.

Palomba, F., Di Nucci, D., Tufano, M., Bavota, G., Oliveto, R., Poshyvanyk, D., & De Lucia, A. (2015). Landfill: An open dataset of code smells with public evaluation. In *Mining Software Repositories (MSR), 2015 IEEE/ACM 12th Working Conference on* (pp. 482-485). IEEE.

Palomba, F., Bavota, G., Di Penta, M., Oliveto, R., De Lucia, A., & Poshyvanyk, D. (2013). Detecting bad smells in source code using change history information. In *Proceedings of the 28th IEEE/ACM International Conference on Automated Software Engineering* (pp. 268-278). IEEE Press. 10.1109/ASE.2013.6693086

Palomba, F., Zanoni, M., Fontana, F. A., De Lucia, A., & Oliveto, R. (2017). Toward a smell-aware bug prediction model. *IEEE Transactions on Software Engineering*, 1. doi:10.1109/TSE.2017.2770122

Park, S., Hussain, I., Taneja, K., Mainul Hossain, B. M., Grechanik, M., & Xie, Q. C. F. (2012). *CarFast: Achieving Higher Statement Coverage Faster.* Retrieved from https://www.cs.uic.edu/~drmark/index_htm_files/CarFast.pdf

Parviainen, P., Takalo, J., Teppola, S., & Tihinen, M. (2009). *Model-driven development processes and practices.* VTT Technical Research Centre of Finland, VTT Working Papers 114.

Patel, P., Bhatt, C., & Talati, D. (2018). Structural Coverage Analysis with DO-178B Standards. In *International Conference on Advanced Computing, Networking and Informatics (ICANI).* Springer.

Pavan, K. P., Sanjay, A., & Zornitza, P. (2012). Comparing Performance of Web Service Interaction Styles : SOAP vs. REST. *Proceedings of the Conference on Information Systems Applied Research*, 1–24.

Peters, R., & Zaidman, A. (2012). Evaluating the lifespan of code smells using software repository mining. In *Software Maintenance and Reengineering (CSMR), 2012 16th European Conference on* (pp. 411-416). IEEE.

Phipps, E., & Pawlowski, R. (2012). Efficient Expression Templates for Operator Overloading-Based Automatic Differentiation. In Recent Advances in Algorithmic Differentiation (pp. 309-319). Academic Press.

Pietrzak, B., & Walter, B. (2006). Leveraging code smell detection with inter-smell relations. In *International Conference on Extreme Programming and Agile Processes in Software Engineering* (pp. 75-84). Springer. 10.1007/11774129_8

Pinkham, R. (2017). *What Is the Difference Between Swagger and OpenAPI?* Retrieved from Swagger: https://swagger.io/blog/difference-between-swagger-and-openapi/

Porubaen, J., Bacikova, M., Chodarev, S., & Nosál, M. (2015). Teaching pragmatic model-driven software development. *Computer Science and Information Systems*, *12*(2), 683–705. doi:10.2298/CSIS140107022P

Preston-Werner, T. (n.d.). *Semantic Versioning 2.0.0.* Retrieved from Semantic Versioning 2.0.0: https://semver.org/spec/v2.0.0.html

RAML. (2018). *The RESTful API Modeling Language (RAML) Spec.* Retrieved from Github: https://github.com/raml-org/raml-spec

Ramsdale, C. (2010). *Building MVP apps: MVP Part I.* Available from http://www.gwtproject.org/articles/mvp-architecture.html

Rani, M., Nayak, R., & Vyas, O. P. (2015). An ontology-based adaptive personalized e-learning system, assisted by software agents on cloud storage. *Knowledge-Based Systems*, *90*, 33–48. doi:10.1016/j.knosys.2015.10.002

RAPITA Systems Ltd. (n.d.). *Seven Roadblocks to 100% Structural Coverage (and how to avoid them)*. Retrieved from https://www.danlawinc.com/wp-content/uploads/2016/12/MC-WP-007-51-LR-Roadblocks-to-100pc-Coverage.pdf

Rapita Systems. (n.d.). Retrieved from https://www.rapitasystems.com/

Reddy, K. R., & Rao, A. A. (2009). Dependency oriented complexity metrics to detect rippling related design defects. *Software Engineering Notes*, *34*(4), 1–7. doi:10.1145/1543405.1543421

Richardson, L. A. (2013). *RESTful Web APIs: Services for a Changing World*. O'Reilly Media, Inc.

Ringert, J., Rumpe, B., Schulze, C., & Wortmann, A. (2017). Teaching agile model-driven engineering for cyber-physical systems. In *Software Engineering: Software Engineering Education and Training Track (ICSE-SEET), 2017 IEEE/ACM 39th International Conference on*. IEEE.

Robillard, M. P., & DeLine, R. (2011). A field study of API learning obstacles. *Empirical Software Engineering*, *16*(6), 703–732. doi:10.100710664-010-9150-8

Robins, A., Rountree, J., & Rountree, N. (2003). Learning and Teaching Programming: A Review and Discussion. *Journal of Computer Science Education, 13*(2), 137-172. Doi:10.1076/csed.13.2.137.14200

Romero, C., González, P., Ventura, S., del Jesús, M. J., & Herrera, F. (2009). Evolutionary algorithms for subgroup discovery in e-learning: A practical application using Moodle data. *Expert Systems with Applications, 36*(2), 1632-1644. Retrieved from http://www.sciencedirect.com/science/article/pii/S0957417407005933

Sahani, A. K. (2015). *A Novel Approach to Improve Concolic Testing* (Master's thesis). National Institute of Technology, Rourkela, India.

Sancho-Thomas, P., Fuentes-Fernández, R., & Fernández-Manjón, B. (2009) Learning teamwork skills in university programming courses. *Computers & Education, 53*(2), 517-531. Retrieved from http://www.sciencedirect.com/science/article/pii/S0360131509000797

Scheidgen, M., Efftinge, S., & Marticke, F. (2016). Metamodeling vs metaprogramming: A case study on developing client libraries for REST APIs. Lecture Notes in Computer Science, 9764, 205–216. doi:10.1007/978-3-319-42061-5_13

Schmidt, A., Kimmig, D., Bittner, K., & Dickerhof, M. (2014). Teaching Model-Driven Software Development: Revealing the "Great Miracle" of Code Generation to Students. *Proceedings of the Sixteenth Australasian Computing Education Conference (ACE2014), 148,* 97–104.

Schreibmann, V., & Braun, P. (2014). Design and Implementation of a Model-Driven Approach for Restful APIs. *5th IEEE Germany Student Conference.* Retrieved from http://www.ieee-student-conference.de/fileadmin/papers/2014/ieeegsc2014_submission_8.pdf

Schreibmann, V., & Braun, P. (2015). Model-driven Development of RESTful APIs. *Proceedings of the 11th International Conference on Web Information Systems and Technologies,* 5–14. 10.5220/0005411200050014

Schreier, S. (2011). Modeling RESTful applications. *Proceedings of the Second International Workshop on RESTful Design - WS-REST '11,* 15. 10.1145/1967428.1967434

Schwichtenberg, S. A. (2017). From Open API to Semantic Specifications and Code Adapters. In *Web Services (ICWS), 2017 IEEE International Conference on* (pp. 484-491). Honolulu, HI: IEEE.

Sedelmaier, Y., & Landes, D. (2014). Practicing soft skills in software engineering: A project-based didactical approach. In Overcoming Challenges in Software Engineering Education: Delivering Non-Technical Knowledge and Skills (pp. 161-179). IGI Global.

Shahid, M., & Ibrahim, S. (2011). An Evaluation of Test Coverage Tools in Software Testing. *International Conference on Telecommunication Technology and Applications, Proc. of CSIT (IACSIT),* 5.

Shannon, C. E. (2001). A mathematical theory of communication. *Mobile Computing and Communications Review, 5*(1), 3–55. doi:10.1145/584091.584093

Sharma, H., & Chug, A. (2015). Dynamic metrics are superior than static metrics in maintainability prediction: An empirical case study. *2015 4th International Conference on Reliability, Infocom Technologies and Optimization: Trends and Future Directions, ICRITO 2015,* 2–7. 10.1109/ICRITO.2015.7359354

Shelke, S., & Nagpure, S. (2014, July 1). The Study of Various Code Coverage Tools. *International Journal of Computer Trends and Technology*, *13*(1), 46–49. doi:10.14445/22312803/IJCTT-V13P110

Simões, A., & Almeida, J. J. (2010). Processing XML: a rewriting system approach. In XATA 2010 --- 8ª Conferência Nacional em XML. Aplicações e Tecnologias Associadas.

Simões, J., Díaz-Redondo, R., & Fernández-Vilas, A. (2013). A social gamification framework for a K-6 learning platform. *Computers in Human Behavior, 29*(2), 345-353. Retrieved from http://www.sciencedirect.com/science/article/pii/S0747563212001574

Singh, G., & Chopra, V. (2013). A study of bad smells in code. *Int J SciEmergTechnol Latest Trends*, *7*(91), 16–20.

SmartBear. (2018). *OpenAPI Specification | Swagger*. Retrieved May 31, 2018, from https://swagger.io/specification/

SOA Work Group. (2016). *Service-Oriented Architecture*. Retrieved January 18, 2018, from http://www.opengroup.org/soa/source-book/soa/index.htm

Sohan, S., Anslow, C., & Maurer, F. (2015). A case study of web API evolution. In *2015 IEEE World Congress on Services* (pp. 245-252). New York: IEEE. 10.1109/SERVICES.2015.43

Somers, J. (2017). *The Coming Software Apocalypse*. Retrieved from http://www.theatlantic.com/technology/archive/2017/09/saving-the-world-from-code/540393/

SonarQube. (2018). *Architecture and Integration - SonarQube Documentation*. Retrieved October 18, 2018, from https://docs.sonarqube.org/display/SONAR/Architecture+and+Integration

SQALE. (2017, July 1). Retrieved October 18, 2018, from https://en.wikipedia.org/wiki/SQALE

Srivastaval, J., & Dwivedi, T. (2015). Software Testing Strategy approach on source code applying conditional coverage method. *International Journal of Software Engineering and Its Applications*, *6*(3), 25–31. doi:10.5121/ijsea.2015.6303

Stahl, T., Völter, M., Bettin, J., Haase, A., & Helsen, S. (2006). *Model-Driven Software Development: Technology, Engineering, Management*. Wiley.

Statement and Branch Coverage Examples. (n.d.). Retrieved from https://www. istqb.guru/how-to-calculate-statement-branchdecision-and-path-coverage-for-istqb- exam-purpose

Statement Coverage in Software Testing. (n.d.). Retrieved from https://www.guru99. com/learn-statement-coverage.html

Structural Coverage Analysis for Safety-Critical Code. (n.d.). Retrieved from http:// mys5.org/Proceedings/2015/Day_3/2015-S5-Day3_1415_Bhattacharya.pdf

Sun, Y., Brain, M., Kroening, D., Hawthorn, A., Wilson, T., Schanda, F., . . . Broster, I. (2017). *Functional Requirements-Based Automated Testing for Avionics.* arXiv:1707.01466v1

Swagger. (2018a). *Swagger Code Generator.* Retrieved from Github: https://github. com/swagger-api/swagger-codegen/tree/3.0.0

Swagger. (2018b). *Swagger UI.* Retrieved from Github: https://github.com/swagger- api/swagger-ui

Szugyi, Z., & Porkolab, Z. (2013). Comparison of DC and MC/ DC Code Coverages. *Proceedings of the Twelfth International Conference on Informatics.* 10.15546/ aeei-2013-0050

Tan, J., Guo, X., Zheng, W., & Zhong, M. (2014). Case-based teaching using the Laboratory Animal System for learning C/C++ programming. *Computers & Education, 77,* 39-49. Retrieved from http://www.sciencedirect.com/science/article/ pii/S0360131514000888

Tassey, G. (2002). *The economic impacts of inadequate infrastructure for software testing.* National Institute of Standards and Technology.

Tekinerdogan, B. (2011). Experiences in teaching a graduate course on model-driven software development. *Computer Science Education, 21*(4), 363–387. doi:10.108 0/08993408.2011.630129

Thakur, M. S. (2017). Review on Structural Software Testing Coverage Approaches. *International Journal of Advance research, Ideas and Innovations in Technology,* 281-286.

The Linux Foundation. (2017a). *Open API Initiative.* Retrieved October 21, 2017, from https://www.openapis.org/

The Linux Foundation. (2017b). *The OpenAPI Specification*. Retrieved October 22, 2017, from https://github.com/OAI/OpenAPI-Specification

Tihomirovs, J., & Grabis, J. (2016). Comparison of SOAP and REST Based Web Services Using Software Evaluation Metrics. *Information Technology and Management Science*, *19*(1), 92–97. doi:10.1515/itms-2016-0017

Torchiano, M., Tomassetti, F., Ricca, F., Tiso, A., & Reggio, G. (2013). Relevance, benefits, and problems of software modelling and model driven techniques - A survey in the Italian industry. *Journal of Systems and Software*, *86*(8), 2110–2126. doi:10.1016/j.jss.2013.03.084

Tufano, M., Palomba, F., Bavota, G., Oliveto, R., Di Penta, M., De Lucia, A., & Poshyvanyk, D. (2015). When and why your code starts to smell bad. In *Software Engineering (ICSE), 2015 IEEE/ACM 37th IEEE International Conference on* (Vol. 1, pp. 403-414). IEEE.

Tuparov, G., Tuparova, D., & Tsarnakova, A. (2012). Using Interactive Simulation-Based Learning Objects in Introductory Course of Programming. *Procedia - Social and Behavioral Sciences, 46*, 2276-2280. Retrieved from http://www.sciencedirect.com/science/article/pii/S1877042812015984

Uddin, G., & Robillard, M. P. (2015). How API documentation fails. *IEEE Software*, *32*(4), 68–75. doi:10.1109/MS.2014.80

Uziak, J. (2016). A Project Based Learning Approach in An Engineering Curriculum. *Global Journal of Engineering Education*, *18*(2), 119–123.

Van Emden, E., & Moonen, L. (2002). Java quality assurance by detecting code smells. In *Reverse Engineering, 2002. Proceedings. Ninth Working Conference on* (pp. 97-106). IEEE.

Vasudevan, K. (2017). *The Importance of Standardized API Design*. Retrieved January 29, 2018, from https://swaggerhub.com/blog/api-design/the-importance-of-standardized-api-design/

VectorCAST Interactive Tutorial. (n.d.). Retrieved from https://www.vectorcast.com/sites/default/files/downloads/pdf/vcast_interactive_tutorials.pdf

Vega, C., Jiménez, C., & Villalobos, J. (2013). A scalable and incremental project-based learning approach for CS1/CS2 courses. *Education and Information Technologies, 18*(2), 309-329. Retrieved from http://link.springer.com/article/10.1007/s10639-012-9242-8#

Verdú, E., Regueras, L. M., Verdú, M. J., Leal, J. P., de Castro, J. P., & Queirós, R. (2012). A distributed system for learning programming on-line. *Computers & Education, 58*(1), 1-10. Doi:10.1016/j.compedu.2011.08.015

Vilkomir, S., Alluri, A., Kuhn, D. R., & Kacker, R. N. (2017). Combinatorial and MC/DC Coverage Levels of Random Testing. *IEEE International Conference*, 61-68. 10.1109/QRS-C.2017.19

Vlissides, J. A. (1995). *Design patterns: Elements of reusable object-oriented software*. Reading, MA: Addison-Wesley.

W3C. (2004). *Web Services Architecture*. Retrieved January 9, 2018, from https://www.w3.org/TR/ws-arch/

Webber, J. A. (2010). *REST in practice: Hypermedia and systems architecture*. O'Reilly Media, Inc. doi:10.1007/978-3-642-15114-9_3

Whittle, J., Hutchinson, J., & Rouncefield, M. (2014). The state of practice in model-driven engineering. *IEEE Software*, *31*(3), 79–85. doi:10.1109/MS.2013.65

Whittle, J., Hutchinson, J., Rouncefield, M., Burden, H., & Heldal, R. (2017). A taxonomy of tool-related issues affecting the adoption of model-driven engineering. *Software & Systems Modeling*, *16*(2), 313–331. doi:10.100710270-015-0487-8

Wikipedia. (2018). *List of tools for static code analysis*. Retrieved October 18, 2018, from https://en.wikipedia.org/wiki/List_of_tools_for_static_code_analysis#Multi-language

World Wide Web Consortium (W3C). (2018a). *Web standards: technical specifications and guidelines*. Available at http://www.w3.org/

World Wide Web Consortium (W3C). (2018b). *Markup validation services*. Available at http://validator.w3.org/

World Wide Web Consortium (W3C). (2018c). *CSS validation services*. Available at http://jigsaw.w3.org/css-validator/

Xavier, J., & Coelho, A. (2011). Computer-based assessment system for e-learning applied to programming education. *Proceedings, ser. 4th International Conference of Education, Research and Innovations*, 3738–3747.

Xin, F., Wei, Z., Feng-yu, Y., & Qi-jun, L. (2015). Test Data Automatic Generation Based on Modified Condition/Decision Coverage Criteria. *International Conference on Computer Science and Intelligent Communication (CSIC)*.

Yusifoğlu, V. G. (2015). Software test-code engineering: A systematic mapping. *Information and Software Technology*, *58*, 123–147. doi:10.1016/j.infsof.2014.06.009

Yusof, N., Zin, N. A. M., & Adnan, N. S. (2012). Java Programming Assessment Tool for Assignment Module in Moodle E-learning System. *Procedia - Social and Behavioral Sciences, 56*, 767-773. Retrieved from http://www.sciencedirect.com/science/article/pii/S1877042812041766

Zampetti, F., Scalabrino, S., Oliveto, R., Canfora, G., & Penta, M. D. (2017). How Open Source Projects Use Static Code Analysis Tools in Continuous Integration Pipelines. *2017 IEEE/ACM 14th International Conference on Mining Software Repositories (MSR), * 334-344.

Zander, J., Schieferdecker, I. K., & Mosterman, P. (2011). Model-Based Testing for Embedded Systems. *Computational Analysis, Synthesis, and Design of Dynamic Systems.*

Zhang, H. P. (2015). Application on the entropy method for determination of weight of evaluating index in fuzzy mathematics for wine quality assessment. *Advance Journal of Food Science and Technology*, *7*(3), 195–198. doi:10.19026/ajfst.7.1293

Zhu, H., Hall, P. A. V., & May, J. H. R. (1997). Software unit test coverage and adequacy. *ACM Computing Surveys*, *29*(4), 366–427. doi:10.1145/267580.267590

Zolotas, C., Diamantopoulos, T., Chatzidimitriou, K. C., & Symeonidis, A. L. (2017). From requirements to source code: A Model-Driven Engineering approach for RESTful web services. *Automated Software Engineering*, *24*(4), 791–838. doi:10.100710515-016-0206-x

Related References

To continue our tradition of advancing information science and technology research, we have compiled a list of recommended IGI Global readings. These references will provide additional information and guidance to further enrich your knowledge and assist you with your own research and future publications.

Aasi, P., Rusu, L., & Vieru, D. (2017). The Role of Culture in IT Governance Five Focus Areas: A Literature Review. *International Journal of IT/Business Alignment and Governance, 8*(2), 42-61. doi:10.4018/IJITBAG.2017070103

Abdrabo, A. A. (2018). Egypt's Knowledge-Based Development: Opportunities, Challenges, and Future Possibilities. In A. Alraouf (Ed.), *Knowledge-Based Urban Development in the Middle East* (pp. 80–101). Hershey, PA: IGI Global. doi:10.4018/978-1-5225-3734-2.ch005

Abu Doush, I., & Alhami, I. (2018). Evaluating the Accessibility of Computer Laboratories, Libraries, and Websites in Jordanian Universities and Colleges. *International Journal of Information Systems and Social Change*, 9(2), 44–60. doi:10.4018/IJISSC.2018040104

Adeboye, A. (2016). Perceived Use and Acceptance of Cloud Enterprise Resource Planning (ERP) Implementation in the Manufacturing Industries. *International Journal of Strategic Information Technology and Applications*, 7(3), 24–40. doi:10.4018/IJSITA.2016070102

Adegbore, A. M., Quadri, M. O., & Oyewo, O. R. (2018). A Theoretical Approach to the Adoption of Electronic Resource Management Systems (ERMS) in Nigerian University Libraries. In A. Tella & T. Kwanya (Eds.), *Handbook of Research on Managing Intellectual Property in Digital Libraries* (pp. 292–311). Hershey, PA: IGI Global. doi:10.4018/978-1-5225-3093-0.ch015

Adhikari, M., & Roy, D. (2016). Green Computing. In G. Deka, G. Siddesh, K. Srinivasa, & L. Patnaik (Eds.), *Emerging Research Surrounding Power Consumption and Performance Issues in Utility Computing* (pp. 84–108). Hershey, PA: IGI Global. doi:10.4018/978-1-4666-8853-7.ch005

Afolabi, O. A. (2018). Myths and Challenges of Building an Effective Digital Library in Developing Nations: An African Perspective. In A. Tella & T. Kwanya (Eds.), *Handbook of Research on Managing Intellectual Property in Digital Libraries* (pp. 51–79). Hershey, PA: IGI Global. doi:10.4018/978-1-5225-3093-0.ch004

Agarwal, R., Singh, A., & Sen, S. (2016). Role of Molecular Docking in Computer-Aided Drug Design and Development. In S. Dastmalchi, M. Hamzeh-Mivehroud, & B. Sokouti (Eds.), *Applied Case Studies and Solutions in Molecular Docking-Based Drug Design* (pp. 1–28). Hershey, PA: IGI Global. doi:10.4018/978-1-5225-0362-0.ch001

Ali, O., & Soar, J. (2016). Technology Innovation Adoption Theories. In L. Al-Hakim, X. Wu, A. Koronios, & Y. Shou (Eds.), *Handbook of Research on Driving Competitive Advantage through Sustainable, Lean, and Disruptive Innovation* (pp. 1–38). Hershey, PA: IGI Global. doi:10.4018/978-1-5225-0135-0.ch001

Alsharo, M. (2017). Attitudes Towards Cloud Computing Adoption in Emerging Economies. *International Journal of Cloud Applications and Computing*, *7*(3), 44–58. doi:10.4018/IJCAC.2017070102

Amer, T. S., & Johnson, T. L. (2016). Information Technology Progress Indicators: Temporal Expectancy, User Preference, and the Perception of Process Duration. *International Journal of Technology and Human Interaction*, *12*(4), 1–14. doi:10.4018/IJTHI.2016100101

Amer, T. S., & Johnson, T. L. (2017). Information Technology Progress Indicators: Research Employing Psychological Frameworks. In A. Mesquita (Ed.), *Research Paradigms and Contemporary Perspectives on Human-Technology Interaction* (pp. 168–186). Hershey, PA: IGI Global. doi:10.4018/978-1-5225-1868-6.ch008

Anchugam, C. V., & Thangadurai, K. (2016). Introduction to Network Security. In D. G., M. Singh, & M. Jayanthi (Eds.), Network Security Attacks and Countermeasures (pp. 1-48). Hershey, PA: IGI Global. doi:10.4018/978-1-4666-8761-5.ch001

Anchugam, C. V., & Thangadurai, K. (2016). Classification of Network Attacks and Countermeasures of Different Attacks. In D. G., M. Singh, & M. Jayanthi (Eds.), Network Security Attacks and Countermeasures (pp. 115-156). Hershey, PA: IGI Global. doi:10.4018/978-1-4666-8761-5.ch004

Anohah, E. (2016). Pedagogy and Design of Online Learning Environment in Computer Science Education for High Schools. *International Journal of Online Pedagogy and Course Design, 6*(3), 39–51. doi:10.4018/IJOPCD.2016070104

Anohah, E. (2017). Paradigm and Architecture of Computing Augmented Learning Management System for Computer Science Education. *International Journal of Online Pedagogy and Course Design, 7*(2), 60–70. doi:10.4018/IJOPCD.2017040105

Anohah, E., & Suhonen, J. (2017). Trends of Mobile Learning in Computing Education from 2006 to 2014: A Systematic Review of Research Publications. *International Journal of Mobile and Blended Learning, 9*(1), 16–33. doi:10.4018/IJMBL.2017010102

Assis-Hassid, S., Heart, T., Reychav, I., & Pliskin, J. S. (2016). Modelling Factors Affecting Patient-Doctor-Computer Communication in Primary Care. *International Journal of Reliable and Quality E-Healthcare, 5*(1), 1–17. doi:10.4018/IJRQEH.2016010101

Bailey, E. K. (2017). Applying Learning Theories to Computer Technology Supported Instruction. In M. Grassetti & S. Brookby (Eds.), *Advancing Next-Generation Teacher Education through Digital Tools and Applications* (pp. 61–81). Hershey, PA: IGI Global. doi:10.4018/978-1-5225-0965-3.ch004

Balasubramanian, K. (2016). Attacks on Online Banking and Commerce. In K. Balasubramanian, K. Mala, & M. Rajakani (Eds.), *Cryptographic Solutions for Secure Online Banking and Commerce* (pp. 1–19). Hershey, PA: IGI Global. doi:10.4018/978-1-5225-0273-9.ch001

Baldwin, S., Opoku-Agyemang, K., & Roy, D. (2016). Games People Play: A Trilateral Collaboration Researching Computer Gaming across Cultures. In K. Valentine & L. Jensen (Eds.), *Examining the Evolution of Gaming and Its Impact on Social, Cultural, and Political Perspectives* (pp. 364–376). Hershey, PA: IGI Global. doi:10.4018/978-1-5225-0261-6.ch017

Banerjee, S., Sing, T. Y., Chowdhury, A. R., & Anwar, H. (2018). Let's Go Green: Towards a Taxonomy of Green Computing Enablers for Business Sustainability. In M. Khosrow-Pour (Ed.), *Green Computing Strategies for Competitive Advantage and Business Sustainability* (pp. 89–109). Hershey, PA: IGI Global. doi:10.4018/978-1-5225-5017-4.ch005

Basham, R. (2018). Information Science and Technology in Crisis Response and Management. In M. Khosrow-Pour, D.B.A. (Ed.), Encyclopedia of Information Science and Technology, Fourth Edition (pp. 1407-1418). Hershey, PA: IGI Global. doi:10.4018/978-1-5225-2255-3.ch121

Batyashe, T., & Iyamu, T. (2018). Architectural Framework for the Implementation of Information Technology Governance in Organisations. In M. Khosrow-Pour, D.B.A. (Ed.), Encyclopedia of Information Science and Technology, Fourth Edition (pp. 810-819). Hershey, PA: IGI Global. doi:10.4018/978-1-5225-2255-3.ch070

Bekleyen, N., & Çelik, S. (2017). Attitudes of Adult EFL Learners towards Preparing for a Language Test via CALL. In D. Tafazoli & M. Romero (Eds.), *Multiculturalism and Technology-Enhanced Language Learning* (pp. 214–229). Hershey, PA: IGI Global. doi:10.4018/978-1-5225-1882-2.ch013

Bennett, A., Eglash, R., Lachney, M., & Babbitt, W. (2016). Design Agency: Diversifying Computer Science at the Intersections of Creativity and Culture. In M. Raisinghani (Ed.), *Revolutionizing Education through Web-Based Instruction* (pp. 35–56). Hershey, PA: IGI Global. doi:10.4018/978-1-4666-9932-8.ch003

Bergeron, F., Croteau, A., Uwizeyemungu, S., & Raymond, L. (2017). A Framework for Research on Information Technology Governance in SMEs. In S. De Haes & W. Van Grembergen (Eds.), *Strategic IT Governance and Alignment in Business Settings* (pp. 53–81). Hershey, PA: IGI Global. doi:10.4018/978-1-5225-0861-8.ch003

Bhatt, G. D., Wang, Z., & Rodger, J. A. (2017). Information Systems Capabilities and Their Effects on Competitive Advantages: A Study of Chinese Companies. *Information Resources Management Journal, 30*(3), 41–57. doi:10.4018/IRMJ.2017070103

Bogdanoski, M., Stoilkovski, M., & Risteski, A. (2016). Novel First Responder Digital Forensics Tool as a Support to Law Enforcement. In M. Hadji-Janev & M. Bogdanoski (Eds.), *Handbook of Research on Civil Society and National Security in the Era of Cyber Warfare* (pp. 352–376). Hershey, PA: IGI Global. doi:10.4018/978-1-4666-8793-6.ch016

Boontarig, W., Papasratorn, B., & Chutimaskul, W. (2016). The Unified Model for Acceptance and Use of Health Information on Online Social Networks: Evidence from Thailand. *International Journal of E-Health and Medical Communications, 7*(1), 31–47. doi:10.4018/IJEHMC.2016010102

Brown, S., & Yuan, X. (2016). Techniques for Retaining Computer Science Students at Historical Black Colleges and Universities. In C. Prince & R. Ford (Eds.), *Setting a New Agenda for Student Engagement and Retention in Historically Black Colleges and Universities* (pp. 251–268). Hershey, PA: IGI Global. doi:10.4018/978-1-5225-0308-8.ch014

Burcoff, A., & Shamir, L. (2017). Computer Analysis of Pablo Picasso's Artistic Style. *International Journal of Art, Culture and Design Technologies*, 6(1), 1–18. doi:10.4018/IJACDT.2017010101

Byker, E. J. (2017). I Play I Learn: Introducing Technological Play Theory. In C. Martin & D. Polly (Eds.), *Handbook of Research on Teacher Education and Professional Development* (pp. 297–306). Hershey, PA: IGI Global. doi:10.4018/978-1-5225-1067-3.ch016

Calongne, C. M., Stricker, A. G., Truman, B., & Arenas, F. J. (2017). Cognitive Apprenticeship and Computer Science Education in Cyberspace: Reimagining the Past. In A. Stricker, C. Calongne, B. Truman, & F. Arenas (Eds.), *Integrating an Awareness of Selfhood and Society into Virtual Learning* (pp. 180–197). Hershey, PA: IGI Global. doi:10.4018/978-1-5225-2182-2.ch013

Carlton, E. L., Holsinger, J. W. Jr, & Anunobi, N. (2016). Physician Engagement with Health Information Technology: Implications for Practice and Professionalism. *International Journal of Computers in Clinical Practice*, 1(2), 51–73. doi:10.4018/IJCCP.2016070103

Carneiro, A. D. (2017). Defending Information Networks in Cyberspace: Some Notes on Security Needs. In M. Dawson, D. Kisku, P. Gupta, J. Sing, & W. Li (Eds.), Developing Next-Generation Countermeasures for Homeland Security Threat Prevention (pp. 354-375). Hershey, PA: IGI Global. doi:10.4018/978-1-5225-0703-1.ch016

Cavalcanti, J. C. (2016). The New "ABC" of ICTs (Analytics + Big Data + Cloud Computing): A Complex Trade-Off between IT and CT Costs. In J. Martins & A. Molnar (Eds.), *Handbook of Research on Innovations in Information Retrieval, Analysis, and Management* (pp. 152–186). Hershey, PA: IGI Global. doi:10.4018/978-1-4666-8833-9.ch006

Chase, J. P., & Yan, Z. (2017). Affect in Statistics Cognition. In *Assessing and Measuring Statistics Cognition in Higher Education Online Environments: Emerging Research and Opportunities* (pp. 144–187). Hershey, PA: IGI Global. doi:10.4018/978-1-5225-2420-5.ch005

Chen, C. (2016). Effective Learning Strategies for the 21st Century: Implications for the E-Learning. In M. Anderson & C. Gavan (Eds.), *Developing Effective Educational Experiences through Learning Analytics* (pp. 143–169). Hershey, PA: IGI Global. doi:10.4018/978-1-4666-9983-0.ch006

Chen, E. T. (2016). Examining the Influence of Information Technology on Modern Health Care. In P. Manolitzas, E. Grigoroudis, N. Matsatsinis, & D. Yannacopoulos (Eds.), *Effective Methods for Modern Healthcare Service Quality and Evaluation* (pp. 110–136). Hershey, PA: IGI Global. doi:10.4018/978-1-4666-9961-8.ch006

Cimermanova, I. (2017). Computer-Assisted Learning in Slovakia. In D. Tafazoli & M. Romero (Eds.), *Multiculturalism and Technology-Enhanced Language Learning* (pp. 252–270). Hershey, PA: IGI Global. doi:10.4018/978-1-5225-1882-2.ch015

Cipolla-Ficarra, F. V., & Cipolla-Ficarra, M. (2018). Computer Animation for Ingenious Revival. In F. Cipolla-Ficarra, M. Ficarra, M. Cipolla-Ficarra, A. Quiroga, J. Alma, & J. Carré (Eds.), *Technology-Enhanced Human Interaction in Modern Society* (pp. 159–181). Hershey, PA: IGI Global. doi:10.4018/978-1-5225-3437-2.ch008

Cockrell, S., Damron, T. S., Melton, A. M., & Smith, A. D. (2018). Offshoring IT. In M. Khosrow-Pour, D.B.A. (Ed.), Encyclopedia of Information Science and Technology, Fourth Edition (pp. 5476-5489). Hershey, PA: IGI Global. doi:10.4018/978-1-5225-2255-3.ch476

Coffey, J. W. (2018). Logic and Proof in Computer Science: Categories and Limits of Proof Techniques. In J. Horne (Ed.), *Philosophical Perceptions on Logic and Order* (pp. 218–240). Hershey, PA: IGI Global. doi:10.4018/978-1-5225-2443-4.ch007

Dale, M. (2017). Re-Thinking the Challenges of Enterprise Architecture Implementation. In M. Tavana (Ed.), *Enterprise Information Systems and the Digitalization of Business Functions* (pp. 205–221). Hershey, PA: IGI Global. doi:10.4018/978-1-5225-2382-6.ch009

Das, A., Dasgupta, R., & Bagchi, A. (2016). Overview of Cellular Computing-Basic Principles and Applications. In J. Mandal, S. Mukhopadhyay, & T. Pal (Eds.), *Handbook of Research on Natural Computing for Optimization Problems* (pp. 637–662). Hershey, PA: IGI Global. doi:10.4018/978-1-5225-0058-2.ch026

De Maere, K., De Haes, S., & von Kutzschenbach, M. (2017). CIO Perspectives on Organizational Learning within the Context of IT Governance. *International Journal of IT/Business Alignment and Governance, 8*(1), 32-47. doi:10.4018/IJITBAG.2017010103

Demir, K., Çaka, C., Yaman, N. D., İslamoğlu, H., & Kuzu, A. (2018). Examining the Current Definitions of Computational Thinking. In H. Ozcinar, G. Wong, & H. Ozturk (Eds.), *Teaching Computational Thinking in Primary Education* (pp. 36–64). Hershey, PA: IGI Global. doi:10.4018/978-1-5225-3200-2.ch003

Deng, X., Hung, Y., & Lin, C. D. (2017). Design and Analysis of Computer Experiments. In S. Saha, A. Mandal, A. Narasimhamurthy, S. V, & S. Sangam (Eds.), Handbook of Research on Applied Cybernetics and Systems Science (pp. 264-279). Hershey, PA: IGI Global. doi:10.4018/978-1-5225-2498-4.ch013

Denner, J., Martinez, J., & Thiry, H. (2017). Strategies for Engaging Hispanic/Latino Youth in the US in Computer Science. In Y. Rankin & J. Thomas (Eds.), *Moving Students of Color from Consumers to Producers of Technology* (pp. 24–48). Hershey, PA: IGI Global. doi:10.4018/978-1-5225-2005-4.ch002

Devi, A. (2017). Cyber Crime and Cyber Security: A Quick Glance. In R. Kumar, P. Pattnaik, & P. Pandey (Eds.), *Detecting and Mitigating Robotic Cyber Security Risks* (pp. 160–171). Hershey, PA: IGI Global. doi:10.4018/978-1-5225-2154-9.ch011

Dores, A. R., Barbosa, F., Guerreiro, S., Almeida, I., & Carvalho, I. P. (2016). Computer-Based Neuropsychological Rehabilitation: Virtual Reality and Serious Games. In M. Cruz-Cunha, I. Miranda, R. Martinho, & R. Rijo (Eds.), *Encyclopedia of E-Health and Telemedicine* (pp. 473–485). Hershey, PA: IGI Global. doi:10.4018/978-1-4666-9978-6.ch037

Doshi, N., & Schaefer, G. (2016). Computer-Aided Analysis of Nailfold Capillaroscopy Images. In D. Fotiadis (Ed.), *Handbook of Research on Trends in the Diagnosis and Treatment of Chronic Conditions* (pp. 146–158). Hershey, PA: IGI Global. doi:10.4018/978-1-4666-8828-5.ch007

Related References

Doyle, D. J., & Fahy, P. J. (2018). Interactivity in Distance Education and Computer-Aided Learning, With Medical Education Examples. In M. Khosrow-Pour, D.B.A. (Ed.), Encyclopedia of Information Science and Technology, Fourth Edition (pp. 5829-5840). Hershey, PA: IGI Global. doi:10.4018/978-1-5225-2255-3.ch507

Elias, N. I., & Walker, T. W. (2017). Factors that Contribute to Continued Use of E-Training among Healthcare Professionals. In F. Topor (Ed.), *Handbook of Research on Individualism and Identity in the Globalized Digital Age* (pp. 403–429). Hershey, PA: IGI Global. doi:10.4018/978-1-5225-0522-8.ch018

Eloy, S., Dias, M. S., Lopes, P. F., & Vilar, E. (2016). Digital Technologies in Architecture and Engineering: Exploring an Engaged Interaction within Curricula. In D. Fonseca & E. Redondo (Eds.), *Handbook of Research on Applied E-Learning in Engineering and Architecture Education* (pp. 368–402). Hershey, PA: IGI Global. doi:10.4018/978-1-4666-8803-2.ch017

Estrela, V. V., Magalhães, H. A., & Saotome, O. (2016). Total Variation Applications in Computer Vision. In N. Kamila (Ed.), *Handbook of Research on Emerging Perspectives in Intelligent Pattern Recognition, Analysis, and Image Processing* (pp. 41–64). Hershey, PA: IGI Global. doi:10.4018/978-1-4666-8654-0.ch002

Filipovic, N., Radovic, M., Nikolic, D. D., Saveljic, I., Milosevic, Z., Exarchos, T. P., ... Parodi, O. (2016). Computer Predictive Model for Plaque Formation and Progression in the Artery. In D. Fotiadis (Ed.), *Handbook of Research on Trends in the Diagnosis and Treatment of Chronic Conditions* (pp. 279–300). Hershey, PA: IGI Global. doi:10.4018/978-1-4666-8828-5.ch013

Fisher, R. L. (2018). Computer-Assisted Indian Matrimonial Services. In M. Khosrow-Pour, D.B.A. (Ed.), Encyclopedia of Information Science and Technology, Fourth Edition (pp. 4136-4145). Hershey, PA: IGI Global. doi:10.4018/978-1-5225-2255-3.ch358

Fleenor, H. G., & Hodhod, R. (2016). Assessment of Learning and Technology: Computer Science Education. In V. Wang (Ed.), *Handbook of Research on Learning Outcomes and Opportunities in the Digital Age* (pp. 51–78). Hershey, PA: IGI Global. doi:10.4018/978-1-4666-9577-1.ch003

García-Valcárcel, A., & Mena, J. (2016). Information Technology as a Way To Support Collaborative Learning: What In-Service Teachers Think, Know and Do. *Journal of Information Technology Research*, 9(1), 1–17. doi:10.4018/JITR.2016010101

Gardner-McCune, C., & Jimenez, Y. (2017). Historical App Developers: Integrating CS into K-12 through Cross-Disciplinary Projects. In Y. Rankin & J. Thomas (Eds.), *Moving Students of Color from Consumers to Producers of Technology* (pp. 85–112). Hershey, PA: IGI Global. doi:10.4018/978-1-5225-2005-4.ch005

Garvey, G. P. (2016). Exploring Perception, Cognition, and Neural Pathways of Stereo Vision and the Split–Brain Human Computer Interface. In A. Ursyn (Ed.), *Knowledge Visualization and Visual Literacy in Science Education* (pp. 28–76). Hershey, PA: IGI Global. doi:10.4018/978-1-5225-0480-1.ch002

Ghafele, R., & Gibert, B. (2018). Open Growth: The Economic Impact of Open Source Software in the USA. In M. Khosrow-Pour (Ed.), *Optimizing Contemporary Application and Processes in Open Source Software* (pp. 164–197). Hershey, PA: IGI Global. doi:10.4018/978-1-5225-5314-4.ch007

Ghobakhloo, M., & Azar, A. (2018). Information Technology Resources, the Organizational Capability of Lean-Agile Manufacturing, and Business Performance. *Information Resources Management Journal*, *31*(2), 47–74. doi:10.4018/IRMJ.2018040103

Gianni, M., & Gotzamani, K. (2016). Integrated Management Systems and Information Management Systems: Common Threads. In P. Papajorgji, F. Pinet, A. Guimarães, & J. Papathanasiou (Eds.), *Automated Enterprise Systems for Maximizing Business Performance* (pp. 195–214). Hershey, PA: IGI Global. doi:10.4018/978-1-4666-8841-4.ch011

Gikandi, J. W. (2017). Computer-Supported Collaborative Learning and Assessment: A Strategy for Developing Online Learning Communities in Continuing Education. In J. Keengwe & G. Onchwari (Eds.), *Handbook of Research on Learner-Centered Pedagogy in Teacher Education and Professional Development* (pp. 309–333). Hershey, PA: IGI Global. doi:10.4018/978-1-5225-0892-2.ch017

Gokhale, A. A., & Machina, K. F. (2017). Development of a Scale to Measure Attitudes toward Information Technology. In L. Tomei (Ed.), *Exploring the New Era of Technology-Infused Education* (pp. 49–64). Hershey, PA: IGI Global. doi:10.4018/978-1-5225-1709-2.ch004

Grace, A., O'Donoghue, J., Mahony, C., Heffernan, T., Molony, D., & Carroll, T. (2016). Computerized Decision Support Systems for Multimorbidity Care: An Urgent Call for Research and Development. In M. Cruz-Cunha, I. Miranda, R. Martinho, & R. Rijo (Eds.), *Encyclopedia of E-Health and Telemedicine* (pp. 486–494). Hershey, PA: IGI Global. doi:10.4018/978-1-4666-9978-6.ch038

Gupta, A., & Singh, O. (2016). Computer Aided Modeling and Finite Element Analysis of Human Elbow. *International Journal of Biomedical and Clinical Engineering*, *5*(1), 31–38. doi:10.4018/IJBCE.2016010104

H., S. K. (2016). Classification of Cybercrimes and Punishments under the Information Technology Act, 2000. In S. Geetha, & A. Phamila (Eds.), *Combating Security Breaches and Criminal Activity in the Digital Sphere* (pp. 57-66). Hershey, PA: IGI Global. doi:10.4018/978-1-5225-0193-0.ch004

Hafeez-Baig, A., Gururajan, R., & Wickramasinghe, N. (2017). Readiness as a Novel Construct of Readiness Acceptance Model (RAM) for the Wireless Handheld Technology. In N. Wickramasinghe (Ed.), *Handbook of Research on Healthcare Administration and Management* (pp. 578–595). Hershey, PA: IGI Global. doi:10.4018/978-1-5225-0920-2.ch035

Hanafizadeh, P., Ghandchi, S., & Asgarimehr, M. (2017). Impact of Information Technology on Lifestyle: A Literature Review and Classification. *International Journal of Virtual Communities and Social Networking*, *9*(2), 1–23. doi:10.4018/IJVCSN.2017040101

Harlow, D. B., Dwyer, H., Hansen, A. K., Hill, C., Iveland, A., Leak, A. E., & Franklin, D. M. (2016). Computer Programming in Elementary and Middle School: Connections across Content. In M. Urban & D. Falvo (Eds.), *Improving K-12 STEM Education Outcomes through Technological Integration* (pp. 337–361). Hershey, PA: IGI Global. doi:10.4018/978-1-4666-9616-7.ch015

Haseski, H. İ., Ilic, U., & Tuğtekin, U. (2018). Computational Thinking in Educational Digital Games: An Assessment Tool Proposal. In H. Ozcinar, G. Wong, & H. Ozturk (Eds.), *Teaching Computational Thinking in Primary Education* (pp. 256–287). Hershey, PA: IGI Global. doi:10.4018/978-1-5225-3200-2.ch013

Hee, W. J., Jalleh, G., Lai, H., & Lin, C. (2017). E-Commerce and IT Projects: Evaluation and Management Issues in Australian and Taiwanese Hospitals. *International Journal of Public Health Management and Ethics*, *2*(1), 69–90. doi:10.4018/IJPHME.2017010104

Hernandez, A. A. (2017). Green Information Technology Usage: Awareness and Practices of Philippine IT Professionals. *International Journal of Enterprise Information Systems*, *13*(4), 90–103. doi:10.4018/IJEIS.2017100106

Hernandez, A. A., & Ona, S. E. (2016). Green IT Adoption: Lessons from the Philippines Business Process Outsourcing Industry. *International Journal of Social Ecology and Sustainable Development, 7*(1), 1–34. doi:10.4018/IJSESD.2016010101

Hernandez, M. A., Marin, E. C., Garcia-Rodriguez, J., Azorin-Lopez, J., & Cazorla, M. (2017). Automatic Learning Improves Human-Robot Interaction in Productive Environments: A Review. *International Journal of Computer Vision and Image Processing, 7*(3), 65–75. doi:10.4018/IJCVIP.2017070106

Horne-Popp, L. M., Tessone, E. B., & Welker, J. (2018). If You Build It, They Will Come: Creating a Library Statistics Dashboard for Decision-Making. In L. Costello & M. Powers (Eds.), *Developing In-House Digital Tools in Library Spaces* (pp. 177–203). Hershey, PA: IGI Global. doi:10.4018/978-1-5225-2676-6.ch009

Hossan, C. G., & Ryan, J. C. (2016). Factors Affecting e-Government Technology Adoption Behaviour in a Voluntary Environment. *International Journal of Electronic Government Research, 12*(1), 24–49. doi:10.4018/IJEGR.2016010102

Hu, H., Hu, P. J., & Al-Gahtani, S. S. (2017). User Acceptance of Computer Technology at Work in Arabian Culture: A Model Comparison Approach. In M. Khosrow-Pour (Ed.), *Handbook of Research on Technology Adoption, Social Policy, and Global Integration* (pp. 205–228). Hershey, PA: IGI Global. doi:10.4018/978-1-5225-2668-1.ch011

Huie, C. P. (2016). Perceptions of Business Intelligence Professionals about Factors Related to Business Intelligence input in Decision Making. *International Journal of Business Analytics, 3*(3), 1–24. doi:10.4018/IJBAN.2016070101

Hung, S., Huang, W., Yen, D. C., Chang, S., & Lu, C. (2016). Effect of Information Service Competence and Contextual Factors on the Effectiveness of Strategic Information Systems Planning in Hospitals. *Journal of Global Information Management, 24*(1), 14–36. doi:10.4018/JGIM.2016010102

Ifinedo, P. (2017). Using an Extended Theory of Planned Behavior to Study Nurses' Adoption of Healthcare Information Systems in Nova Scotia. *International Journal of Technology Diffusion, 8*(1), 1–17. doi:10.4018/IJTD.2017010101

Ilie, V., & Sneha, S. (2018). A Three Country Study for Understanding Physicians' Engagement With Electronic Information Resources Pre and Post System Implementation. *Journal of Global Information Management, 26*(2), 48–73. doi:10.4018/JGIM.2018040103

Inoue-Smith, Y. (2017). Perceived Ease in Using Technology Predicts Teacher Candidates' Preferences for Online Resources. *International Journal of Online Pedagogy and Course Design*, 7(3), 17–28. doi:10.4018/IJOPCD.2017070102

Islam, A. A. (2016). Development and Validation of the Technology Adoption and Gratification (TAG) Model in Higher Education: A Cross-Cultural Study Between Malaysia and China. *International Journal of Technology and Human Interaction*, 12(3), 78–105. doi:10.4018/IJTHI.2016070106

Islam, A. Y. (2017). Technology Satisfaction in an Academic Context: Moderating Effect of Gender. In A. Mesquita (Ed.), *Research Paradigms and Contemporary Perspectives on Human-Technology Interaction* (pp. 187–211). Hershey, PA: IGI Global. doi:10.4018/978-1-5225-1868-6.ch009

Jamil, G. L., & Jamil, C. C. (2017). Information and Knowledge Management Perspective Contributions for Fashion Studies: Observing Logistics and Supply Chain Management Processes. In G. Jamil, A. Soares, & C. Pessoa (Eds.), *Handbook of Research on Information Management for Effective Logistics and Supply Chains* (pp. 199–221). Hershey, PA: IGI Global. doi:10.4018/978-1-5225-0973-8.ch011

Jamil, G. L., Jamil, L. C., Vieira, A. A., & Xavier, A. J. (2016). Challenges in Modelling Healthcare Services: A Study Case of Information Architecture Perspectives. In G. Jamil, J. Poças Rascão, F. Ribeiro, & A. Malheiro da Silva (Eds.), *Handbook of Research on Information Architecture and Management in Modern Organizations* (pp. 1–23). Hershey, PA: IGI Global. doi:10.4018/978-1-4666-8637-3.ch001

Janakova, M. (2018). Big Data and Simulations for the Solution of Controversies in Small Businesses. In M. Khosrow-Pour, D.B.A. (Ed.), Encyclopedia of Information Science and Technology, Fourth Edition (pp. 6907-6915). Hershey, PA: IGI Global. doi:10.4018/978-1-5225-2255-3.ch598

Jha, D. G. (2016). Preparing for Information Technology Driven Changes. In S. Tiwari & L. Nafees (Eds.), *Innovative Management Education Pedagogies for Preparing Next-Generation Leaders* (pp. 258–274). Hershey, PA: IGI Global. doi:10.4018/978-1-4666-9691-4.ch015

Jhawar, A., & Garg, S. K. (2018). Logistics Improvement by Investment in Information Technology Using System Dynamics. In A. Azar & S. Vaidyanathan (Eds.), *Advances in System Dynamics and Control* (pp. 528–567). Hershey, PA: IGI Global. doi:10.4018/978-1-5225-4077-9.ch017

Kalelioğlu, F., Gülbahar, Y., & Doğan, D. (2018). Teaching How to Think Like a Programmer: Emerging Insights. In H. Ozcinar, G. Wong, & H. Ozturk (Eds.), *Teaching Computational Thinking in Primary Education* (pp. 18–35). Hershey, PA: IGI Global. doi:10.4018/978-1-5225-3200-2.ch002

Kamberi, S. (2017). A Girls-Only Online Virtual World Environment and its Implications for Game-Based Learning. In A. Stricker, C. Calongne, B. Truman, & F. Arenas (Eds.), *Integrating an Awareness of Selfhood and Society into Virtual Learning* (pp. 74–95). Hershey, PA: IGI Global. doi:10.4018/978-1-5225-2182-2.ch006

Kamel, S., & Rizk, N. (2017). ICT Strategy Development: From Design to Implementation – Case of Egypt. In C. Howard & K. Hargiss (Eds.), *Strategic Information Systems and Technologies in Modern Organizations* (pp. 239–257). Hershey, PA: IGI Global. doi:10.4018/978-1-5225-1680-4.ch010

Kamel, S. H. (2018). The Potential Role of the Software Industry in Supporting Economic Development. In M. Khosrow-Pour, D.B.A. (Ed.), Encyclopedia of Information Science and Technology, Fourth Edition (pp. 7259-7269). Hershey, PA: IGI Global. doi:10.4018/978-1-5225-2255-3.ch631

Karon, R. (2016). Utilisation of Health Information Systems for Service Delivery in the Namibian Environment. In T. Iyamu & A. Tatnall (Eds.), *Maximizing Healthcare Delivery and Management through Technology Integration* (pp. 169–183). Hershey, PA: IGI Global. doi:10.4018/978-1-4666-9446-0.ch011

Kawata, S. (2018). Computer-Assisted Parallel Program Generation. In M. Khosrow-Pour, D.B.A. (Ed.), Encyclopedia of Information Science and Technology, Fourth Edition (pp. 4583-4593). Hershey, PA: IGI Global. doi:10.4018/978-1-5225-2255-3.ch398

Khanam, S., Siddiqui, J., & Talib, F. (2016). A DEMATEL Approach for Prioritizing the TQM Enablers and IT Resources in the Indian ICT Industry. *International Journal of Applied Management Sciences and Engineering*, 3(1), 11–29. doi:10.4018/IJAMSE.2016010102

Khari, M., Shrivastava, G., Gupta, S., & Gupta, R. (2017). Role of Cyber Security in Today's Scenario. In R. Kumar, P. Pattnaik, & P. Pandey (Eds.), *Detecting and Mitigating Robotic Cyber Security Risks* (pp. 177–191). Hershey, PA: IGI Global. doi:10.4018/978-1-5225-2154-9.ch013

Related References

Khouja, M., Rodriguez, I. B., Ben Halima, Y., & Moalla, S. (2018). IT Governance in Higher Education Institutions: A Systematic Literature Review. *International Journal of Human Capital and Information Technology Professionals*, 9(2), 52–67. doi:10.4018/IJHCITP.2018040104

Kim, S., Chang, M., Choi, N., Park, J., & Kim, H. (2016). The Direct and Indirect Effects of Computer Uses on Student Success in Math. *International Journal of Cyber Behavior, Psychology and Learning*, 6(3), 48–64. doi:10.4018/IJCBPL.2016070104

Kiourt, C., Pavlidis, G., Koutsoudis, A., & Kalles, D. (2017). Realistic Simulation of Cultural Heritage. *International Journal of Computational Methods in Heritage Science*, 1(1), 10–40. doi:10.4018/IJCMHS.2017010102

Korikov, A., & Krivtsov, O. (2016). System of People-Computer: On the Way of Creation of Human-Oriented Interface. In V. Mkrttchian, A. Bershadsky, A. Bozhday, M. Kataev, & S. Kataev (Eds.), *Handbook of Research on Estimation and Control Techniques in E-Learning Systems* (pp. 458–470). Hershey, PA: IGI Global. doi:10.4018/978-1-4666-9489-7.ch032

Köse, U. (2017). An Augmented-Reality-Based Intelligent Mobile Application for Open Computer Education. In G. Kurubacak & H. Altinpulluk (Eds.), *Mobile Technologies and Augmented Reality in Open Education* (pp. 154–174). Hershey, PA: IGI Global. doi:10.4018/978-1-5225-2110-5.ch008

Lahmiri, S. (2018). Information Technology Outsourcing Risk Factors and Provider Selection. In M. Gupta, R. Sharman, J. Walp, & P. Mulgund (Eds.), *Information Technology Risk Management and Compliance in Modern Organizations* (pp. 214–228). Hershey, PA: IGI Global. doi:10.4018/978-1-5225-2604-9.ch008

Landriscina, F. (2017). Computer-Supported Imagination: The Interplay Between Computer and Mental Simulation in Understanding Scientific Concepts. In I. Levin & D. Tsybulsky (Eds.), *Digital Tools and Solutions for Inquiry-Based STEM Learning* (pp. 33–60). Hershey, PA: IGI Global. doi:10.4018/978-1-5225-2525-7.ch002

Lau, S. K., Winley, G. K., Leung, N. K., Tsang, N., & Lau, S. Y. (2016). An Exploratory Study of Expectation in IT Skills in a Developing Nation: Vietnam. *Journal of Global Information Management*, 24(1), 1–13. doi:10.4018/JGIM.2016010101

Lavranos, C., Kostagiolas, P., & Papadatos, J. (2016). Information Retrieval Technologies and the "Realities" of Music Information Seeking. In I. Deliyannis, P. Kostagiolas, & C. Banou (Eds.), *Experimental Multimedia Systems for Interactivity and Strategic Innovation* (pp. 102–121). Hershey, PA: IGI Global. doi:10.4018/978-1-4666-8659-5.ch005

Lee, W. W. (2018). Ethical Computing Continues From Problem to Solution. In M. Khosrow-Pour, D.B.A. (Ed.), Encyclopedia of Information Science and Technology, Fourth Edition (pp. 4884-4897). Hershey, PA: IGI Global. doi:10.4018/978-1-5225-2255-3.ch423

Lehto, M. (2016). Cyber Security Education and Research in the Finland's Universities and Universities of Applied Sciences. *International Journal of Cyber Warfare & Terrorism, 6*(2), 15–31. doi:10.4018/IJCWT.2016040102

Lin, C., Jalleh, G., & Huang, Y. (2016). Evaluating and Managing Electronic Commerce and Outsourcing Projects in Hospitals. In A. Dwivedi (Ed.), *Reshaping Medical Practice and Care with Health Information Systems* (pp. 132–172). Hershey, PA: IGI Global. doi:10.4018/978-1-4666-9870-3.ch005

Lin, S., Chen, S., & Chuang, S. (2017). Perceived Innovation and Quick Response Codes in an Online-to-Offline E-Commerce Service Model. *International Journal of E-Adoption, 9*(2), 1–16. doi:10.4018/IJEA.2017070101

Liu, M., Wang, Y., Xu, W., & Liu, L. (2017). Automated Scoring of Chinese Engineering Students' English Essays. *International Journal of Distance Education Technologies, 15*(1), 52–68. doi:10.4018/IJDET.2017010104

Luciano, E. M., Wiedenhöft, G. C., Macadar, M. A., & Pinheiro dos Santos, F. (2016). Information Technology Governance Adoption: Understanding its Expectations Through the Lens of Organizational Citizenship. *International Journal of IT/Business Alignment and Governance, 7*(2), 22-32. doi:10.4018/IJITBAG.2016070102

Mabe, L. K., & Oladele, O. I. (2017). Application of Information Communication Technologies for Agricultural Development through Extension Services: A Review. In T. Tossy (Ed.), *Information Technology Integration for Socio-Economic Development* (pp. 52–101). Hershey, PA: IGI Global. doi:10.4018/978-1-5225-0539-6.ch003

Manogaran, G., Thota, C., & Lopez, D. (2018). Human-Computer Interaction With Big Data Analytics. In D. Lopez & M. Durai (Eds.), *HCI Challenges and Privacy Preservation in Big Data Security* (pp. 1–22). Hershey, PA: IGI Global. doi:10.4018/978-1-5225-2863-0.ch001

Margolis, J., Goode, J., & Flapan, J. (2017). A Critical Crossroads for Computer Science for All: "Identifying Talent" or "Building Talent," and What Difference Does It Make? In Y. Rankin & J. Thomas (Eds.), *Moving Students of Color from Consumers to Producers of Technology* (pp. 1–23). Hershey, PA: IGI Global. doi:10.4018/978-1-5225-2005-4.ch001

Mbale, J. (2018). Computer Centres Resource Cloud Elasticity-Scalability (CRECES): Copperbelt University Case Study. In S. Aljawarneh & M. Malhotra (Eds.), *Critical Research on Scalability and Security Issues in Virtual Cloud Environments* (pp. 48–70). Hershey, PA: IGI Global. doi:10.4018/978-1-5225-3029-9.ch003

McKee, J. (2018). The Right Information: The Key to Effective Business Planning. In *Business Architectures for Risk Assessment and Strategic Planning: Emerging Research and Opportunities* (pp. 38–52). Hershey, PA: IGI Global. doi:10.4018/978-1-5225-3392-4.ch003

Mensah, I. K., & Mi, J. (2018). Determinants of Intention to Use Local E-Government Services in Ghana: The Perspective of Local Government Workers. *International Journal of Technology Diffusion*, 9(2), 41–60. doi:10.4018/IJTD.2018040103

Mohamed, J. H. (2018). Scientograph-Based Visualization of Computer Forensics Research Literature. In J. Jeyasekar & P. Saravanan (Eds.), *Innovations in Measuring and Evaluating Scientific Information* (pp. 148–162). Hershey, PA: IGI Global. doi:10.4018/978-1-5225-3457-0.ch010

Moore, R. L., & Johnson, N. (2017). Earning a Seat at the Table: How IT Departments Can Partner in Organizational Change and Innovation. *International Journal of Knowledge-Based Organizations*, 7(2), 1–12. doi:10.4018/IJKBO.2017040101

Mtebe, J. S., & Kissaka, M. M. (2016). Enhancing the Quality of Computer Science Education with MOOCs in Sub-Saharan Africa. In J. Keengwe & G. Onchwari (Eds.), *Handbook of Research on Active Learning and the Flipped Classroom Model in the Digital Age* (pp. 366–377). Hershey, PA: IGI Global. doi:10.4018/978-1-4666-9680-8.ch019

Mukul, M. K., & Bhattaharyya, S. (2017). Brain-Machine Interface: Human-Computer Interaction. In E. Noughabi, B. Raahemi, A. Albadvi, & B. Far (Eds.), *Handbook of Research on Data Science for Effective Healthcare Practice and Administration* (pp. 417–443). Hershey, PA: IGI Global. doi:10.4018/978-1-5225-2515-8.ch018

Na, L. (2017). Library and Information Science Education and Graduate Programs in Academic Libraries. In L. Ruan, Q. Zhu, & Y. Ye (Eds.), *Academic Library Development and Administration in China* (pp. 218–229). Hershey, PA: IGI Global. doi:10.4018/978-1-5225-0550-1.ch013

Nabavi, A., Taghavi-Fard, M. T., Hanafizadeh, P., & Taghva, M. R. (2016). Information Technology Continuance Intention: A Systematic Literature Review. *International Journal of E-Business Research*, 12(1), 58–95. doi:10.4018/IJEBR.2016010104

Nath, R., & Murthy, V. N. (2018). What Accounts for the Differences in Internet Diffusion Rates Around the World? In M. Khosrow-Pour, D.B.A. (Ed.), Encyclopedia of Information Science and Technology, Fourth Edition (pp. 8095-8104). Hershey, PA: IGI Global. doi:10.4018/978-1-5225-2255-3.ch705

Nedelko, Z., & Potocan, V. (2018). The Role of Emerging Information Technologies for Supporting Supply Chain Management. In M. Khosrow-Pour, D.B.A. (Ed.), Encyclopedia of Information Science and Technology, Fourth Edition (pp. 5559-5569). Hershey, PA: IGI Global. doi:10.4018/978-1-5225-2255-3.ch483

Ngafeeson, M. N. (2018). User Resistance to Health Information Technology. In M. Khosrow-Pour, D.B.A. (Ed.), Encyclopedia of Information Science and Technology, Fourth Edition (pp. 3816-3825). Hershey, PA: IGI Global. doi:10.4018/978-1-5225-2255-3.ch331

Nozari, H., Najafi, S. E., Jafari-Eskandari, M., & Aliahmadi, A. (2016). Providing a Model for Virtual Project Management with an Emphasis on IT Projects. In C. Graham (Ed.), *Strategic Management and Leadership for Systems Development in Virtual Spaces* (pp. 43–63). Hershey, PA: IGI Global. doi:10.4018/978-1-4666-9688-4.ch003

Nurdin, N., Stockdale, R., & Scheepers, H. (2016). Influence of Organizational Factors in the Sustainability of E-Government: A Case Study of Local E-Government in Indonesia. In I. Sodhi (Ed.), *Trends, Prospects, and Challenges in Asian E-Governance* (pp. 281–323). Hershey, PA: IGI Global. doi:10.4018/978-1-4666-9536-8.ch014

Odagiri, K. (2017). Introduction of Individual Technology to Constitute the Current Internet. In *Strategic Policy-Based Network Management in Contemporary Organizations* (pp. 20–96). Hershey, PA: IGI Global. doi:10.4018/978-1-68318-003-6.ch003

Okike, E. U. (2018). Computer Science and Prison Education. In I. Biao (Ed.), *Strategic Learning Ideologies in Prison Education Programs* (pp. 246–264). Hershey, PA: IGI Global. doi:10.4018/978-1-5225-2909-5.ch012

Olelewe, C. J., & Nwafor, I. P. (2017). Level of Computer Appreciation Skills Acquired for Sustainable Development by Secondary School Students in Nsukka LGA of Enugu State, Nigeria. In C. Ayo & V. Mbarika (Eds.), *Sustainable ICT Adoption and Integration for Socio-Economic Development* (pp. 214–233). Hershey, PA: IGI Global. doi:10.4018/978-1-5225-2565-3.ch010

Related References

Oliveira, M., Maçada, A. C., Curado, C., & Nodari, F. (2017). Infrastructure Profiles and Knowledge Sharing. *International Journal of Technology and Human Interaction*, *13*(3), 1–12. doi:10.4018/IJTHI.2017070101

Otarkhani, A., Shokouhyar, S., & Pour, S. S. (2017). Analyzing the Impact of Governance of Enterprise IT on Hospital Performance: Tehran's (Iran) Hospitals – A Case Study. *International Journal of Healthcare Information Systems and Informatics*, *12*(3), 1–20. doi:10.4018/IJHISI.2017070101

Otunla, A. O., & Amuda, C. O. (2018). Nigerian Undergraduate Students' Computer Competencies and Use of Information Technology Tools and Resources for Study Skills and Habits' Enhancement. In M. Khosrow-Pour, D.B.A. (Ed.), Encyclopedia of Information Science and Technology, Fourth Edition (pp. 2303-2313). Hershey, PA: IGI Global. doi:10.4018/978-1-5225-2255-3.ch200

Özçınar, H. (2018). A Brief Discussion on Incentives and Barriers to Computational Thinking Education. In H. Ozcinar, G. Wong, & H. Ozturk (Eds.), *Teaching Computational Thinking in Primary Education* (pp. 1–17). Hershey, PA: IGI Global. doi:10.4018/978-1-5225-3200-2.ch001

Pandey, J. M., Garg, S., Mishra, P., & Mishra, B. P. (2017). Computer Based Psychological Interventions: Subject to the Efficacy of Psychological Services. *International Journal of Computers in Clinical Practice*, *2*(1), 25–33. doi:10.4018/IJCCP.2017010102

Parry, V. K., & Lind, M. L. (2016). Alignment of Business Strategy and Information Technology Considering Information Technology Governance, Project Portfolio Control, and Risk Management. *International Journal of Information Technology Project Management*, *7*(4), 21–37. doi:10.4018/IJITPM.2016100102

Patro, C. (2017). Impulsion of Information Technology on Human Resource Practices. In P. Ordóñez de Pablos (Ed.), *Managerial Strategies and Solutions for Business Success in Asia* (pp. 231–254). Hershey, PA: IGI Global. doi:10.4018/978-1-5225-1886-0.ch013

Patro, C. S., & Raghunath, K. M. (2017). Information Technology Paraphernalia for Supply Chain Management Decisions. In M. Tavana (Ed.), *Enterprise Information Systems and the Digitalization of Business Functions* (pp. 294–320). Hershey, PA: IGI Global. doi:10.4018/978-1-5225-2382-6.ch014

Paul, P. K. (2016). Cloud Computing: An Agent of Promoting Interdisciplinary Sciences, Especially Information Science and I-Schools – Emerging Techno-Educational Scenario. In L. Chao (Ed.), *Handbook of Research on Cloud-Based STEM Education for Improved Learning Outcomes* (pp. 247–258). Hershey, PA: IGI Global. doi:10.4018/978-1-4666-9924-3.ch016

Paul, P. K. (2018). The Context of IST for Solid Information Retrieval and Infrastructure Building: Study of Developing Country. *International Journal of Information Retrieval Research*, 8(1), 86–100. doi:10.4018/IJIRR.2018010106

Paul, P. K., & Chatterjee, D. (2018). iSchools Promoting "Information Science and Technology" (IST) Domain Towards Community, Business, and Society With Contemporary Worldwide Trend and Emerging Potentialities in India. In M. Khosrow-Pour, D.B.A. (Ed.), Encyclopedia of Information Science and Technology, Fourth Edition (pp. 4723-4735). Hershey, PA: IGI Global. doi:10.4018/978-1-5225-2255-3.ch410

Pessoa, C. R., & Marques, M. E. (2017). Information Technology and Communication Management in Supply Chain Management. In G. Jamil, A. Soares, & C. Pessoa (Eds.), *Handbook of Research on Information Management for Effective Logistics and Supply Chains* (pp. 23–33). Hershey, PA: IGI Global. doi:10.4018/978-1-5225-0973-8.ch002

Pineda, R. G. (2016). Where the Interaction Is Not: Reflections on the Philosophy of Human-Computer Interaction. *International Journal of Art, Culture and Design Technologies*, 5(1), 1–12. doi:10.4018/IJACDT.2016010101

Pineda, R. G. (2018). Remediating Interaction: Towards a Philosophy of Human-Computer Relationship. In M. Khosrow-Pour (Ed.), *Enhancing Art, Culture, and Design With Technological Integration* (pp. 75–98). Hershey, PA: IGI Global. doi:10.4018/978-1-5225-5023-5.ch004

Poikela, P., & Vuojärvi, H. (2016). Learning ICT-Mediated Communication through Computer-Based Simulations. In M. Cruz-Cunha, I. Miranda, R. Martinho, & R. Rijo (Eds.), *Encyclopedia of E-Health and Telemedicine* (pp. 674–687). Hershey, PA: IGI Global. doi:10.4018/978-1-4666-9978-6.ch052

Qian, Y. (2017). Computer Simulation in Higher Education: Affordances, Opportunities, and Outcomes. In P. Vu, S. Fredrickson, & C. Moore (Eds.), *Handbook of Research on Innovative Pedagogies and Technologies for Online Learning in Higher Education* (pp. 236–262). Hershey, PA: IGI Global. doi:10.4018/978-1-5225-1851-8.ch011

Related References

Radant, O., Colomo-Palacios, R., & Stantchev, V. (2016). Factors for the Management of Scarce Human Resources and Highly Skilled Employees in IT-Departments: A Systematic Review. *Journal of Information Technology Research, 9*(1), 65–82. doi:10.4018/JITR.2016010105

Rahman, N. (2016). Toward Achieving Environmental Sustainability in the Computer Industry. *International Journal of Green Computing, 7*(1), 37–54. doi:10.4018/IJGC.2016010103

Rahman, N. (2017). Lessons from a Successful Data Warehousing Project Management. *International Journal of Information Technology Project Management, 8*(4), 30–45. doi:10.4018/IJITPM.2017100103

Rahman, N. (2018). Environmental Sustainability in the Computer Industry for Competitive Advantage. In M. Khosrow-Pour (Ed.), *Green Computing Strategies for Competitive Advantage and Business Sustainability* (pp. 110–130). Hershey, PA: IGI Global. doi:10.4018/978-1-5225-5017-4.ch006

Rajh, A., & Pavetic, T. (2017). Computer Generated Description as the Required Digital Competence in Archival Profession. *International Journal of Digital Literacy and Digital Competence, 8*(1), 36–49. doi:10.4018/IJDLDC.2017010103

Raman, A., & Goyal, D. P. (2017). Extending IMPLEMENT Framework for Enterprise Information Systems Implementation to Information System Innovation. In M. Tavana (Ed.), *Enterprise Information Systems and the Digitalization of Business Functions* (pp. 137–177). Hershey, PA: IGI Global. doi:10.4018/978-1-5225-2382-6.ch007

Rao, Y. S., Rauta, A. K., Saini, H., & Panda, T. C. (2017). Mathematical Model for Cyber Attack in Computer Network. *International Journal of Business Data Communications and Networking, 13*(1), 58–65. doi:10.4018/IJBDCN.2017010105

Rapaport, W. J. (2018). Syntactic Semantics and the Proper Treatment of Computationalism. In M. Danesi (Ed.), *Empirical Research on Semiotics and Visual Rhetoric* (pp. 128–176). Hershey, PA: IGI Global. doi:10.4018/978-1-5225-5622-0.ch007

Raut, R., Priyadarshinee, P., & Jha, M. (2017). Understanding the Mediation Effect of Cloud Computing Adoption in Indian Organization: Integrating TAM-TOE- Risk Model. *International Journal of Service Science, Management, Engineering, and Technology, 8*(3), 40–59. doi:10.4018/IJSSMET.2017070103

Regan, E. A., & Wang, J. (2016). Realizing the Value of EHR Systems Critical Success Factors. *International Journal of Healthcare Information Systems and Informatics*, *11*(3), 1–18. doi:10.4018/IJHISI.2016070101

Rezaie, S., Mirabedini, S. J., & Abtahi, A. (2018). Designing a Model for Implementation of Business Intelligence in the Banking Industry. *International Journal of Enterprise Information Systems*, *14*(1), 77–103. doi:10.4018/IJEIS.2018010105

Rezende, D. A. (2016). Digital City Projects: Information and Public Services Offered by Chicago (USA) and Curitiba (Brazil). *International Journal of Knowledge Society Research*, *7*(3), 16–30. doi:10.4018/IJKSR.2016070102

Rezende, D. A. (2018). Strategic Digital City Projects: Innovative Information and Public Services Offered by Chicago (USA) and Curitiba (Brazil). In M. Lytras, L. Daniela, & A. Visvizi (Eds.), *Enhancing Knowledge Discovery and Innovation in the Digital Era* (pp. 204–223). Hershey, PA: IGI Global. doi:10.4018/978-1-5225-4191-2.ch012

Riabov, V. V. (2016). Teaching Online Computer-Science Courses in LMS and Cloud Environment. *International Journal of Quality Assurance in Engineering and Technology Education*, *5*(4), 12–41. doi:10.4018/IJQAETE.2016100102

Ricordel, V., Wang, J., Da Silva, M. P., & Le Callet, P. (2016). 2D and 3D Visual Attention for Computer Vision: Concepts, Measurement, and Modeling. In R. Pal (Ed.), *Innovative Research in Attention Modeling and Computer Vision Applications* (pp. 1–44). Hershey, PA: IGI Global. doi:10.4018/978-1-4666-8723-3.ch001

Rodriguez, A., Rico-Diaz, A. J., Rabuñal, J. R., & Gestal, M. (2017). Fish Tracking with Computer Vision Techniques: An Application to Vertical Slot Fishways. In M. S., & V. V. (Eds.), Multi-Core Computer Vision and Image Processing for Intelligent Applications (pp. 74-104). Hershey, PA: IGI Global. doi:10.4018/978-1-5225-0889-2.ch003

Romero, J. A. (2018). Sustainable Advantages of Business Value of Information Technology. In M. Khosrow-Pour, D.B.A. (Ed.), Encyclopedia of Information Science and Technology, Fourth Edition (pp. 923-929). Hershey, PA: IGI Global. doi:10.4018/978-1-5225-2255-3.ch079

Romero, J. A. (2018). The Always-On Business Model and Competitive Advantage. In N. Bajgoric (Ed.), *Always-On Enterprise Information Systems for Modern Organizations* (pp. 23–40). Hershey, PA: IGI Global. doi:10.4018/978-1-5225-3704-5.ch002

Rosen, Y. (2018). Computer Agent Technologies in Collaborative Learning and Assessment. In M. Khosrow-Pour, D.B.A. (Ed.), Encyclopedia of Information Science and Technology, Fourth Edition (pp. 2402-2410). Hershey, PA: IGI Global. doi:10.4018/978-1-5225-2255-3.ch209

Rosen, Y., & Mosharraf, M. (2016). Computer Agent Technologies in Collaborative Assessments. In Y. Rosen, S. Ferrara, & M. Mosharraf (Eds.), *Handbook of Research on Technology Tools for Real-World Skill Development* (pp. 319–343). Hershey, PA: IGI Global. doi:10.4018/978-1-4666-9441-5.ch012

Roy, D. (2018). Success Factors of Adoption of Mobile Applications in Rural India: Effect of Service Characteristics on Conceptual Model. In M. Khosrow-Pour (Ed.), *Green Computing Strategies for Competitive Advantage and Business Sustainability* (pp. 211–238). Hershey, PA: IGI Global. doi:10.4018/978-1-5225-5017-4.ch010

Ruffin, T. R. (2016). Health Information Technology and Change. In V. Wang (Ed.), *Handbook of Research on Advancing Health Education through Technology* (pp. 259–285). Hershey, PA: IGI Global. doi:10.4018/978-1-4666-9494-1.ch012

Ruffin, T. R. (2016). Health Information Technology and Quality Management. *International Journal of Information Communication Technologies and Human Development*, *8*(4), 56–72. doi:10.4018/IJICTHD.2016100105

Ruffin, T. R., & Hawkins, D. P. (2018). Trends in Health Care Information Technology and Informatics. In M. Khosrow-Pour, D.B.A. (Ed.), Encyclopedia of Information Science and Technology, Fourth Edition (pp. 3805-3815). Hershey, PA: IGI Global. doi:10.4018/978-1-5225-2255-3.ch330

Safari, M. R., & Jiang, Q. (2018). The Theory and Practice of IT Governance Maturity and Strategies Alignment: Evidence From Banking Industry. *Journal of Global Information Management*, *26*(2), 127–146. doi:10.4018/JGIM.2018040106

Sahin, H. B., & Anagun, S. S. (2018). Educational Computer Games in Math Teaching: A Learning Culture. In E. Toprak & E. Kumtepe (Eds.), *Supporting Multiculturalism in Open and Distance Learning Spaces* (pp. 249–280). Hershey, PA: IGI Global. doi:10.4018/978-1-5225-3076-3.ch013

Sanna, A., & Valpreda, F. (2017). An Assessment of the Impact of a Collaborative Didactic Approach and Students' Background in Teaching Computer Animation. *International Journal of Information and Communication Technology Education*, *13*(4), 1–16. doi:10.4018/IJICTE.2017100101

Savita, K., Dominic, P., & Ramayah, T. (2016). The Drivers, Practices and Outcomes of Green Supply Chain Management: Insights from ISO14001 Manufacturing Firms in Malaysia. *International Journal of Information Systems and Supply Chain Management*, *9*(2), 35–60. doi:10.4018/IJISSCM.2016040103

Scott, A., Martin, A., & McAlear, F. (2017). Enhancing Participation in Computer Science among Girls of Color: An Examination of a Preparatory AP Computer Science Intervention. In Y. Rankin & J. Thomas (Eds.), *Moving Students of Color from Consumers to Producers of Technology* (pp. 62–84). Hershey, PA: IGI Global. doi:10.4018/978-1-5225-2005-4.ch004

Shahsavandi, E., Mayah, G., & Rahbari, H. (2016). Impact of E-Government on Transparency and Corruption in Iran. In I. Sodhi (Ed.), *Trends, Prospects, and Challenges in Asian E-Governance* (pp. 75–94). Hershey, PA: IGI Global. doi:10.4018/978-1-4666-9536-8.ch004

Siddoo, V., & Wongsai, N. (2017). Factors Influencing the Adoption of ISO/IEC 29110 in Thai Government Projects: A Case Study. *International Journal of Information Technologies and Systems Approach*, *10*(1), 22–44. doi:10.4018/IJITSA.2017010102

Sidorkina, I., & Rybakov, A. (2016). Computer-Aided Design as Carrier of Set Development Changes System in E-Course Engineering. In V. Mkrttchian, A. Bershadsky, A. Bozhday, M. Kataev, & S. Kataev (Eds.), *Handbook of Research on Estimation and Control Techniques in E-Learning Systems* (pp. 500–515). Hershey, PA: IGI Global. doi:10.4018/978-1-4666-9489-7.ch035

Sidorkina, I., & Rybakov, A. (2016). Creating Model of E-Course: As an Object of Computer-Aided Design. In V. Mkrttchian, A. Bershadsky, A. Bozhday, M. Kataev, & S. Kataev (Eds.), *Handbook of Research on Estimation and Control Techniques in E-Learning Systems* (pp. 286–297). Hershey, PA: IGI Global. doi:10.4018/978-1-4666-9489-7.ch019

Simões, A. (2017). Using Game Frameworks to Teach Computer Programming. In R. Alexandre Peixoto de Queirós & M. Pinto (Eds.), *Gamification-Based E-Learning Strategies for Computer Programming Education* (pp. 221–236). Hershey, PA: IGI Global. doi:10.4018/978-1-5225-1034-5.ch010

Sllame, A. M. (2017). Integrating LAB Work With Classes in Computer Network Courses. In H. Alphin Jr, R. Chan, & J. Lavine (Eds.), *The Future of Accessibility in International Higher Education* (pp. 253–275). Hershey, PA: IGI Global. doi:10.4018/978-1-5225-2560-8.ch015

Smirnov, A., Ponomarev, A., Shilov, N., Kashevnik, A., & Teslya, N. (2018). Ontology-Based Human-Computer Cloud for Decision Support: Architecture and Applications in Tourism. *International Journal of Embedded and Real-Time Communication Systems*, 9(1), 1–19. doi:10.4018/IJERTCS.2018010101

Smith-Ditizio, A. A., & Smith, A. D. (2018). Computer Fraud Challenges and Its Legal Implications. In M. Khosrow-Pour, D.B.A. (Ed.), Encyclopedia of Information Science and Technology, Fourth Edition (pp. 4837-4848). Hershey, PA: IGI Global. doi:10.4018/978-1-5225-2255-3.ch419

Sohani, S. S. (2016). Job Shadowing in Information Technology Projects: A Source of Competitive Advantage. *International Journal of Information Technology Project Management*, 7(1), 47–57. doi:10.4018/IJITPM.2016010104

Sosnin, P. (2018). Figuratively Semantic Support of Human-Computer Interactions. In *Experience-Based Human-Computer Interactions: Emerging Research and Opportunities* (pp. 244–272). Hershey, PA: IGI Global. doi:10.4018/978-1-5225-2987-3.ch008

Spinelli, R., & Benevolo, C. (2016). From Healthcare Services to E-Health Applications: A Delivery System-Based Taxonomy. In A. Dwivedi (Ed.), *Reshaping Medical Practice and Care with Health Information Systems* (pp. 205–245). Hershey, PA: IGI Global. doi:10.4018/978-1-4666-9870-3.ch007

Srinivasan, S. (2016). Overview of Clinical Trial and Pharmacovigilance Process and Areas of Application of Computer System. In P. Chakraborty & A. Nagal (Eds.), *Software Innovations in Clinical Drug Development and Safety* (pp. 1–13). Hershey, PA: IGI Global. doi:10.4018/978-1-4666-8726-4.ch001

Srisawasdi, N. (2016). Motivating Inquiry-Based Learning Through a Combination of Physical and Virtual Computer-Based Laboratory Experiments in High School Science. In M. Urban & D. Falvo (Eds.), *Improving K-12 STEM Education Outcomes through Technological Integration* (pp. 108–134). Hershey, PA: IGI Global. doi:10.4018/978-1-4666-9616-7.ch006

Stavridi, S. V., & Hamada, D. R. (2016). Children and Youth Librarians: Competencies Required in Technology-Based Environment. In J. Yap, M. Perez, M. Ayson, & G. Entico (Eds.), *Special Library Administration, Standardization and Technological Integration* (pp. 25–50). Hershey, PA: IGI Global. doi:10.4018/978-1-4666-9542-9.ch002

Sung, W., Ahn, J., Kai, S. M., Choi, A., & Black, J. B. (2016). Incorporating Touch-Based Tablets into Classroom Activities: Fostering Children's Computational Thinking through iPad Integrated Instruction. In D. Mentor (Ed.), *Handbook of Research on Mobile Learning in Contemporary Classrooms* (pp. 378–406). Hershey, PA: IGI Global. doi:10.4018/978-1-5225-0251-7.ch019

Syväjärvi, A., Leinonen, J., Kivivirta, V., & Kesti, M. (2017). The Latitude of Information Management in Local Government: Views of Local Government Managers. *International Journal of Electronic Government Research*, *13*(1), 69–85. doi:10.4018/IJEGR.2017010105

Tanque, M., & Foxwell, H. J. (2018). Big Data and Cloud Computing: A Review of Supply Chain Capabilities and Challenges. In A. Prasad (Ed.), *Exploring the Convergence of Big Data and the Internet of Things* (pp. 1–28). Hershey, PA: IGI Global. doi:10.4018/978-1-5225-2947-7.ch001

Teixeira, A., Gomes, A., & Orvalho, J. G. (2017). Auditory Feedback in a Computer Game for Blind People. In T. Issa, P. Kommers, T. Issa, P. Isaías, & T. Issa (Eds.), *Smart Technology Applications in Business Environments* (pp. 134–158). Hershey, PA: IGI Global. doi:10.4018/978-1-5225-2492-2.ch007

Thompson, N., McGill, T., & Murray, D. (2018). Affect-Sensitive Computer Systems. In M. Khosrow-Pour, D.B.A. (Ed.), Encyclopedia of Information Science and Technology, Fourth Edition (pp. 4124-4135). Hershey, PA: IGI Global. doi:10.4018/978-1-5225-2255-3.ch357

Trad, A., & Kalpić, D. (2016). The E-Business Transformation Framework for E-Commerce Control and Monitoring Pattern. In I. Lee (Ed.), *Encyclopedia of E-Commerce Development, Implementation, and Management* (pp. 754–777). Hershey, PA: IGI Global. doi:10.4018/978-1-4666-9787-4.ch053

Triberti, S., Brivio, E., & Galimberti, C. (2018). On Social Presence: Theories, Methodologies, and Guidelines for the Innovative Contexts of Computer-Mediated Learning. In M. Marmon (Ed.), *Enhancing Social Presence in Online Learning Environments* (pp. 20–41). Hershey, PA: IGI Global. doi:10.4018/978-1-5225-3229-3.ch002

Tripathy, B. K. T. R., S., & Mohanty, R. K. (2018). Memetic Algorithms and Their Applications in Computer Science. In S. Dash, B. Tripathy, & A. Rahman (Eds.), Handbook of Research on Modeling, Analysis, and Application of Nature-Inspired Metaheuristic Algorithms (pp. 73-93). Hershey, PA: IGI Global. doi:10.4018/978-1-5225-2857-9.ch004

Turulja, L., & Bajgoric, N. (2017). Human Resource Management IT and Global Economy Perspective: Global Human Resource Information Systems. In M. Khosrow-Pour (Ed.), *Handbook of Research on Technology Adoption, Social Policy, and Global Integration* (pp. 377–394). Hershey, PA: IGI Global. doi:10.4018/978-1-5225-2668-1.ch018

Unwin, D. W., Sanzogni, L., & Sandhu, K. (2017). Developing and Measuring the Business Case for Health Information Technology. In K. Moahi, K. Bwalya, & P. Sebina (Eds.), *Health Information Systems and the Advancement of Medical Practice in Developing Countries* (pp. 262–290). Hershey, PA: IGI Global. doi:10.4018/978-1-5225-2262-1.ch015

Vadhanam, B. R. S., M., Sugumaran, V., V., V., & Ramalingam, V. V. (2017). Computer Vision Based Classification on Commercial Videos. In M. S., & V. V. (Eds.), Multi-Core Computer Vision and Image Processing for Intelligent Applications (pp. 105-135). Hershey, PA: IGI Global. doi:10.4018/978-1-5225-0889-2.ch004

Valverde, R., Torres, B., & Motaghi, H. (2018). A Quantum NeuroIS Data Analytics Architecture for the Usability Evaluation of Learning Management Systems. In S. Bhattacharyya (Ed.), *Quantum-Inspired Intelligent Systems for Multimedia Data Analysis* (pp. 277–299). Hershey, PA: IGI Global. doi:10.4018/978-1-5225-5219-2.ch009

Vassilis, E. (2018). Learning and Teaching Methodology: "1:1 Educational Computing. In K. Koutsopoulos, K. Doukas, & Y. Kotsanis (Eds.), *Handbook of Research on Educational Design and Cloud Computing in Modern Classroom Settings* (pp. 122–155). Hershey, PA: IGI Global. doi:10.4018/978-1-5225-3053-4.ch007

Wadhwani, A. K., Wadhwani, S., & Singh, T. (2016). Computer Aided Diagnosis System for Breast Cancer Detection. In Y. Morsi, A. Shukla, & C. Rathore (Eds.), *Optimizing Assistive Technologies for Aging Populations* (pp. 378–395). Hershey, PA: IGI Global. doi:10.4018/978-1-4666-9530-6.ch015

Wang, L., Wu, Y., & Hu, C. (2016). English Teachers' Practice and Perspectives on Using Educational Computer Games in EIL Context. *International Journal of Technology and Human Interaction*, *12*(3), 33–46. doi:10.4018/IJTHI.2016070103

Watfa, M. K., Majeed, H., & Salahuddin, T. (2016). Computer Based E-Healthcare Clinical Systems: A Comprehensive Survey. *International Journal of Privacy and Health Information Management*, *4*(1), 50–69. doi:10.4018/IJPHIM.2016010104

Weeger, A., & Haase, U. (2016). Taking up Three Challenges to Business-IT Alignment Research by the Use of Activity Theory. *International Journal of IT/Business Alignment and Governance, 7*(2), 1-21. doi:10.4018/IJITBAG.2016070101

Wexler, B. E. (2017). Computer-Presented and Physical Brain-Training Exercises for School Children: Improving Executive Functions and Learning. In B. Dubbels (Ed.), *Transforming Gaming and Computer Simulation Technologies across Industries* (pp. 206–224). Hershey, PA: IGI Global. doi:10.4018/978-1-5225-1817-4.ch012

Williams, D. M., Gani, M. O., Addo, I. D., Majumder, A. J., Tamma, C. P., Wang, M., ... Chu, C. (2016). Challenges in Developing Applications for Aging Populations. In Y. Morsi, A. Shukla, & C. Rathore (Eds.), *Optimizing Assistive Technologies for Aging Populations* (pp. 1–21). Hershey, PA: IGI Global. doi:10.4018/978-1-4666-9530-6.ch001

Wimble, M., Singh, H., & Phillips, B. (2018). Understanding Cross-Level Interactions of Firm-Level Information Technology and Industry Environment: A Multilevel Model of Business Value. *Information Resources Management Journal, 31*(1), 1–20. doi:10.4018/IRMJ.2018010101

Wimmer, H., Powell, L., Kilgus, L., & Force, C. (2017). Improving Course Assessment via Web-based Homework. *International Journal of Online Pedagogy and Course Design, 7*(2), 1–19. doi:10.4018/IJOPCD.2017040101

Wong, Y. L., & Siu, K. W. (2018). Assessing Computer-Aided Design Skills. In M. Khosrow-Pour, D.B.A. (Ed.), Encyclopedia of Information Science and Technology, Fourth Edition (pp. 7382-7391). Hershey, PA: IGI Global. doi:10.4018/978-1-5225-2255-3.ch642

Wongsurawat, W., & Shrestha, V. (2018). Information Technology, Globalization, and Local Conditions: Implications for Entrepreneurs in Southeast Asia. In P. Ordóñez de Pablos (Ed.), *Management Strategies and Technology Fluidity in the Asian Business Sector* (pp. 163–176). Hershey, PA: IGI Global. doi:10.4018/978-1-5225-4056-4.ch010

Yang, Y., Zhu, X., Jin, C., & Li, J. J. (2018). Reforming Classroom Education Through a QQ Group: A Pilot Experiment at a Primary School in Shanghai. In H. Spires (Ed.), *Digital Transformation and Innovation in Chinese Education* (pp. 211–231). Hershey, PA: IGI Global. doi:10.4018/978-1-5225-2924-8.ch012

Yilmaz, R., Sezgin, A., Kurnaz, S., & Arslan, Y. Z. (2018). Object-Oriented Programming in Computer Science. In M. Khosrow-Pour, D.B.A. (Ed.), Encyclopedia of Information Science and Technology, Fourth Edition (pp. 7470-7480). Hershey, PA: IGI Global. doi:10.4018/978-1-5225-2255-3.ch650

Yu, L. (2018). From Teaching Software Engineering Locally and Globally to Devising an Internationalized Computer Science Curriculum. In S. Dikli, B. Etheridge, & R. Rawls (Eds.), *Curriculum Internationalization and the Future of Education* (pp. 293–320). Hershey, PA: IGI Global. doi:10.4018/978-1-5225-2791-6.ch016

Yuhua, F. (2018). Computer Information Library Clusters. In M. Khosrow-Pour, D.B.A. (Ed.), Encyclopedia of Information Science and Technology, Fourth Edition (pp. 4399-4403). Hershey, PA: IGI Global. doi:10.4018/978-1-5225-2255-3.ch382

Zare, M. A., Taghavi Fard, M. T., & Hanafizadeh, P. (2016). The Assessment of Outsourcing IT Services using DEA Technique: A Study of Application Outsourcing in Research Centers. *International Journal of Operations Research and Information Systems*, 7(1), 45–57. doi:10.4018/IJORIS.2016010104

Zhao, J., Wang, Q., Guo, J., Gao, L., & Yang, F. (2016). An Overview on Passive Image Forensics Technology for Automatic Computer Forgery. *International Journal of Digital Crime and Forensics*, 8(4), 14–25. doi:10.4018/IJDCF.2016100102

Zimeras, S. (2016). Computer Virus Models and Analysis in M-Health IT Systems: Computer Virus Models. In A. Moumtzoglou (Ed.), *M-Health Innovations for Patient-Centered Care* (pp. 284–297). Hershey, PA: IGI Global. doi:10.4018/978-1-4666-9861-1.ch014

Zlatanovska, K. (2016). Hacking and Hacktivism as an Information Communication System Threat. In M. Hadji-Janev & M. Bogdanoski (Eds.), *Handbook of Research on Civil Society and National Security in the Era of Cyber Warfare* (pp. 68–101). Hershey, PA: IGI Global. doi:10.4018/978-1-4666-8793-6.ch004

About the Contributors

Ricardo Peixoto de Queirós holds a PhD in Computer Science and is an assistant professor of Computer Science at the Polytechnic Institute of Porto. He is also a researcher in the field of e-learning interoperability and programming languages learning at the Center for Research in Advanced Computing Systems (CRACS) research group of INESC TEC Porto. He is one of the development team members that created Enki, a gamified IDE for learning computer programming powered by Mooshak (a system for managing online programming contests often used in the IEEEXtreme competitions). He is also the author of 5 books regarding Android development and has almost 100 scientific publications focused on computer science education.

Alberto Simões has a PhD in Artificial Inteligence, area of Natural Language Processing, is a lecturer at Polytechnic Institute of Cávado and Ave, in Barcelos, and a researcher at Algoritmi Center and Center for Humanistic Studies, both from University of Minho. Main Interests: Natural Language Processing: Bilingual Resources Extraction, Machine Translation and Ontologies; Languages Processing, Domain Specific Languages; Digital Preservation, namely music scores; Artificial Intelligence in Computer Games Development.

Mário Teixeira Pinto has a PhD in Computer Science at Portucalense University, Master of Electronics, and Computer Engineering at Faculty of Engineering - Porto University, and degree in Computer Science. Professor in Informatics Department, at the Polytechnic Institute of Porto. Coordinator of the Degree in Technology and Information Systems for the Web, Polytechnic Institute of Porto. President of the Scientific-Technical Council of ESEIG and member of the General Council of the Polytechnic Institute of Porto. Author of 11 books by the publisher Atlantic Center, in Informatics. Develops research activity in the areas of knowledge management systems; e-learning systems and mobile learning; e-assessment; several publications (over 30) in proceedings of international conferences, international journals and chapter books in Springer and IGI Global publishers. Member of the Scientific

Committee of several international conferences, including: European Conference on Knowledge Management; European Conference on e-learning; Iberian Systems and Information Technologies Conference; World Conference on Information Systems and Technologies; Conferencia Iberica de Sistemas y Tecnologias de Information; Member of the International Society for Professional Innovation Management (ISPIM).

$$* * *$$

Miguel Andrade has been working professionally with IT since 1989. Starting as a coder, he worked across several industries managing IT both as an internal and as an independent consultant, reaching the position of head of IT for an international company. Around 2000 he started to specialize in Open Source Software from an enterprise perspective (support availability, code quality, legal aspects) and also from a social perspective, leading to the creation of Neoscopio SA in 2007, after completing an advanced entrepreneurship training programme at the University of Porto. He graduated from FEUP with a degree in electrotechnical engineering, specializing in telecommunications and computers. Later he obtained an MBA/MSc from the University of Porto Business School (PBS) specialized in Quantitative Methods Applied to Management. He's Currently CEO at Neoscopio SA and is also teaching Web Programming and Software Engineering at the Polytechnic Institute of Porto, School of Management and Technology.

Míriam Antón-Rodríguez received the M.S. and Ph.D. degrees in telecommunication engineering from the University of Valladolid, Spain, in 2003 and 2008, respectively. Since 2004, she is a professor in the Telecommunication Engineering School and a researcher in the Telematics & Imaging Group of the Department of Signal Theory, Communications and Telematics Engineering. Her teaching and research interests includes both applications on the Web and mobile applications mainly in learning, health, and socio-legal fields, bio-inspired algorithms for data mining, and neural networks for artificial vision. She is author or co-author of many publications in journals and of contributions to conferences.

Isabel Azevedo holds a Ph.D. in Informatics Engineering from the Faculty of Engineering of the University of Porto (FEUP). She is an Associate Professor in the Department of Informatics Engineering of ISEP, and a researcher at the Games, Interaction and Learning Technologies (GILT) research group at ISEP. Isabel Azevedo previously worked in the area of Technological Infrastructures at FEUP, and in the Documentation Service of Aveiro University. Her main research topics include model-driven engineering, decentralized applications, and learning technologies.

Nuno Bettencourt holds a Ph.D. in Informatics Engineering from the Universidade de Trás-os-Montes e Alto Douro (UTAD). He is an Associate Professor for the Department of Informatics Engineering at Instituto Superior de Engenharia do Porto (ISEP). He nourishes special interest for software engineering and systems architecture, model driven engineering, software quality assurance and adoption of agile methodologies for the development and management of IT projects. In addition to lecturing, he is also a researcher and has authored several articles and chapters. His main research interests are Semantic Web, Information Privacy, Content Sharing on the Internet and Software Development Quality.

Chintan Bhatt is currently working as an Assistant Professor in Computer Engineering department, Chandubhai S. Patel Institute of Technology, Charusat. He is a member of IEEE, EAI, ACM, CSI, AIRCC and IAENG (International Association of Engineers). His areas of interest include Internet of Things, Data Mining, Web Mining, Networking, Security Mobile Computing, Big Data and Software Engineering. He has more than 5 years of teaching experience and research experience, having good teaching and research interests. He has chaired a track in CSNT 2015 and ICTCS 2014. He has been working as Reviewer in Wireless Communications, IEEE (Impact Factor-6.524) and Internet of Things Journal, IEEE, Knowledge-Based Systems, Elsevier (Impact Factor-2.9) Applied Computing and Informatics, Elsevier and Mobile Networks and Applications, Springer. He has delivered an expert talk on Internet of Things at Broadcast Engineering Society Doordarshan, Ahmedabad on 30/09/2015. He has been awarded Faculty with Maximum Publication in CSIC Award and Paper Presenter Award at International Conference in CSI-2015, held at New Delhi.

Alexandre Bragança holds a Ph.D. in Information Systems and Technologies in the knowledge field of Programming Engineering and Information Systems from the University of Minho, Portugal. He has more than 20 years of industry experience managing software development teams and projects. He holds a position of Adjunct Professor at the Department of Informatics Engineering of ISEP (Instituto Superior de Engenharia do Porto). His main research topics are model-driven engineering and software product lines.

Francisco Díaz Pernas received the Ph.D. degree in industrial engineering from Valladolid University, Valladolid, Spain, in 1993. From 1988 to 1995, he joined the Department of System Engineering and Automatics, Valladolid University, Spain, where he has worked in artificial vision systems for industry applications as quality control for manufacturing. Since 1996 he has been a professor in the School of Telecommunication Engineering and a Senior Researcher in Telematics & Imaging Group of the Department of Signal Theory, Communications, and Telematics Engineering. His main research interests are applications on the Web, intelligent transportation system, and neural networks for artificial vision. He is author or coauthor of many publications in journals and of contributions to conferences.

Rafael Gonçalves received his BSc in Informatics Engineering from the Polytechnic Institute of Porto - School of Engineering (ISEP) in 2016. He is currently attending the last year of the MS in Informatics Engineering, in the field of Software Engineering. During the BSc Rafael worked in two startups, focused on the development of back-end engineering processes. Currently he works as a Software Engineer at CEiiA, building solutions for the deployment and management of smart mobility services.

David Gonzalez-Ortega has been an associate professor in the Telecommunications Engineering School at the University of Valladolid (Spain) since 2010 after being an assistant professor from 2005. He received his M.S. and Ph.D. degrees in Telecommunications Engineering from the University of Valladolid in 2002 and 2009, respectively. Since 2003 he has been a researcher in the Imaging and Telematics Group of the Department of Signal Theory, Communications and Telematics Engineering at the University of Valladolid. His research interests include computer vision, image analysis, pattern recognition, neural networks, real-time applications, and driving simulators.

María Jiménez-Gómez received the M.S. and Ph.D. degrees in telecommunication engineering from the University of Valladolid, Spain, in 2003 and 2009, respectively. She is working as assistant professor at that University since October 2005. She has large experience in digital signal processing, and specifically in radar systems. Also, she is researching in teaching innovative projects, collaborating with different researching groups. Recently, she has been incorporated in Industrial Engineering School at the same University of Valladolid, as a teacher and researcher, in the area of manufacturing processes engineering. She is author or co-author of various publications in journals and of contributions to conferences.

Mario Martinez-Zarzuela received the M.S. and Ph.D. degrees in telecommunication engineering from the University of Valladolid, Spain, in 2004 and 2009, respectively. Since 2005 he has been an assistant professor in the School of Telecommunication Engineering and a researcher in the Telematics & Imaging Group of the Department of Signal Theory, Communications and Telematics Engineering. His research interests include Artificial Intelligence, Deep Learning, Parallel processing on GPUs, Virtual and Augmented Reality and Bio-inspired architectures for Computer Vision and Image Processing. He is author of more than 50 publications in international journals.

Deepti Mehrotra is a gold medalist and received PhD from Lucknow University. Currently she is working as Professor, Amity School of Engineering and Technology, Amity University, NOIDA, India. She has more than 18 years of experience in teaching, research and content writing. She had published more than 50 papers in international refereed Journals and conference Proceedings. Her research interests are information security, data mining and knowledge management.

Parnasi Patel was born in 1995 in India. She received her BE degree from Gujarat Technological University, India in 2016 and MTech degree from Charotar University of Science and Technology in 2018.

Ivo Pereira is currently Head of Innovation and Research at E-goi, a Portuguese company that owns a multichannel marketing automation platform with the same name. He is also an Invited Adjunct Professor at ISEP P.Porto, Portugal. In 2016 he was a Research Associate in Loughborough University, UK. In 2014, he finished his PhD at UTAD, Portugal, with the title "Intelligent system for scheduling assisted by learning". Before, he concluded a Masters and a Bachelor's degrees at ISEP, Portugal, in 2009 and 2006 respectively. He was a researcher at GECAD, ISEP, Portugal for several years, between 2007 and 2014.

María A. Pérez received the M.S. and Ph.D. degrees in telecommunication engineering from the University of Valladolid, Spain, in 1996 and 1999, respectively. She has been working as a lecturer at that University since October 1996. She has experience in coordinating projects related to telematics applications for the Information Society, mainly concerning the application of ICT (Information and Communication Technologies) to the learning process (e-learning). She has also experience in the evaluation of pre-proposals, proposals and final reports of projects co-funded by the European Commission. She is author or co-author of various publications in journals and of contributions to conferences.

Ricardo Santos finished his bachelor's degree in Informatics Engineering in ISEP, P. Porto, Portugal. He is currently concluding his master's degree in Graphic Systems and Multimedia in the same institution, and he is working as back-end developer in E-goi, which is a company whose main product is a multichannel marketing automation, also called E-goi.

Rajni Sehgal is a postgraduate from Banasthali Vidyapeeth and pursuing Ph.D. in Computer Science and Engineering from Amity University, Noida. Currently she is working as Assistant Professor, Amity School of Engineering and Technology, Amity University, NOIDA, India. . She has more than 10 years of experience in teaching and industry. She had published about 5 papers in national and international conference proceedings and Journal. Her research areas are software engineering and software reliability.

Index

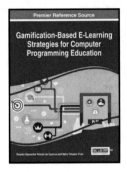
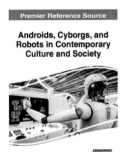

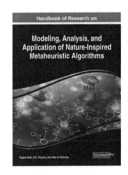

Ensure Quality Research is Introduced to the Academic Community

Become an IGI Global Reviewer for Authored Book Projects

The overall success of an authored book project is dependent on quality and timely reviews.

In this competitive age of scholarly publishing, constructive and timely feedback significantly expedites the turnaround time of manuscripts from submission to acceptance, allowing the publication and discovery of forward-thinking research at a much more expeditious rate. Several IGI Global authored book projects are currently seeking highly qualified experts in the field to fill vacancies on their respective editorial review boards:

Applications may be sent to:
development@igi-global.com

Applicants must have a doctorate (or an equivalent degree) as well as publishing and reviewing experience. Reviewers are asked to write reviews in a timely, collegial, and constructive manner. All reviewers will begin their role on an ad-hoc basis for a period of one year, and upon successful completion of this term can be considered for full editorial review board status, with the potential for a subsequent promotion to Associate Editor.

If you have a colleague that may be interested in this opportunity, we encourage you to share this information with them.